# The New Urban Politics

# The New
# Urban Politics

edited by
**Louis H. Masotti**
and
**Robert L. Lineberry**

**CENTER FOR URBAN AFFAIRS**
**NORTHWESTERN UNIVERSITY**

**Ballinger Publishing Company** ● **Cambridge, Mass.**
*A Subsidiary of J.B. Lippincott Company*

Copyright © 1976 by Ballinger Publishing Company. All rights reserved. No part of this publication may be reproduced, stored in a retrieval system, or transmitted in any form or by any means, electronic mechanical photocopy, recording or otherwise, without the prior written consent of the publisher.

International Standard Book Number: 0-88410-422-2

Library of Congress Catalog Card Number: 76-5869

Printed in the United States of America

**Library of Congress Cataloging in Publication Data**
Main entry under title:

The New urban politics.

Includes bibliographical references
1. Municipal government—United States— Addresses, essays, lectures.
I. Lineberry, Robert L.  II. Masotti, Louis H.
JS341.N48    301.5'92'9073    76-5869
ISBN 0-88410-422-2

# ✳ Contents

v

**List of Figures**

## ✳ List of Tables

**Preface**

This book of original essays on the new urban politics grew out of our continuing interest in the politics of the city and our concern with the efficacy and accuracy of the how social scientists, and particularly political scientists, conceptualize and analyze urban phenomena. Since we knew that many of our professional colleagues shared this concern and interest, we approached some of them to prepare papers on new perspectives on urban politics for a panel at the 1975 Midwest Political Science Association meetings. The papers in this volume by Jones and Yates are revisions of papers originally presented at that panel. Katznelson and Lupsha, each of whom gave papers at the MPSA panel, subsequently decided to submit different papers for this collection; Lupsha's was originally presented at the 1975 American Political Science Association meetings. Preston, a discussant for the MPSA panel, was asked to write the paper on black politics.

The other contributors—Newton, Wirt, Antunes and Mladenka, Bingham and Haider—were identified as thoughtful political scientists with a fresh perspective that would add to the scope and purpose of the book. We are pleased that they agreed to accept our invitation to contribute papers.

We feel that the original objective of the project, to assemble a variety of new perspectives on the politics of, and in, cities by a group of insightful urban scholars, has been achieved. The volume is designed to assist academicians, professionals and laymen alike in understanding the changing nature of urban issues and political actors. We are hopeful that those who read and use the book will find it as stimulating to them as assembling it has been to us.

We are deeply grateful to the staff of the Center of Urban Affairs, Northwestern University, and especially Deborah Ellis Dennis and Joy Charlton, for their considerable assistance in preparing the manuscripts for publication.

L.H.M.
R.L.L.

Evanston, Illinois
January, 1976.

*xv*

For Angela and Julia

**Introduction**

# The New Urban Politics

**ROBERT L. LINEBERRY**
**LOUIS H. MASOTTI**

The state of urban political analysis today is almost—not quite—as disquieting as the state of the cities themselves. Political scientists can lend sympathetic ears, but they have not yet developed the capacity to understand and explain the new urban politics. Underlying the rationale for this volume is our belief that the changes in the city politic and in urban political analysis have not kept pace with one another. If anything, the disjuncture between what political scientists know about the city and what is happening in it grows wider.

The 1960s saw an outpouring of literature and commentary on the sorry state of the city, code-named the "urban crisis," which generated more moral fervor than exacting analysis. It provided an empty vessel into which the whole battery of urban ills, from ghettos to garbage collection, from housing shortages to housing abandonments, could be poured. It generated more metaphors than explanations. To George Sternlieb the city (Newark was his case in point) is like a "sandbox" where people were given things to do when they could not be productive.[1] To Norton Long the city was a "reservation," where contemporary society walled in its urban dependents.[2] To Edward C. Banfield, whose *Unheavenly City* was greeted with critical response ranging from the mildly hostile to the wildly hostile, the principal difficulty with the city was that we had set our expectations ahead of our capacities, like the mechanical rabbit at the dog track, so that we had no hope of bringing the two into line.[3]

Today, it is distinctly unfashionable to discuss such overarching conceptions of the city in crisis. And this is scarcely related to Richard M. Nixon's presidential pronouncement in 1972 that the urban crisis was over. There is now more effort to look first at the parts before we piece them together into a whole. It is now clear that the pieces of the urban political jigsaw cannot be reconstructed into a puzzle compatible with the understandings of the 1960s. This is true for two reasons; first, because the American city has witnessed some important political transformations, and second, because our modes of understanding the urban political process have changed just as rapidly. Unfortunately, it is difficult to get somewhere when both the terrain and the road map are changing simultaneously, especially if those changes are not congruent. The purpose of this volume of original essays is, therefore, to reconceptualize those pieces of the urban puzzle and in doing so to subject a set of new actors and issues in urban politics to more careful scrutiny.

### The Changing Study of Urban Governance

**The Reformist Paradigm and Its Critics.** In one of the most widely quoted works on the history and philosophy of science, Thomas Kuhn develops the concept of "paradigmatic" inquiry.[4] Scientific revolutions occur when a prevailing paradigm, which contains not the right *answers,* but the right *questions,* begins to break down. The paradigm controls the kind of inquiry going on in a discipline so that most "normal science" is little more than puzzle solving. The beauty of a paradigm, of course, is that it tells you what you are looking for even before you find it. Kuhn's theory of scientific revolutions has frequently been applied to the social sciences, though usually in the process of criticizing the allegedly preparadigmatic state of social scientific inquiry.

The study of urban politics, however, was born with a remarkably consensual paradigm and held fast to its puzzles for more than half a century. That paradigm, of course, was the reformist theory of urban governance. Though ultimately prescriptive rather than merely descriptive, the reformist model provided a set of explanations about how city politics operated and how it would change under specified conditions. Explanations were offered for the emergence of political corruption and for how political change took place, and predictions (not just prescriptions) were suggested for the consequences of adopting the baker's dozen municipal reforms of manager government, nonpartisanship, civil service systems, at-large elections, and so forth. The paradigm was, like all paradigms, diffused through the community of scholars not only through professional organs (particularly the *National Municipal*—now *Civic—Review*) but especially through the textbooks in the field of municipal government and administration.

What happened to the reformist paradigm is what happens ultimately to all paradigms: disquieting evidence which could not be incorporated into the predictions of the conventional wisdom began to erode it. Generally, that evidence came from two bodies of inquiry. The first was the power-structure literature and the other was the work which showed that reformed institutions had not lessened the amount of "politics" in the city but merely transformed its character.

The power-structure literature was never directly counterposed to the reformist paradigm. This is not uncommon, as proponents of alternate paradigms frequently talk past one another because they operate on very different assumptions. Floyd Hunter's *Community Power Structure* is credited with being the first major work to address the power question.[5] If Hunter's elitist theory of power was correct, and if most of the critical decisions of urban governance were made outside the formal structure of municipal institutions, then reforming municipal institutions counted for little in the larger scheme of things. Honesty and efficiency on small matters hardly made a difference if dominance on the larger ones was in the hands of a self-perpetuating elite.

Robert Dahl in *Who Governs?* created a countervailing political science paradigm to Hunter's stratificationist paradigm.[6] The political scientist's approach to power traveled under various flags, but most (including Dahl himself) called it simply "pluralism." It, too, pretty much talked past the reformist paradigm, but the tension between the stratificationist and the pluralist paradigms spurred a massive outpouring of research and writing on the structure of power in American cities. Crane has shown that bodies of inquiry in the disciplines frequently develop "invisible colleges," so that the growth of research follows the familiar S-shaped curve of the diffusion-of-innovation literature.[7] That is exactly what happened with the explosion of writings on power, which grew exponentially after Hunter's book, continued even after *Who Governs?* and began to decline only in the late 1960s. By then it was clear that, except for occasional forays by spokesmen for either the stratificationist or the pluralist approaches, the power structure paradigm had played out its options.

Indeed, if at the beginning of the 1960s it was possible for Dahl to ask "who governs?", by the end of the decade many were asking "who cares who governs?" A pluralist sharing-of-power model obviously could not have explained how cities, including Dahl's New Haven, erupted into the riots of the 1960s. Nor was the critical link between power on the one hand and policy outputs on the other very well established. The ties between power structures and issues like school busing, zoning and residential patterning, law enforcement, and service allocations have never been made explicit. We might even speculate that such ties are weak and that both pluralist and elitist power structures play less decisive roles in the allocation of public goods and services than the furious debate about power implied.

Neither paradigm paid much attention to the powerful role played in policy making by that creation of the reform paradigm, the urban public bureaucracy. If, to borrow from Lawrence Herson's oft-cited paper on "The Lost World of Municipal Government," urban governance was generally an under-studied phenomenon, then urban bureaucratic decision making was at the darkest epicenter of the dark continent.[8] The emergence of the bureaucratic city-state has virtually overwhelmed the conventional debates about mayor-centered coalitions vs. the dominance of local economic elites.

Also at the beginning of the 1960s, scholars began to chip away at the reformist paradigm's assumptions regarding the political consequences of reform. While reform may have produced efficiency, it traded off other values, including representativeness and responsiveness. If public bureaucracies paved the streets more economically than political machines, they were also less responsive to citizen demands than precinct captains. If they promoted efficiency, they also reduced the participation of lower class groups in elections. If city managers displaced council members and mayors as loci of power, the possibility of citizen control was eroded.

The attack on the reform paradigm effectively inaugurated the contemporary study of urban politics. In retrospect, it is remarkable how long it took political scientists to resuscitate their interest in the politics of urban governance and particularly the politics of municipal reform.

It was another book, also published in the early 1960s, which "deinstitutionalized" the study of urban government. Banfield and Wilson's *City Politics* was among the first to focus on mayors instead of mayor-council government, managers instead of city manager government, voting patterns instead of nonpartisan elections, and bureaucratic politics instead of the civil service.[9] The "theory" of *City Politics* proved subsequently to be its weakest link, of course. The notion that there is a recognized "public-regarding" and "private-regarding" ethos strained even the capacity of its authors to demonstrate.[10] That the "ethos theory" was no theory at all, but only a provocative metaphor, is now clear. But it is also clear that *City Politics* reopened the possibility of studying politics within and between institutions without the excess baggage of the reformist paradigm.

**Recovering from the All-Too-Successful Moratorium on Theory**. In 1963, Robert Wood wrote a paper on the "Contributions of Political Science to Urban Form." There he issued a call for a "moratorium on theory" arguing that "the temptation of more theory should be resisted, at least until we work through the round of present hypotheses."[11] Exactly what sort of theories Wood wanted to see less of was, unfortunately, not clear. It was clear that the period of the 1960s saw a virtual hiatus of theoretical development and paradigmatic transformation. The result was that the study of urban politics has been, at best, pretheoretical or atheoretical and, at worst, antitheoretical.

If a theory is a generalized explanation of a set of related phenomena, then there was little of it in the study of urban politics. There may be some critical differences between theories and paradigms which would trouble historians of science, but students of urban politics need not concern themselves with such niceties. Since the demise of the reformist and the power paradigms, urban political scientists have largely been adrift upon an atheoretical sea. One testimonial to such a state of affairs is that perhaps the only serious effort by a political scientist to provide a holistic treatment of the city is Banfield's *Unheavenly City*.[12] And one of the several remarkable aspects of that effort is how few of the conventional actors and issues figure in the argument. There is an inexorable and deterministic cast to the thinking, as if groups, mayors, power structures, the press, the bureaucrats and the voters made little difference in working out the dynamics of metropolitan growth and class culture in the city. Curiously, for an author who wrote widely about city politics, the subjects of politics, power and policy play little role in Banfield's argument.

Indeed, in the 1960s, urban political scientists were clearly "between paradigms," developing mostly what might be called, following Robert Merton, "middle-range" theory. The emergent critique of the reformist paradigm had coalesced with a mushrooming literature on power and process in the city, but the conjunction had failed to provide a holistic approach to the subject of urban politics. There is nothing wrong, we emphasize, with middle-range theory. A body of research that is forever "between paradigms" cannot, however, long survive.

Fortunately, there are several harbingers of unifying precepts in the study of urban politics, and we attempt to incorporate some of them into this volume. We think of three: the policy approach to the city, the emergent sociospatial focus, and a more amorphous perspective which we will call the "critical" approach.

**The Policy Approach.** The words "public policy" have a galvanizing effect on the social sciences today. New journals—*Public Policy, Policy Science, Policy Analysis, Policy Studies Journal,* and others—have appeared with much of their focus on the urban field. A policy approach is said to give unification to the social sciences and to fuse the scientific and action-oriented propensities of the social scientific community.[13] Unquestionably, there will be some unification of focus in the urban sciences through the policy approach. We have not, however, explicitly incorporated chapters on urban policy in this volume, for several reasons.[14] First, the study of urban policy is already well advanced and much less in need of reassessment than the study of urban politics per se. Second, precisely because the policy paradigm is so thoroughly diffused through the urban disciplines, no study of urban politics could be complete without due attention to the policy implications of a political analysis. Thus, most of the papers in the present volume—certainly those by Wirt, Jones, Yates and Lupsha—though manifestly about changing dimensions of urban politics, contain "public policy" as their principal dependent variable.

**The Emergence of a Sociospatial Perspective.** One other theoretical straw in the wind is a resurgent attention to the spatial dimensions of urbanism and an application of ecological thinking to urban politics. Because urban political scientists have never taken seriously the maxim to "neither a borrower nor a lender be," there have been importations from both sociology and geography. Political scientists like Williams and Kaufman[15] and geographers like Cox,

Harvey and Smith have all urged a conceptualization of urban politics as the conflict of values in finite space.[16] Williams suggests that urban politics is a large sociospatial turf where the principal driving force is a motivation to secure and protect accessibility to valued cultural and technological locales. Such a perspective would contribute significantly to an understanding of why the old demand for metropolitan integration, a critical component of the reform paradigm, met so much headwind. To the degree that the politics of busing is more than raw racism—and reasonable arguments could be made on both sides of that question—the erosion of spatial dominance on the part of white urban neighborhoods contributes fuel to the fire of the busing issue. One touchstone of a spatial conception of urban politics is that the single policy most thoroughly dominated by urban institutions is land use and zoning. Correlatively, it is a measure of the degree to which local autonomy has eroded that the idea of national land-use planning is being taken seriously.

Spatial thinking offers, it seems to us, at least one additional advantage in addition to tying urban political science more closely to allied inquiries in sociology, geology and even economics: it permits an explicit fusion of the inputs or "politics" side of inquiry with the outputs or "policy" side. It seemed for a while that there would be yet another fissure developing between those studying urban politics and those studying urban policy. There is a unifying nexus, though, in the idea that sociospatial conflict produces differential access to valued outputs of the city. Thinking spatially encourages, even demands, that we integrate the input and output sides of the urban system. The politics of urban services, which Antunes and Mladenka discuss in this volume, is a part of the politics of spatial advantage and deprivation. The black mayor must assiduously cultivate cross-sectional coalitions and deliver public services with perhaps even more care than the white mayor; otherwise only an overwhelming black electorate will return him to office.

**A "Critical" Paradigm for the Study of Urban Politics.** There is a third emergent focus in the study of urban politics whose label is the most difficult to assign but whose impact may in the long run be the greatest. We call it, for lack of better terminology, a "critical" approach to the study of the city. There is a need, though, to distinguish it sharply from the urban crisis literature of the 1960s. Urbanists have never been able to resist decrying the state of the cities, an observation confirmed in any linear examination of writings from Lord Bryce to the Kerner Commission and beyond. During the 1960s the decrying rose to a fever pitch. Even perusing the book titles of the decade—*Cities in a Race with Time, Metropolis in Crisis, The Death and Life of Great American Cities, The Urban Dilemma, The Metropolitan Enigma, The State of the Cities, The Unheavenly City*—provides a sense of the "gloom and doom" atmosphere. The "urban crisis" was the fashionable crisis of the last decade, sandwiched in between the missile crisis and the energy crisis. It was an umbrella so large that everything from gouging by ghetto merchants to auto fumes, from bulging welfare rolls to school busing, from riots to exclusionary zoning, could comfortably fit underneath. It was the "big bang" approach to urban analysis and the explosions in the urban ghettos seemed to confirm how relevant was its description. But partly because there was no theory of political urbanism, every element could assume coequal emphasis and weight.

The emergent critical paradigm in the 1970s is quite different. It begins by explicitly evaluating the urban condition against a set of articulated premises about urban life in capitalist or noncapitalist societies. It is also holistic in that the urban condition in both the public and private spheres is the focus of attention. Some of the critical perspective derives from a neo-Marxian perspective and much of that is strongly influenced by European urban sociologists.[17] Perhaps the best example of the critical approach to the city and its political system broadly defined is David Harvey's *Social Justice and the City*.[18] Harvey is by profession a geographer, and the spatial emphasis in his thinking is greater than in that of other writers of the genre. The city as he conceives it is an income distribution system, with income being defined as "real" income and not merely "pecuniary" income. The working out of the distributive process is the basic social, economic and political process in the capitalist city. Such a perspective addresses issues of equity, equality and social justice, rather than the economic and political efficiency arguments of more mainstream political scientists and economists. Obviously, a full blown Marxist perspective is hardly a *sine qua non* for a concern with those issues; the city in either a capitalist or a socialist state functions as a mechanism of social control and as an economic device for distributing goods and services to social groupings. In this volume, such issues are addressed in the papers by Katznelson and Newton.

### Toward the 1980s: Some Transformations
### In Urban Politics

If the study of urban politics has undergone some important transformations in the past decade, it is also true that the substance of urban politics has not remained fixed. Whether these changes are congruent and whether it is possible to calibrate them is difficult to say. This volume represents, of course, our best efforts to understand these changes in substance, mediated by the changes in approaches. At this point it may be useful to set out our own views on the principal axes of transformation in the substance of urban political life as we approach the 1980s.

**The Fractionalization of the Race Issue and the Emergence of the Equality Issue.** If there was any central thread to the urban crisis literature of the 1960s, it was the fact of race. Fortified by the conflagrations of the middle and later years of the decade, the racial dimension became the one common denominator of the crisis scenario. It figured prominently in the pronouncements of both the right and the left. In Banfield's *Unheavenly City* there was the development of the "blacks are like the Irish" hypothesis. As blacks were the latest immigrant group to árrive in the city, they would expect upward mobility as they were caught up in the process of metropolitan growth. Now, says Banfield,

> The Negro's *main* disadvantage is the same as the Puerto Rican's and the Mexican's: namely, that he is the most recent unskilled and hence relatively low-income, migrant to reach the city from a backward rural area. The city is not the end of his journey but the start of it . . . . Like earlier immigrants, the Negro has reason to expect that his children will have increases of opportunity even greater than his.[19]

Writing from the other end of the political spectrum, Frances Fox Piven attributes much of the political turbulence of the city in the 1960s to the fact that "federal dollars and federal authority were used to resuscitate the functions of the political machine, on the one hand *by spurring local service agencies to respond to the black newcomers,* and on the other by spurring *blacks to make demands upon city services.*"[20] Interestingly, of the three principal actors in Piven's theory—the service bureaucracies, the black organized interests in the cities and the liberal Democratic regime—only the first survived intact into the 1970s.

Linking the fate of the city to the rise and fall of black fortunes within it meant that the social health of the city could be fairly approximated by measuring trends toward or away from racial equality. The impact of the spate of black-oriented policies in the 1960s has never fully been measured, but the gap between white and black incomes did narrow appreciably during the period. Between 1959 and 1970 black family income grew from 51 to 61 percent of white family income. But if the fate of the city is to be measured by that gap, it must be noted that things have worsened since 1970, because by 1973 the same ratio had slipped back to 58 percent. Whether a vigorous economy or a vigorous national policy (both of which subsequently decelerated) explains the slippage is not clear.

Yet the race issue had become fractionalized in the early 1970s. While busing and, to a lesser degree, crime and housing have heavy racial components, numerous racial issues have melted into larger questions of schooling, servicing, bureaucratic responsiveness and the panoply of urban problems on which blacks may be quantitatively but not qualitatively different than other groups.

One factor in defusing the race issue, as Michael Preston shows in this volume, is the election of several black mayors. This is true for two reasons. First, black candidates have had to build fairly broad-based constituencies even where black voters constituted a very large share of the electorate. Second, in the post-election period, black mayors have faced much the same set of constraints as white mayors and have handled them in similar ways. There are, to be sure, other reasons for the fractionalization of the race issue, but the cluster of urban problems once called "civil rights" now factors out on such dimensions as the "politics of urban services," the "politics of representation," or the "politics of crime and law enforcement."

In a larger sense, the new factor displacing civil rights policy may be dimly seen as a growing concern for the political—as opposed to the ideological—questions of equity and equality. John K. Galbraith wrote in 1958 that "inequality has ceased to preoccupy men's minds."[21] The accuracy of such a remark today is doubtful, unless we take quite literally the phrase about "preoccupy men's minds." S.M. Miller and Pamela Roby, writing at the peak of the era of poverty policy, argued forcefully that most of the issues conventionally defined as poverty-related were in fact questions of inequality.[22] Since then a sort of hidden redefinition of numerous conventional questions has transpired. Coleman's famous report started out as an inquiry into minority schooling, but sparked a debate about the impact of schooling on equality, a debate most recently joined again by Christopher Jencks, *et al.*[23]

If Lasswell's aphorism about "who gets what how" once applied almost exclusively to which groups won elections and got legislation passed, it has recently been expanded to income distribution and the larger issue of the distributive and redistributive impacts of public policy. Urban public services were once the domain of public administration specialists. Their equity aspects, however, have provoked concern both by scholars and by citizen groups challenging the distribution of neighborhood service levels.[24]

**From Metropolitanization to Federalization.** The 1960s also witnessed the winding down of metropolitanization as a political issue. It was an issue whose time never came. Part and parcel of the reform paradigm was the assertion that the plethora of governmental units within the metropolis was both inefficient and inequitable. It was inefficient because scores or hundreds of local governments could not produce coordinated, optimal choices about problems which ignored local borders. Pollution in community A or high crime rates in community B nonetheless affected community C. It was inequitable because different governments had access to widely differing tax bases. They also had widely varying service needs, and all too frequently weak tax bases went together with high service needs. The solution of a generation of metropolitan reformers was to regionalize or metropolitanize urban governance. The effort, except in a few, mostly Southern, metropolitan areas, came to naught. As Oliver Williams observed,

> Through the second quarter of this century, political scientists were writing on why metropolitan areas needed to be politically integrated through local government consolidation. Thus far, in the third quarter, a major theme has been documentation of how thoroughly this advice has been rejected by the American people.[25]

There were several reasons why the metropolitan reform drive never got far. Intellectually, the reform paradigm was under attack from two quite different sources by the end of the 1960s, the one from the left and the other from the right. At such times, the turf occupied by the hitherto consensual middle always shrinks. From the left came the call for community control—essentially for more governments within the metropolis rather than fewer.[26] The new governments were to be composed of autonomous urban communities, particularly minority communities within the central city. Their formalities and financing were not always clearly spelled out, but the movement for neighborhood government was simultaneous with—even spurred by—the "maximum feasible participation" requirements of the Economic Opportunity legislation. Participation of the poor in governing their own affairs became more important as a mode of insuring responsiveness than tinkering with the abstractions of metropolitics. Political scientists even accumulated evidence that participation in neighborhood political organizations resuscitated citizen trust and efficacy.[27]

There also emerged, though, a challenge to metropolitanizing assumptions from the right, specifically the "public choice theorists." Political economists like Bish and Ostrom argued that fragmentation of the metropolis maximized citizen choice about what mix of taxes and services one preferred to "purchase."[28] Larger governments, instead of increasing efficiency, would merely incur severe diseconomies of scale. Like all economic theories built upon assumptions of "easy mobility," the public choice approach had problems with those groups too poor or politically powerless to take advantage of the "metropolitan marketplace." Nevertheless, it constituted a different sort of intellectual challenge to the largely unexamined assumptions of metropolitan reform.

Politically, of course, metropolitan reorganization simply never got off the ground in most places. Among the major United States cities, only Nashville, Jacksonville, Miami, Indianapolis and a few others inaugurated any form of metropolitan government. The Southern concentration of such innovations even fueled the charge that metropolitanizing was not exactly neutral in its racial impacts, submerging incipient black central city majorities into new metropolitan electorates dominated by suburban whites. In most places, though, rationalizing the multiplicity of metropolitan governments was simply an issue whose time never came.

Perhaps more important, the massive federalization of urban programs in the 1960s meant that cities established new suprametropolitan ties which reduced the pressure for metropolitan solutions. The federal government poured money into cities as rapidly as new schemes for doing so could be implemented and grant applications processed. Model cities, sewer construction, library aid, law enforcement assistance moneys, poverty funds and, finally, the logical extension—revenue sharing—marked a new dependence of the city on a rich benefactor. For the poorer central city, it was no longer so necessary to gaze longingly at the suburban tax base; for the richer suburb, federal moneys eased the need to consider intrametropolitan issues of equity. Social services and social policy were essentially federalized. This left the city autonomous only within the most narrow domains of conventional service provision. Lingering issues of equity were solved—as they usually are in the American system—by making the size of the pie bigger. As cities got more resources from the federal government, they undertook more social service policies. Problems arose, however, when the pie threatened to stop growing.

### The City in a Society of Scarcity

By the 1970s, America slowly came to the realization that there may be limits to our natural resources, to the growth of the GNP, to technological breakthroughs and even to the capacity of our service economy. The recognition of real and potential scarcity comes slowly to a nation which has known only surplus in recent decades, since it undermines the historic assumptions about "bigger is better" and the "goodness of growth."

Politically we have been concerned with the process of distributing more yet now are confronted with the necessary politics of dividing up less. It's a new ball game with new rules and very likely new outcomes. As Haider points out in his contribution to this collection, fiscal scarcity and the brink of bankruptcy in New York City have already traumatized the internal politics of that city (and put every large city in the country on alert), threatened the economic stability of New York State, and challenged the responsiveness of the New Federalism of Nixon and Ford.

Militant municipal labor organizations whose net demands in the past have done much to jeopardize the urban economy are beginning to pay the price of scarcity. Big city mayors around the nation are cutting payrolls and reducing services on the one hand and inventing new taxes and increasing old ones on the other, in an effort to eliminate revenue shortfalls. Although the problem is most acute in New York, big cities everywhere have begun to respond to "stag-flation," always reluctantly, sometimes heroically, and the forced result in each case is painful austerities. Lasswell's "who gets what?" question may need to be rephrased as "who keeps, and who loses, what?"

Urban austerity threatens to erode an already diminished quality of life, and a disproportionate cost of the loss is as usual being paid by those least able to afford it—the have-nots. Demands for justice and equality tend to fade along with fiscal surplus. Who will pay the political price of welfare cuts, reductions in police and fire protection, unavailable health care, uncollected garbage, closed schools, and the loss of amenities like libraries, museums and parks is a question to which urban political science offers no answers. No doubt we will witness the formation of new alliances and coalitions across racial, ethnic and class lines in an effort to influence the allocation of very scarce resources, but most likely they will operate with a considerably reduced set of expectations.

To the extent that the new politics of scarcity accepts limits and attempts to work within them, the fiscal crisis may have some redeeming urban value. It will, for example, give the cities an opportunity to reassess their priorities, and perhaps more important, to consider whether their programs have been getting enough bang for the bucks expended on them; to consider in other words, whether the problem is *really* money, or merely that dollars have come to represent a relatively easy way to measure both program commitment and performance. It is no coincidence that a resurgent concern for "productivity" began first in New York City. Cities seem to spend more and get less from their service institutions; perhaps the fiscal crisis provides an opportunity to reconsider the basic causes of the urban condition and to reconsider viable alternatives to those institutions responsible for such areas as education, health, neighborhood renewal and civic order. Such an effort is encouraged by the new fiscal limits and politically possible because of the concurrent appraisals being made of our urban institutions, both public and private.

Absent a massive New Deal-like urban bailout by the federal or state governments, urban politics of the late 70s and into the 80s might well require a decrease in urban dependency on external resources and force a consideration of "do-it-yourselves or else" strategies.[29] The politics of reconstituting the community to accommodate new fiscal limits and to approximate old life-style standards represents another dimension of the transfiguration of urban politics and policy.

It is a commonplace of the urbanism literature that cities have always been at the cutting edge of American social change. In an era of *Limits to Growth*, cities will presumably be the first elements of the society to experience such limits.[30] Reviewing New York City's peculiar fiscal plight, Irving Kristol was moved to remark that "New York symbolizes a scaling-down of services, in all of our institutions, which have been inflated to an extraordinary degree."[31] In this volume, Haider analyzes the grinding fiscal constraints on the American city and assesses the New York experience in light of some critical demographic and economic processes affecting urban governance.

### The Rise of the New Urban Governors and the Demise of Legitimacy

Cities have not, in recent years, behaved as though there were impending limits on growth. To the contrary, urban costs, taxes and budgets have increased more rapidly than the growth of the Gross National Product. It is well known that a large share of these increases have been prompted and absorbed by the growing service bureaucracies in urban governments. These are the institutions which Theodore Lowi once labeled the "new machines."[32] Contrasting them with the old machines, he suggested that the new ones nonetheless shared certain features in common with their predecessors. They were relatively irresponsible centers of power, insulated from the direct control of mayors and councils and the indirect power of citizens. The contemporary city has thus become the "bureaucratic city state," which was, Lowi suggested, "well run but badly governed."

Such a dominance by professional, bureaucratic regimes was, to be sure, the logical outgrowth of the triumph of the reformist paradigm. If there was neither a Republican nor a Democratic way to pave a street (or collect garbage or teach children to read or fight crime), there was presumably a *right* way to do it. Unfortunately, it is no longer entirely clear that cities, whether governable or not, are even well run. When Louis Harris surveyed a sample of the population for the Senate Committee on Government Operations to ascertain confidence levels in basic institutions, local governments ranked sixteenth out of twenty-two.[33] Considerable survey evidence exists at the local level to show that citizens perceive the quality of urban services as deteriorating. Douglas Yates, writing of the principal changes in the urban political climate, remarks that

> Now that the urban crisis has been discovered, debated and in some quarters dismissed, government officials and academic analysts have increasingly come to focus on "service delivery" as the central issue and problem of urban policy . . . delivery is itself highly interesting . . . . For one thing, it is difficult to see how a government can solve its dramatic problems if it cannot solve its routine ones.[34]

Recent social science has supported vague citizen suspicions that the best-laid schemes of policy makers frequently go awry. The assault upon the educational system is perhaps the most well known.[35] But the discovery that policing and law enforcement resources may have little to do with crime, citizen attitudes or civic order is equally troubling.[36] And the accumulating literature on the difficulty of "policy implementation" suggests that the slippage between policy intent and policy actualization is often great.[37] Given the thrust of research findings about the state of the city, it is little wonder that citizen attitudes toward urban governance have become more hostile. The outcroppings of this demise of legitimacy are evident in the near-impossibility of passing tax increases and even once-sancrosanct school referenda, in the short life span of urban mayors, and in the continued rumblings of neighborhood political action groups.

The challenge to the legitimacy and effectiveness of urban governance is perhaps the most profound transformation in urban politics and the one whose implications are most difficult to explain. It is most certainly the principal ingredient which makes the new urban politics different from the old.

## NOTES

1. George Sternlieb, "The City as Sandbox," *The Public Interest,* 25 (Fall, 1971), pp. 14–21.

2. Norton Long, "The City as Reservation," *The Public Interest,* 25 (Fall,

1971), pp. 22–38. But see also Alexander Ganz and Thomas O'Brien, "The City: Sandbox, Reservation, or Dynamo?" *Public Policy,* 21 (Winter, 1973), pp. 107–123.

3. Edward C. Banfield, *Unheavenly City* (Boston: Little, Brown, 1968).

4. Thomas Kuhn, *The Structure of Scientific Revolutions* (Chicago: University of Chicago Press, 1962).

5. Floyd Hunter, *Community Power Structure* (Chapel Hill: University of North Carolina Press, 1953).

6. Robert Dahl, *Who Governs?* (New Haven: Yale University Press, 1961).

7. Diana Crane, *Invisible Colleges* (Chicago: University of Chicago Press, 1972).

8. Lawrence Herson, "The Lost World of Municipal Government," *American Political Science Review,* 51 (June, 1957), pp. 330–345.

9. Edward C. Banfield and James Q. Wilson, *City Politics* (Cambridge: Harvard University Press, 1963).

10. James Q. Wilson and Edward C. Banfield, "Public-Regardingness as a Value Premise in Voting Behavior," *American Political Science Review,* 58 (December, 1964), pp. 876–887; "Political Ethos Revisited," *American Political Science Review,* 65 (December, 1971), pp. 1048–1062.

11. Robert C. Wood, "The Contributions of Political Science to Urban Form," in Werner Z. Hirsch, ed., *Urban Life and Form* (New York: Holt, Rinehart and Winston, 1963), p.122.

12. Banfield, *Unheavenly City.*

13. See the discussion in James C. Charlesworth, ed., *Integration of the Social Sciences through Policy Analysis,* monograph 14 (Philadelphia: American Academy of Political and Social Science, 1972).

14. See, however, the collection of papers in Robert L. Lineberry and Louis H. Masotti, eds., *Urban Problems and Public Policy* (Lexington, Mass.: D.C. Heath, Lexington Books, 1975).

15. Oliver P. Williams, *Metropolitan Political Analysis* (New York: The Free Press, 1971); Clifford Kaufman, "Political Urbanism: Urban Spatial Organization, Policy and Politics," *Urban Affairs Quarterly,* 9 (June, 1974), pp. 421–436.

16. Kevin Cox, *Conflict, Power and Politics in the City* (New York: McGraw-Hill, 1973); David Harvey, *Social Justice and the City* (Baltimore: Johns Hopkins University Press, 1973); David M. Smith, "Who Gets What Where and How: A Welfare Focus for Human Geography," *Geography,* 59 (November, 1974), pp. 289–297.

17. See e.g., the papers in C. G. Pickvance, ed., *Urban Sociology: Critical Essays* (London: Methuen, 1976), and the papers by Pickvance, Castells and Walton in John Walton and Louis H. Masotti, eds., *The City in Comparative Perspective* (Beverly Hills, Calif.: Sage Publications, Inc., 1976).

18. Harvey, *Social Justice and the City.*

19. Edward C. Banfield, *The Unheavenly City Revisited* (Boston: Little, Brown, 1974), p. 78.

20. "The Urban Crisis: Who Got What and Why" in Robert Paul Wolff, ed.,

*1984 Revisited* (New York: Alfred A. Knopf, 1973), p. 175. Emphasis in the original.

21. John K. Galbraith, *The Affluent Society* (New York: New American Library, 1958), p. 72.

22. S.M. Miller and Pamela Roby, *The Future of Inequality* (New York: Basic Books, 1970).

23. Christopher Jencks et al., *Inequality: A Reassessment of the Effect of Family and Schooling in America* (New York: Basic Books, 1972).

24. On the issue of service equity and distribution see Frank S. Levy, Arnold J. Meltsner and Aaron Wildavsky, *Urban Outcomes: Schools, Streets, and Libraries* (Berkeley: University of California Press, 1974); Robert L. Lineberry, "Mandating Urban Equality: The Distribution of Municipal Public Services," *Texas Law Review,* 53 (December, 1974), pp. 26–59; and Miller and Roby, chap. 5.

25. Oliver Williams, "Life Style Values and Political Decentralization in Metropolitan Areas," *Social Science Quarterly,* 48 (December, 1967), p. 299.

26. See e.g., Alan Altshuler, *Community Control* (New York: Pegasus, 1970); and Milton Kotler, *Neighborhood Government* (Indianapolis: Bobbs-Merrill, 1969).

27. Richard L. Cole, *Citizen Participation and the Urban Policy Process* (Lexington, Mass.: D.C. Heath, 1974).

28. Robert L. Bish and Vincent Ostrom, *Understanding Urban Government: Metropolitan Reform Reconsidered* (Washington: American Enterprise Institute for Public Policy Research, 1973).

29. Thus a *New York Magazine* editorial (November 17, 1975, pp. 48–49), optimistically suggested that New Yorkers should mobilize themselves "to assume—voluntarily—public responsibilities for which there is no money."

30. Donella Meadows et al., *The Limits to Growth* (New York: Universe Books, 1971).

31. Irving Kristol, quoted in the *New York Times,* December 29, 1975, p. 42.

32. Theodore Lowi, "Machine Politics—Old and New," *The Public Interest,* (Fall, 1967), pp. 83–92.

33. Louis Harris, "Confidence and Concern: Citizens View American Government," a report of the Subcommittee on Intergovernmental Relations of the Committee on Government Operations, United States Senate, December 3, 1973, pp. 37–38.

34. Douglas Yates, "Service Delivery and the Urban Political Order," in Willis D. Hawley and David Rogers, eds., *Improving the Quality of Urban Management* (Beverly Hills, Calif.: Sage Publications, Inc., 1974), p. 213.

35. See Jencks, *Inequality.*

36. See the experimental analysis of police patrol practices in *The Kansas City Preventive Patrol Experiment: A Summary Report* (Washington, D.C.: The Police Foundation, 1974).

37. Jeffrey Pressman and Aaron Wildavsky, *Implementation* (Berkeley: University of California Press, 1973).

Part One

# Reconceptualizing Urban Politics

Chapter One

# Class Capacity and Social Cohesion in American Cities

IRA KATZNELSON

On the eve of capitalist industrialization, English literature maintained a rigid distinction between the processes of rural exploitation—which were dissolved in idyllic portraits of landscapes and green fields—and urban wickedness. The country was innocent and sublime; the city was the dwelling-place of iniquity of all kinds, including moral and material cupidity.[1]

This portrait, of course, was a mystification. The 17th and 18th century English town was the agent and the reflection of a mode of production still predominantly rural. This kind of artificial divide continues to haunt us still, and in so doing tends to promote only partial interpretations of urban realities. In ordinary discourse and in too many scholarly presentations, the city continues to be portrayed as the locale of a myriad of social ills, as if these shortcomings were uniquely or inherently urban and as if cities and their problems were not condensed versions of the relations that characterize the society as a whole.

The city, including its politics, is not a thing in itself that can be studied in a contextual and relational vacuum. Cities may be the loci of distinctive patterns of action, but by themselves they do not provide a sufficient frame of analysis. From this starting point, this essay examines two periods of social unrest in American cities—the transformation of the Eastern port cities from a predominantly mercantile to industrial base in the years preceding the Civil War, and the era of intense racial conflict in the 1960s, when the same cities were losing their major industrial functions. In both periods major innovations in urban institutional forms were attempted. The essay thus explores the impact of

This essay's discussion of "class capacity" benefitted from the discussion of a working paper at the Institute for Policy Studies in May 1975. Especially helpful were critical comments by Nancy Hartsock and Alan Wolfe.—I.K.

*19*

these innovations on urban social cohesion; to do so, it first discusses a number of shortcomings in the ways liberal and Marxist scholarship have addressed problems of social control and suggests ways of conceptualizing matters of social control as issues of competing class capacities.

## Class Capacities

Conceptually, we are concerned with how to approach the study of social control, and in so doing to contribute to developing work on the state. Taken on its own terms, the liberal sociological tradition which portrays matters of social control in terms of the clash between the thoughts and actions of free and equal *individuals* and the imperative of social order at the level of *society* is terribly constrained by its failure to specify the place of individuals (and clusters of individuals) *in* society. As George Gurvich has noted, the liberal approach sees order and social reality itself "in a nominalistic way, as rather an assemblage of isolated individuals, whose connection and emergence in a whole stems from social control."[2] Since the approach lacks a convincing theory of social structure and of the material bases of social and political behavior, the liberal literature on social control has tended, normatively, to assert the paramount importance of order and, scientifically, to reify society and leave unexamined the sources of threat to social cohesion.

Park and Burgess, for example, who self-consciously linked their work on the city to questions of order, saw social control as "the central fact and the central problem of sociology," which they viewed as "a point of view and a method for investigating the process by which individuals are induced to cooperate in some sort of permanent corporate existence we call society."[3] But, as Marx usefully cautioned, it is an illusion to portray "society" or "population" as concrete entities without much further specification:

> The population is an abstraction if I leave out, for example, the classes of which it is composed. These classes, in turn, are an empty phrase if I am not familiar with the elements on which they rest. E.g. wage labour, capital, etc. . . . Thus if I were to begin with the population, this would be a chaotic conception of the whole.[4]

At a minimum, the analysis of social control depends on a prior conceptualization of the concrete elements and relations of "society." To the question, "whose control?" the answer, "society's" hardly suffices, since the calculus of cohesion is one of the social relations between corporate constituents of the social structure.

Since Max Weber's concern in this regard is with how a market capitalist society can cohere in the face of profound distributional inequalities, his work on social control is much more illuminating than that of his American interpreters. He made an important distinction between the agents and the mechanisms of control; and he recognized that power and authority relations are instrumental *and* imperative, integrative *and* coercive at the same time.[5] Nevertheless, Weber's work (as well as that of some of his most prominent interpreters) is constrained by its emphasis on authority relationships as things in themselves.[6] As a result, it often eludes issues of the social and material bases of authority.

A complementary shortcoming has characterized much Marxist work on politics and social cohesion (or, perhaps more precisely, the absence of such work). Whereas liberal scholars have often neglected to specify concretely the constituent and relational elements of society, many Marxists have collapsed matters of social control and the state into a rather mechanical class analysis. Too often, as Theda Skocpol has emphasized in her critique of Barrington Moore, " 'Ruling class' explanations . . . tend to argue from class interests to intentions to political outcomes," while missing the point that political arrangements may act as independent constraints on the capacity of a dominant class (or subordinate class) to realize its interests.[7] Thus Poulantzas defines political power as "the *capacity* of a class to realize specific objective interests."[8]

This formulation provides the potential to connect the structural and the volitional in political analysis and to integrate a Weberian agenda into an essentially Marxist analysis of society. For at any given moment the political capacity of a class to secure its interests depends not only on its position with respect to production and on the nature and scope of the contradictions generated by the accumulation process, but also on the heritage of previous political decisions (the English gentry of 1832, for example, was ill-placed to resist reform precisely because its victory in the 17th century had produced a weak central state), the relative capacities of competing ideologies and meaning systems, available mechanisms of physical coercion, and the pattern of political institutionalization by which subordinate and dominant classes are connected. It is in this sense that I have argued elsewhere that

the social control apparatus of the society may be conceptualized as an interlocking set of coercive, symbolic and institutional buffers which soften the impact of basic social contradictions and which induce or compel people to act against their interests (often by not acting at all). In a capitalist political economy, stability, in this view, does not imply the absence of structurally rooted conflicts, but reflects the operation of the buffering mechanisms that shape and limit behavior. The state's function of social control consists in managing the consequences of making capitalism work, and can best be understood as an attempt to manage but not overcome the contradictions of the capitalist system.[9]

The dimensions of social control, seen this way, are neither givens nor outcomes but parts of an ongoing process. The state is not simply the instrument of a dominant class that always prevails or the carrier of the structural imperatives of capital for accumulation and reproduction.[10] Because of the degree of structural autonomy the state has from the economy, and because the liberal state confers citizenship to all the population within its territorial and authoritative embrace, class conflict occurs in distinctive ways within the state in the form of competing class capacities. Anderson and Friedland's formulation is appealing: it is in the interest of the dominant classes to utilize the state to increasingly socialize the operation of the economy (while keeping its fruits in private hands) without socializing political control; conversely, it is in the interest of the relatively subordinate to maximize their political capacities in order to socialize political authority to be able to transform structural economic relations.[11]

The terms of the process of the clash of competing political class capacities, moreover, are established by the scope, activities and institutions of the state. The regulation of aggregate consumer demand by the use of Keynesian economic tools, for example, has contributed mightily to the politicization of issues concerning the distribution of income and wealth. The development of welfare-state programs has produced a politics of bureau-client antagonism. The ward organization of cities provided an important basis for the emergence of ethnic groups as local interest groups. But while these definitions and forms of conflict are distinctive, they revolve directly around the cohesion of the social order and hence the reproduction of capital itself. For this reason the analysis of the politics of social control in terms of competing class capacities provides compelling mediating bridges between the liberal and Marxist traditions of social analysis.

**Agendas of Control**

Since states everywhere try to make their economies grow (if only to secure sufficient revenues to reproduce the state itself), and since capitalist states can only do so by reproducing capital, it follows that the state is of necessity heavily implicated in the maintenance and reproduction of contradictory class relations. From this point of departure, much of the developing Marxist work on the state has given content to functionalist approaches by defining "function" with regard to the reproduction of the forces and social relations of capitalist production.[12] The two fundamental functions of the state are thus those of accumulation (making the economy work) and cohesion (securing the order necessary for accumulation). This approach suggests a vast research agenda, of which the study of urban politics is a part: the analysis of the precise and concrete functioning of these functions.

Since urban social peace contributes to the reproduction of the capitalist order, an analysis of the processes of social control in American cities is a study of competing class capacities in the state. And since managing discontent is widely acknowledged to be a major task of municipal government, we can address the issues of class capacity by exploring the urban political terrain of social control.[13]

While the mechanisms of cohesion may be distinctively local, the agenda of social control is posed in the first instance by factors and relationships which transcend the city. The most important of these largely external factors is the nature and direction of development of the national economy, and the place of the city within it. In the two decades preceding the Civil War, the port cities of Boston, Baltimore, New York and Philadelphia grew explosively and were fundamentally transformed in character under the impact of the shift from an economy dominated by merchant capital to one increasingly under the hegemony of industrial capital. While these cities were at the very core of the process of rapid economic development, they paradoxically found themselves palpably caught in a nexus of forces over which they had little control. In the shift from mercantile to industrial capital, the largest cities of the period lost the sense that they were in control of their fates.

The developing mode of production caused basic changes in their spatial configurations. Although most offices and large factories were yet to come, by 1860 the cities were unmistakably divided into distinctive districts of work and home. No longer a single social, functional or spatial community, the emerging industrial city contained a mosaic of residence communities defined by space, class, ethnicity and race. The strains of the transition were experienced in both the workplace and in class and ethnic specific residence communities in distinctive ways, thus setting the period's agenda of social control.

There was much agitation in the factories, especially by former artisans resisting the devaluation of their labor. The creation of citywide union federations in New York, Baltimore, Philadelphia and Boston in the 1830s; the rapid increase in union membership in the face of legal constraints; the large number of strikes in the period—including a general strike in Philadelphia in 1835; and the establishment of significant workingmen's parties attest to the intensity of the tensions generated by the transformation.

As capitalist development also entailed the segmentation of work from residence, the new realities were experienced in terms of ethnic and racial conflicts over scarce space as well. German and Irish immigrants became the tangible symbols of the shift to the dominance of industrial capital. Native born protestant artisans who had the most to lose expressed their rebellion at the community level by resisting residential incursions. The result was much bloody disorder—between nativists and immigrants, protestants and catholics, blacks and whites. In Philadelphia, as in the other merchant port cities, social peace remained precarious throughout this period. In May and July of 1844 Philadelphia was shaken by particularly intensive rioting that brought about a virtual collapse of public order. After still another riot—this time racial in content—in 1849, the city's businessmen and lawyers held a meeting whose chairman, a former mayor, put the case for a reorganization of the city's boundaries, institutions, and political arrangements: "We have a common interest to protect life and property . . . it has been also been made manifest that our property is not secure . . . property is rendered valueless, comparatively speaking, by popular outbreaks and riots."[14] Though community-based violence was not directed against the ruling classes, it tangibly threatened their interests.

The social control agenda of cities in the 1960s and 1970s has largely been posed by the uneven material and spatial development of American capitalism. Since the Second World War, the boundaries of a dual economy (and related dual labor markets) divided between behemoth firms of large capital concentrations employing roughly a third of the workforce and approximately 12 million small capital firms employing still another third of American workers (either the state at all levels or state-dependent industries like defense employing the rest) have developed with remarkable clarity as the cumulative qualitative impact of uneven development has yielded qualitative results. Aided by the state, the primary sector of large capital has grown relatively richer and the small capital sector poorer as those who control the investment of capital have reinvested in products, machinery, workers and geographic areas that yield the highest returns.[15] As production has been increasingly deconcentrated to the suburbs (New York City alone has lost 300,000 manufacturing jobs since 1970), the bureaucratic conception functions of management have been increasingly concentrated in a small number of significant downtown cores. For this reason, the very large city remains functionally important for capital. But the private production economy and labor markets of the city increasingly have become those of the declining small capital sector.

Most of the social problems of American cities are the result of this process of uneven development. As the cities have become the repositories of the small capital sector work force (most of whom are poor and black or Hispanic), they have also become the locales of poverty-related substantive problems like crime, drugs, educational difficulties and severe health pathologies. All have to be dealt with by city governments, yet all are quite obviously generated by causes external to the cities in which their impact is felt.

These contextual economic realities provide the predisposing conditions, if not always the actual triggering events, for urban unrest. In the past fifteen years the community, not the workplace, has been the principal locus of urban political action. The main target has been the state; particularly the service bureaucracies which deal directly with captive clienteles.[16] And the issues have largely been those posed by an economy increasingly dominated by private small capital (and by government employment)—the collective consumption of housing, schools, education, health care and justice. The recent agenda of urban social control has been set by four overlapping and distinctive clusters of activity. First, and most visible, is remarkable black political ferment; second, ethnic groups act assertively on behalf of an agenda of neighborhood stabilization and preservation; third, patterns of conflict have emerged between mayors who have fashioned pro-growth coalitions and anti-growth alliances which have resisted such programs as urban renewal and expressway construction; and, fourth, the 1960s witnessed a dramatic increase in the pattern of municipal employee behavior Margaret Levi calls bureaucratic insurgency.[17]

Thus there are clear similarities, if also obvious differences, between the two periods. Both were eras of rapid change in the place of the city with respect to the developing national political economy. In both, large sectors of the cities' population experienced and/or perceived either a decline in their relative economic position personally, or with respect to significant others. In both, as well, discontent was lived and resisted not just at the workplace, but in ascriptive and spatial terms as well. In both periods, in short, the political topography within cities came to have less to do with substantive problem-solving, and more to do with managing, controlling and defusing discontent.

### The Franchise of
### Political Incorporation

These agendas of social control may usefully be seen as condensed and intensified moments of the central problem of social cohesion facing liberal capitalist democracies. Order in such societies must be fashioned in spite of the wide distance between formal legal equality (citizenship and the franchise) and the structural inequities produced by the routine operation of the economic system. Managing this task of cohesion is one of the principal functions of the liberal state.

The franchise itself, of course, has been a central means of managing the problem of order. Its exercise defines the political (as distinct from the economic or social) community. Nineteenth century western European politics, for example focused on this problem of definition. At stake was the issue of whether capitalism could be made stable.

Ironically, the expansion of legal rights and equality had made workers terribly vulnerable to exploitation. Freedom from feudal fetters was also the freedom to enter into wage contracts without the traditional paternal protections. For this reason, civil rights are essential to a market economy. The equality of citizenship generally followed the equality of contract. After the French Revolution made the individual voting citizen the unit of representation, politics came to be defined in both its peaceful and violent moments as a set of strategies about political incorporation. "The critical political problem," Bendix has noted, "was whether and to what extent social protest would be accommodated through the extension of citizenship to the lower classes." Established elites feared the franchise, but were also attracted by its possibilities for "strengthening the powers of the nation-state through the mobilization of the working-class in its service."[18]

The politics of incorporation by franchise by focusing on legal as opposed to economic citizenship, had primarily conservative consequences. Indeed, 19th Century European history may be read from one vantage point as the history of a strategy of managed incorporation. The franchise was expanded in fits and starts; expansion was accompanied into the 20th Century by elaborate property, household and residence criteria. The century was marked by a wide array of transitional compromises:

> The basic strategy was to underscore the structural differentiation within the wage-earning strata. Some varieties of *regime censitaire* in fact admitted the better paid wage workers, particularly if they had houses of their own. The householder and lodger franchise in Britain similarly served to integrate the better-off working class within the system and to keep out only the 'real proletariat,' migrants and marginal workers without established local ties.[19]

In the United States in the two decades before the Civil War these elite strategies of gradual incorporation as tools of social control were not available as a result of the earlier universalization of white male suffrage. The battleground of competing class capacities thus had to do not with the extension of formal citizenship but with the management of the contradiction between formal and substantive citizenship.[20] This feature of the polity has been a centerpiece of the recent "urban crisis" as well.

The dual challenge to the social order of the mid 19th Century of work and community conflicts called into question the political capacity of mercantile and industrial capital to rule. As the traditional urban politics of mercantile vs. mechanic interests broke down, urban economic elites in the older cities sought to organize the emerging politics of race and ethnicity to domesticate it and render it predictable. In outline, their response was twofold. They withdrew from the direct governance of their cities and sponsored emerging machine politicians who could organize the political potential of congestion in the cities' new working-class ethnic communities; and they created a new polity at the municipal level. Cities were consolidated, modern police forces and educational bureaucracies created. It is reasonable to conclude that from the outset modern urban politics has been a politics of social control.

Let us explore this process of genesis and its consequences in more detail. The process of urban institutionalization of the period was directed self-consciously to contribute to the cohesion of the new capitalist order by providing for coherent and predictable channels for the expression of discontent and for political bargaining. These goals required the emergence of the specialist politician as well as the development of new mass party linkages at the urban level. The first was facilitated by the thrust of national economic forces; the second by the creation of a new national party system.

From the Revolution into the age of Jackson, most cities were ruled by unified anglo-protestant merchant elite. These gentlemen-politicians correctly saw their cities as pivotal politico-economic units. Indeed, as Richard Wade has stressed, the cities were in incessant competition with each other for the expansion and control of markets.[21] With the transition to an industrial base, local elites found themselves increasingly at odds with each other, as more and more entrepreneurs found their primary reference group among industrialists—including those in other cities—rather than in a shared local elite community.[22] Moreover, both business and governmental affairs became too demanding to be worked at part time. This was particularly the case as cities expanded their boundaries and created new service-bureaucracies to cope with the emerging social stresses of the time. In Cleveland, for example,

> in 1850, the City was spending about three times as much as it had spent in 1837, the year of its incorporation. The 1860 expenditures were seven times those of 1850 and the 1870 expenditures were again seven times those of 1860. Even in this broad way, we can be sure sure that it was no longer quite so easy to play politics with one hand and expect to have a truly major influence.[23]

Perhaps even more to the point is the fact that the old protestant elite simply could not directly manage the new patterns of corrosive ethnic conflict. Their withdrawal from city politics to make way for the ethnic political specialist was thus doubly self-interested. The rewards of money lay with private capital; and social cohesion depended on the forging of new mass links which they could not themselves fashion. The result may well have been, as Dahl has stressed, the democratization of elite recruitment; but the substantive impact was the encapsulation of urban conflict within the embrace of a new city politics that protected capital.[24]

The landmark Chambers-Burnham volume on American parties stresses that historians and social scientists focus too often on individual parties and on contests between parties. Instead, it treats the party system of a given period as the critical unit of analysis. Within this frame of reference, there were two main party systems in the United States before the Civil War. The first lasted only to the mid-1820s (and had severely deteriorated by 1815). The second party system, of which the creation of early urban machines was a part, had its origins in the presidential election of 1824 and reached its full competitive dimensions in 1840.[25] Its hallmarks were a significant expansion in the franchise (as well as turnout rates), the replacement of caucus nomination procedures for president by conventions, and elaborate *decentralized* party organizations with a high degree of uniformity in both major parties and in all sections. Though this party system could not contain the conflicting interests that produced the Civil War, it did innovate ways of making mass suffrage compatible with an order of increasing substantive inequalities by institutionalizing, channeling and socializing "conflict over the control of the regime."[26]

The parties which emerged at the national level were electoral organizations rather than policy-interested associations. And in this period there were suddenly many more electoral opportunities around which to mobilize voters. Among other relevant changes, there were the popular election of governors and presidential electors, the rapid increase in the number of locally elected officials, the creation of small voting districts, the adoption of printed ballots, and the consolidation of elections on a single day.

Quite obviously, the development of early local party machines was facilitated by these national-party and procedural changes. In turn, the character of local machines helped shape and reinforce emerging national party patterns. For though part of a national apparatus, the machines were *local* institutions. The importance of the municipal level of the American federal system is the direct result of what Huntington has labeled the Tudor inheritance.[27] The differentiation of American political authority is unique in the West; this tendency, as Lowi has noted, is reinforced by the interests of state and local party politicians who use the nodal points of the federal system to aggregate local power to become significant national political actors.[28]

The machines replicated this pattern in microcosm at the local level. They were instruments for the selective centralization *and* decentralization of politics and governance. They combined a centralized locus of control with decentralized particularistic political bonds.[29] This combination significantly increased the political capacities of dominant urban classes in the mid 19th Century, and beyond. At the city level of policymaking, the machines used their power to ride with, rather than challenge, the configurations of social and economic forces they found. Not only did the machines insulate the policy process from locally based conflicts, they were involved in the elaboration of the modern urban polity whose principal bureaucratic elements included new citywide modern police forces and primary schools for the masses—the two most consequential urban agencies of social control. And, of course, machines distributed significant economic favors to businessmen in the form of licenses, contracts and tax breaks.

At the local level of mass linkage, the machines also contributed to a definition and practice of local politics that helped cement the new order. The machines stressed ethnicity, not class; community, not work; concrete rewards, not ideology. They exercised their social control function over their followers by organizing both the input and output sides of politics; they provided the only coherent direct access links to government, and acted as the key distributor of political rewards.

The consequences were shifts in the definition and expectations of public policy, and the disaggregation of conflict. As David Protess has argued, a major hallmark of party machines is that they facilitate the expression of potentially explosive redistributive issues in distributive terms; a machine city is "a local polity whose political actors expect almost all political policies which affect it to have a distributive impact; i.e., to be convertible to patronage."[30] In this way, basic social conflicts could be made functional in systemic terms.[31]

Perhaps even more important, the emergence of machines facilitated the continued political separation of work and community. In Europe, by the late 19th Century, mass working class parties of differing ideological hues self-consciously linked the two domains in their appeal. By contrast, the spatial and ethnic bases of machine politics made the machines the adversaries of socialist and laborist parties. In the 1830s and 1840s they were opponents of local workingmens' parties. Later, when unions sought to create local political instruments of their own, as in the New York mayoral election in 1886, the machines usually opposed them with success.

## New Linkages

Writing in the late 1930s, Gosnell sought to construct a balance sheet of machine politics. In the midst of the century's major crisis of the capitalist order, he found that in Chicago the machine was a vital element in the maintenance of social cohesion:

> From the standpoint of the business leaders, this function of parties has been very useful. Some of the submerged groups may not be so appreciative; but the fact remains that during the years 1930–36 the city was comparatively free from violent labor disputes, hunger riots and class warfare. The decentralized, chaotic, and inadequate character of the governmental organization of the city has discouraged far-reaching demands upon local authorities.[32]

In the Chicago of the 1960s as well, the machine proved a useful instrument of social cohesion. But in most cities, where the mass linkage features of machine politics had withered away, local governing elites were not so insulated.[33] Rather, they had to manage the social peace largely within an institutional context that actually exacerbated urban conflict.

The shift in the locus of urban power in the vast majority of older American cities to service bureaucracies weakened the social control position of authorities, for unlike the machines bureaucratic control mechanisms deal only with the output side of politics. They have taken over the machines' functions of distributing services and benefits without assuming the control function of the organization of participation in politics. Moreover, the bureaucracies themselves became basic causes and targets of urban discontent. As Michael Lipsky has stressed, contacts between clients and street-level bureaucrats (teachers, policemen, social workers, nurses, clerks, lower court judges) are fraught with tension.[34] This process of interaction has taken on a dynamic of its own that has enlarged the urban agenda of social control, and in so doing has threatened dominant class capacities.

Urban authorities have responded in two principal ways: by utilizing the available mechanisms of bureaucratic control (including police repression) and by attempting to create functional substitutes for the largely defunct political machines.

Like the party organizations they have come to replace, bureaucratic agencies yield up a whole variety of benefits, and, as Francis Piven has stressed,

> it is by distributing, redistributing and adapting these payoffs that urban political leaders manage to keep peace and build allegiances among diverse groups in the city. In other words, the jobs, contracts, perquisites, as well as the actual services of the municipal housekeeping agencies are just as much the grist of urban politics as they ever were.[35]

The costs of maintaining urban cohesion this way, reflected in the rapidly escalated welfare expenditures and budgets for the salaries of municipal workers in the last fifteen years, have been very high. The most dramatic outcome has been a serious financial crisis in virtually all American cities, most notably, of course, in New York.

The second response in cities marked by the atrophy of party mechanisms of control has been the creation of new participatory mechanisms to anchor and canalize discontent. Indeed, only ten years ago, a whole genre of urban institutions was virtually unknown. Today, little city halls, offices of neighborhood government, community planning boards, decentralized school boards and neighborhood service delivery cabinets are visible features of the urban political landscapes of Boston, Los Angeles, Houston, New York, Columbus and numerous other large cities. How have these new institutions altered the existing web of social and political relationships between public officials and neighborhood residents?

Since the Lindsay administration's institutional innovations in this regard were the nation's most extensive, let us explore this question in the case of New York. "What we saw in early 1966," Lindsay has written,

> was that within the ghetto discontent and alienation were at the breaking point. We saw that a basic commitment to ending that alienation through greater contact was essential. And we knew that words alone would not do the job. . . . Thus, throughout the fall of 1966 and into the spring of 1967 we made plans for a structured, formal link between the neighborhoods and the city.[36]

By 1970, New York had a decentralized structure of elected school boards, a citywide program of Community Planning Boards with advisory powers over land use decisions and, in some neighborhoods, the rudiments of a new multifunctional government, the Neighborhood Action Program. Taken collectively, they performed much as the traditional machines did. They divided arenas of conflict from each other, and they came to define politics in distributional terms.

Judged in terms of the city's educational establishment as a whole, the local school boards had limited powers. The most consequential policy decisions remained centralized. But from the vantage point of competing class capacities, the boards' major functions were never intended to be those of policy. They disaggregated conflict by providing thirty-two, rather than one, foci of protest. In many districts, school board meetings were regularly marked by disruption, including physical violence. But the central board and bureaucracy were now able to proceed in an atmosphere of relative calm. Moreover, from the perspective of neighborhood politics, the local boards have loomed large. In a reform city, they have shifted considerable patronage opportunities (hiring nonprofessional staff, influencing the selection of some teachers and supervisory personnel) to visible neighborhood units. In this way, the volatility of school conflicts has been softened by a redefinition of their content. This feature of urban politics, of course, was a major hallmark of the machine.

The impact of the Neighborhood Action Programs proved much the same, if more ephemeral. In mid-1970, the Lindsay administration began to set up pilot programs of political decentralization in selected planning districts. Under the terms of the program, a local storefront office was established in each affected neighborhood to assist residents in their dealing with city agencies. Area executive directors, appointed by the mayor, headed these offices, and developed community advisory committees in the major policy areas of safety, education, health, housing, etc. to draw up capital budget proposals to be financed from annual allocations of approximately $500,000 to each district. As in the case of the school board, from a city perspective these funds were paltry indeed; for the neighborhood, the funds were large enough to produce competing claimants.

With the election of Mayor Beame, the neighborhood government programs of the Lindsay years were terminated. The new mayor, a product of the Brooklyn regular clubhouses, viewed the program as a threat to the remaining weak Democratic party organizations in the area. Although its life was rather brief, the Neighborhood Action Program did illustrate that very small sums of money and the form of representation at the local level (even where it lacked mass roots and substantive powers of major consequence) were sufficient to engage large numbers of people in the activities of writing grant proposals, preparing budgetary requests, testifying before committees and lobbying neighborhood officials. These activities, which cost individuals and groups much time and effort, complemented the disaggregative impact the school boards had on city unrest. The politics of neighborhood life were defined distributionally; and the targets of distributional demands were now in the neighborhoods, not downtown.

## Context and Consequences

While there may be important scholarly debate as to whether machines have actually withered away, there can be no doubt that the institutional solutions of the mid-19th Century to the problem of order in developing capitalist cities— geographical consolidation, the creation of municipal police and education bureaucracies, and the fashioning of party machines—largely succeeded for over a century in maximizing the class capacities of dominant local and national elites. The bureaucratic and participatory elite solutions of the past two decades are not likely to endure in the same fashion. The reasons have less to do with specifically urban factors as with contextual economic and political realities.

The Nineteenth Century political formula was nurtured by supportive national party arrangements and, more important, by the dynamism of the developing capitalist economy. To be sure, the process of capitalist development itself gave rise to the most pressing urban problems of cohesion; but the very bounty of the process made distributional solutions to redistributive problems possible. The bountiful patronage as well as the rakeoffs of the Tweed ring in New York, for example, hinged on the city's ability to sell bonds in the United States and abroad to finance extensive public improvements and extensions of Manhattan's street grid. In this enterprise Tweed had the support of local entrepreneurs and workers alike, as each group shared in the bounty. And even after the fall of Tweed (whose graft, once exposed, compelled bankers to refuse to extend further credit to the city), following a brief period of local austerity, the dynamics of rapid growth reasserted themselves. With the new bounty of capital and jobs, Tammany emerged even more strongly as a coordinated, centralized, integrative political force. At least until the New Deal, the machines fattened on what seemed to be the unceasing growth of private capital; and with private capital, the great cities of the day.

In more general terms, the most efficient way for the state to secure the social peace, if not the willing obedience of its citizens, is to make the accumulation process work. As Charles Maier has observed about the period after the Second World War, "Growth served as the great conservative idea for a generation: conservative in that it forstalled claims for redistribution on the left or an authoritarian search for power on the part of the right."[37] But as the American dual economy has developed, the cities have become the major losers even in periods of sustained high rates of economic growth (a situation that now seems less and less likely to be renewed without the costs of severe inflation). For this reason, social cohesion in cities—and the urban dynamic of competing class capacities—must be increasingly secured by mechanisms segmented from the direct logic of accumulation, and by programs no longer supported by bounty of growth.

The results are easy to discern. The social control agenda for elites continues to increase, yet existing forms of response themselves become sources of instability and contradiction. Bureaucratic distributive strategies have produced major fiscal dilemmas because of the declining place of the cities within the national economy. And the available solutions to these growing fiscal problems are stopgaps at best, and in the longer run contribute to the declining place of older cities. Raising tax revenues locally to pay for the strategy of bureaucratic distribution provides incentives for individuals and firms who can afford to do so to move out of the cities to escape onerous tax burdens. State and federal aid has not kept up with the rate of increase in the size of municipal deficits, and is even less likely to do so in the future. Borrowing to pay expenses is at best a short-term expedient, and a long-term recipe for financial collapse. Moreover, municipal borrowing has severe consequences for large capital as well. A heavy dependence on capital markets by cities drives up the cost of money for private capital and thus reinforces the underinvestment pathologies of American industry. In this way, the quest for cohesion at the urban level has increased the reproduction costs of American capital as a whole.

Strategies of control that rely on new participatory institutions are also vulnerable to fiscal crises. Many of the new institutions—including CAPs and Model Cities—have directly depended on federal monies that no longer exist. And the mayorally created institutions are terribly vulnerable in periods of budgetary scarcity. Though cosmetic neighborhood government programs are relatively cheap, they are politically difficult to justify when the jobs of policemen and firemen are threatened. And genuine neighborhood government undoubtedly increases the costs of service delivery because efficiencies of cost and standarization are lost. While most of the participatory programs were born in the era of expected growth surpluses and war-fired governmental expansion, they are not likely to survive wars on cost and inflation and fiscal crises.

As the New York case indicates as well, they are not likely to survive because they are not organically attached to national political arrangements. Whereas the machines were rooted in national party systems, the "new machines" have principally been fashioned by mayors who lack party organizations and are embedded in a national party system in advanced decay. And the very constituencies of the new urban organizations have increasingly questioned their legitimacy and functions.

In the late 1960s, after successive summers of major ghetto violence, the problems of urban cohesion seemed to threaten the American configuration of class capacities in potentially revolutionary ways. As the period of riot came to a close, the President of the United States declared the urban crises to be at an end. But as the older cities become increasingly bound up with the fate of small capital, as their services decline in quantity and quality, as the proportion of local capital and labor productively in use is reduced, as the urban fiscal crisis produces financial solutions that worsen the relative economic status of the city, and as the participatory reforms of the 1960s atrophy or are discontinued, the dynamics of urban social cohesion again may become the central battleground of competing American class capacities.

## NOTES

1. See Raymond Williams, *The Country and the City* (London: Oxford University Press, 1973), chapter 5.

2. George Gurvich, "Social Control," in George Gurvich and Wilbert Moore, eds., *Twentieth Century Sociology* (New York: Philosophical Library, 1945), p. 272.

3. Cited in ibid., p. 278.

4. Karl Marx, *Grundrisse* (London: Penguin, 1973), p. 100.

5. For a useful corrective to the usual secondary readings of Weber on these points, see Anthony Giddens, *Capitalism and Social Theory* (London: Cambridge University Press, 1971), chapters 9, 11, 12.

6. See Ralf Dahrendorf, *Class and Class Conflict in Industrial Society* (Stanford: Stanford University Press, 1959); and Reinhard Bendix, *Max Weber: An Intellectual Portrait* (New York: Doubleday Anchor, 1962).

7. Theda Skocpol, "A Critical Review of Barrington Moore's Social Origins of Dictatorship and Democracy," *Politics and Society*, 4 (1973), p. 21.

8. Nicos Poulantzas, *Political Power and Social Classes* (London: New Left Books, 1973), p. 107.

9. Ira Katznelson, "The Crisis of the Capitalist City: Urban Politics and Social Control," in Willis Hawley and Michael Lipsky, eds., *Theoretical Perspectives on Urban Politics* (Englewood Cliffs, New Jersey: Prentice-Hall, 1976), p. 220.

10. For a fine critical overview of the instrumentalist and structuralist positions see David Gold, Clarence Lo and Erik Olin Wright, "Some Recent Developments in Marxist Theories of the Capitalist State," *Monthly Review,* forthcoming.

11. Gosta Esping Anderson and Roger Friedland, "Class Structure, Class Politics, and the Capitalist State," unpublished manuscript.

12. See James O'Connor, *The Fiscal Crisis of the State* (New York: St. Martin's Press, 1973).

13. See Edward C. Banfield and James Q. Wilson, *City Politics* (New York: Vintage, 1963), p. 18.

14. Sam Bass Warner, Jr., *The Private City: Philadelphia in Three Stages of its Growth* (Philadelphia: University of Pennsylvania Press, 1968), p. 155.

15. See Barry Bluestone, "Economic Crisis and the Law of Uneven Development," *Politics and Society*, 3 (1972), pp. 65–82.

16. See Michael Lipsky, "Toward a Theory of Street Level Bureaucracy," in Hawley and Lipsky, *Theoretical Perspectives.*

17. Margaret Levi, "Bureaucratic Insurgency," unpublished manuscript.

18. Reinhard Bendix, *Nation-Building and Citizenship* (New York: Doubleday Anchor, 1969), pp. 67, 114.

19. Ibid., p. 119.

20. For an extended discussion, see Ira Katznelson and Mark Kesselman, *The Politics of Power: A Critical Introduction to American Government* (New York: Harcourt Brace Jovanovich, 1975), chapter 2.

21. Richard Wade, "Urban Life in Western American, 1790–1830," *American Historical Review,* (October 1958), pp. 14–30.

22. Compare Warner, *The Private City*; Robert Dahl, *Who Governs?* (New Haven: Yale University Press, 1961); and Matthew Holden, "Ethnic Accommodation in a Historical Case," *Comparative Studies in Society and History,* 8 (January, 1966).

23. Warner, pp. 175–176.

24. For a more extended discussion, see Ira Katznelson, "Community Conflict and Capitalist Development," unpublished manuscript.

25. See Richard P. McCormick, "Political Development and the Second Party System," in William Nisbet Chambers and Walter Dean Burnham, eds., *The American Party Systems* (New York: Oxford University Press, 1967), pp. 90–116.

26. Theodore J. Lowi, *"Party, Policy and Constitution in America,"* in Chambers and Barnham, p. 239.

27. Samuel P. Huntington, *Political Order in Changing Societies* (New Haven: Yale University Press, 1968), chapter 3.

28. Lowi, pp. 243ff.

29. Martin Shefter, "The Emergence of the Political Machine: An Alternative View," in Hawley and Lipsky, *Theoretical Perspectives.*

30. David Protess, "Banfield's Chicago Revisited: The Conditions for the Transformation of a Political Machine," unpublished manuscript.

31. That is, in the sense of Lewis Coser's *The Functions of Social Conflict* (New York: The Free Press, 1956).

32. Harold F. Gosnell, *Machine Politics* (Chicago: University of Chicago Press, 1968), p. 183.

33. For a discussion that challenges the conventional wisdom that machine functions at the elite level have withered away, see Raymond Wolfinger, *The Politics of Progress* (Englewood Cliffs, New Jersey: Prentice-Hall, 1974), chapter 4.

34. Lipsky, "Toward a Theory."

35. Frances Piven, "The Urban Crisis: Who Got What and Why," in Robert Paul Wolff, ed., *1984 Revisited* (New York: Random House, 1972), p. 171.

36. John V. Lindsay, *The City* (New York: Signet, 1970), pp. 87, 95.

37. Charles Maier, "Beyond Revolution? Resistance and Vulnerability to Radicalism in Advanced Western Societies," unpublished manuscript.

Chapter Two

# Feeble Governments and Private Power: Urban Politics and Policies in the United States

### KENNETH NEWTON

It is a common assumption among contemporary sociologists and political scientists that there is a special and necessary link between decentralized power and democracy such that, all other things being equal, the more diffused and fragmented the power of a government, the more democratic it is. Conversely it follows that a centralized and powerful government, all other things being equal, is likely to be elitist, undemocratic and unresponsive to its citizens. These suppositions are especially common among students of American urban politics, and, indeed, have influenced a whole era of urban research, often with important consequences for the sorts of questions asked and the conclusions drawn about politics and public policy in American cities. L.J. Sharpe draws attention to these rather odd assumptions in the following way: "The prolonged community power debate between the 'elitists' and the 'pluralists' over 'who governs?' neatly reflects the extent to which dispersed power is seen as a central distinguishing characteristic of United States democracy. The underlying assumption, explicitly or implicitly, of both sides of the debate was that the measure of democracy is the extent to which power is dispersed: if it is not dispersed it is elitist and therefore not democratic; if it is dispersed it is pluralist and therefore democratic."[1]

The ready equation of dispersed power structures with pluralist democracy is, of course, much too simple; but it is rooted in a strong American tradition which

This is a revised version of a paper which was written for the Conference on Politics, Policy, and the Quality of Urban Life, Villa Serbelloni, Bellagio, Italy, June 20–24, 1975. I would like to thank David Price, Jim Sharpe, Sidney Tarrow and Philip Williams for comments which greatly improved the original version. Much of the groundwork for the paper was done while I held an American Council of Learned Societies Fellowship at the Department of Sociology, the University of Wisconsin, Madison, 1973–4.

rightly emphasizes the danger to democracy of governments which are too powerful. The same tradition tends to gloss over the equally considerable danger of governments which are too weak and ineffective and which, as a result, are easy prey for well organized, private groups which can readily control the government and use it for their own ends. Edmund Burke recognized this danger when in contrast to the oppressiveness of strong governments he argued that "a feeble government which gives free rein to factious nongovernmental groups may be just as oppressive."[2] Some of the founders of the American constitution also recognized that democracy consists of a delicate balance between too much and too little public and private power. James Wilson remarked that "Bad governments are of two sorts. 1. that which does too little. 2. that which does too much: that which fails through weakness; and that which destroys through oppression. Under which of these evils do the United States at present groan? Under the weakness and inefficiency of its Government. To remedy this weakness we have been sent to this convention."[3]

The purpose of this paper is to show that things have not changed all that much since James Wilson's time and that the weakness of modern urban government in the United States results in private interests gaining considerable power within the system, with far reaching consequences for the whole style and content of urban politics and public policy. In other words, it is claimed that the urban political system of the United States can be characterized in terms of two dimensions which refer to the relative power of publicly accountable authorities. on the one hand, and of private interests and organizations, such as business concerns, formally organized voluntary associations and informal social groups on the other. Put in its starkest form, the argument is that the feeble and fragmented governments found in must urban areas in the United States have helped the excessive concentration of political power in the hands of a narrow section of the population who have proceeded to rule in their own interests. As the opening paragraph argues, the possibility of highly diffused formal authority being accompanied by a highly centralized power system has not been fully recognized in the United States, even though Banfield's classic analysis of Chicago shows how it can be done. More usually, American scholars have assumed that the fragmentation and decentralization of public authority means the diffusion of power which, in turn, has been equated with pluralist democracy. In an attempt to go beyond these assumptions, Figure 2–1 lays out in an oversimplified manner, four analytical types of political system according to the relative power of public and private bodies. The figure suggests that the American system must be distinguished from the more complete forms of liberal democracy which one finds in, for example, the Scandinavian countries.

I have discussed some of the political and economic consequences of weak and fragmented government in metropolitan areas in a previous article and will not cover the same ground again, although that article and this one are essentially complementary in dealing with different aspects of the phenomenon.[4] The two

**Figure 2-1.** Public Authority and Private Power

|  |  | *Public authorities are:* | |
|  |  | *Strong* | *Weak* |
| *Private Interests are:* | *Strong* | Liberal democracies | Free enterprise systems |
|  | *Weak* | Totalitarian systems | Parochial and developing systems |

papers can be read independently of each other, but their arguments, it is hoped, are mutually reinforcing. For the moment I am concerned to show that:

1. urban government in the United States is weak, fragmented and ineffective;
2. its weakness means that private bodies and organizations have inordinate political power;
3. since middle and upper class strata are most powerfully organized, they exercise the greatest influence in the urban political system;
4. the power and influence of these strata may be measured in terms of who gets what, when and how;
5. it is in the interests of the middle and upper class to keep urban government weak, fragmented and ineffective;
6. the very structure and rules of the urban political game which keep government weak and ineffective have been strongly influenced, not to say intentionally or unintentionally created, by middle and upper class values, goals and activities;
7. and that these values are often rationalized by a self-regarding ideology which has been dubbed a "public-regarding ethos."

### The Weak and Fragmented Nature of American Urban Government

That urban government in the United States is fragmented, weak and ineffective is scarcely disputed even by the system's most ardent apologists. Robert Dahl finds it more corrupt, less efficient and less innovative than the federal government, and observes that the worst units in the system are appalling.[5] And in a recent article Edward Banfield states that "In many important respects the American city is a great success, but there are certainly many things about it that are thoroughly unpleasant, and some that are—or ought to be—intolerable." He goes on to point out "one of the great ironies of history—that the Founding Fathers created a political system whose essential character turned out to be the very opposite of what most of them intended," and continues with a discussion of "the problem of metropolitan organization" as one of a multiplicity of more or less overlapping jurisdictions, and the absence of general purpose governments.[6] Almost every other writer on the subject is less conservative and more outspoken than these two in his criticism, and the literature is now so full of various accounts of "the metropolitan problem," that the point needs no more laboring.[7] The balkanization and overlapping of multiple units of local government are usually taken to be the root causes of the failure.

### The Power of Private Interests

Because there is a strong sentiment in the United States which holds that private institutions are both more efficient and somehow morally superior to public ones, the public domain is much narrower in scope than in many other western societies, and consequently there is greater reliance on private bodies to supply services. Even within the realm of legitimate government action, the relative powerlessness of public officials often means that they are unwilling or unable to make decisions which, as a consequence, are hammered out between private interests. According to Kaplan, big cities in the United States are characterized by a broker leadership system, the hallmark of which is "the pervasive and highly influential role of interest groups in policy making and the more passive role played by elected officials. Issues are generally raised and defined by private groups. The political officials put off a commitment on the issues, waiting to see what the alignment of groups on any particular issue will be and whether any decision at all will be required. Sometimes the city politicians insist that the interest groups work out an informal accord on policy, to which the city council will add its formal ratification."[8] Williams and Adrian's study of four small council-manager cities confirms this general picture. They write that ". . . under most conditions, persons outside the legislative body must be depended upon to make the essential policy decisions in all but a formal sense. . . . The typical pattern of policy development was for a group outside the council to take the initiative, with the council reserving judgement until very late in the negotiations that took place between the group and the administration, or between the group and other groups."[9]

Even some research which challenges the prevailing view that city mayors are relatively powerless comes up with the finding that newspapers, bankers, industrialists and merchants form the most influential groups in city politics,[10] and thereby supports Matthew Holden's conclusion that "A good deal of the capacity for urban governance is actually private, even in what is theoretically the realm of public governance."[11] The American system is a veto group system in which, to quote Edward Banfield's lecture again, "it is remarkably easy for a small number of persons, especially if they are organized, to prevent an American local government from carrying out undertakings which are alleged to be—and which may in fact be—in the interests of the large majority."[12] According to Banfield and Wilson this sort of situation is justified by the prevailing ideology of American society: "In the United States, the public takes the view that the elected official ought not to make and impose a policy of his own; instead he should preside over and exercise final authority in a struggle among private and partial interests in which they try to get their policies adopted."[13]

### The Pluralist Heaven

Many, perhaps most, Americans find nothing disturbing about public officials and bodies simply holding the ring as a referee in the fight between private interests, ensuring fair play according to the established rules of the game, and then signaling the winner when the fight is over. On the contrary such a system is often believed to have great merit in that it avoids the possibility of oppression by dictatorial government while, at the same time, allowing maximum room for manoeuvre for different interests and groups to play themselves out. Of course, a corollary of this position is the widely held view that urban society in the United States contains an enormous range, number and diversity of private organizations. But there is no problem here. After all, Tocqueville himself said that "Americans of all ages, all conditions, and all dispositions constantly form associations"[14] and Lord Bryce observed that "association are created, extended, and worked in the United States more quickly and effectively than in any other country."[15] A little later Louis Wirth's remarkably influential essay on urbanism as a way of life remarks upon "the enormous multiplication of voluntary organizations" in urban America.[16] Most recently of all, even the critical Lowi states that social (i.e. group) pluralism "is an undeniable fact about America."[17]

The almost entirely unquestioned view that urban America is teeming with tens of thousands of citizen organizations, associations and groups is ripe for challenge. In the first place, no systematic research on urban organizations seems ever to have been done. It is certainly true that a great deal is known about the people who join voluntary associations, but precious little is known about the organizations they join. There are numerous case studies of issues involving a small number of pressure groups—fluoridation, busing, city charter campaigns and metropolitan reform—and there are studies of particular groups—the League of Women Voters, Chambers of Commerce, the Y.M.C.A., etc.—and, while these are undoubtedly useful, they almost invariably deal with the most newsworthy, partisan and emotional issues or with the best organized, most powerful and most conspicuous groups. It is not clear that this most visible tenth of the pressure group iceberg offers the best basis for generalizations about most groups and most issues; and so little is known about the world of citizen organizations that one can only hazard guesses about their role and function in urban political systems.[18] As one recent, thorough and comprehensive review of the literature concludes: "The available statistics on voluntary organizations in the United States and elsewhere are highly unsatisfactory. No one knows with any real degree of accuracy how many or what kinds of voluntary organizations there are."[19]

What makes this state of affairs all the more curious is that pluralist theorists have not done much systematic empirical work on citizen organizations, even though these are at the heart of the theory. Consider the cities studied by the pluralists, and by other schools of sociology and political science, for that matter—New Haven, Chicago, New York, Oberlin, Miami, Syracuse, Nashville, Oakland, Los Angeles, Atlanta, Levittown, or the pseudonymous Bigtown, Oretown, Border City, and Pacific City—and ask a few elementary questions about their voluntary organizations, that is about their churches, sports clubs, social clubs, trade unions and professional associations, civic societies, community associations, youth clubs, social welfare organizations, cultural associations, P.T.A.s and so on. How many voluntary organizations are there in each city? Is it in the order of tens or hundreds, or thousands? I have put the questions to dozens of urban experts on both sides of the Atlantic and get answers varying from fifty to two thousand per hundred thousand population.

Then go beyond mere head counting and ask questions about the realtionship between city size and type and the number of organizations. What sorts of resources (money, members, property, duplicating machines and office staff) do different kinds of organizations control? What are the different kinds of organization? What are their main kinds of activity and how are these related, if at all, to political activity? What sections of the community are well organized, poorly organized, or unorganized? One could go on elaborating these sorts of questions at length and, although these are no more than preliminary steps to an understanding of urban society and politics, the interesting thing is not the lack of answers, but the fact that the questions have never even been asked in the first place.

Even if one knew the rough contours of the group world, one could still not assess pluralist theory, for one would have to know something about the political activity of these organizations and under what sorts of circumstances they engage in political activity, if at all. What proportion of voluntary organizations are active in local politics in, say, a twelve-month period, and how does the proportion vary between different types of political structures and cultures? How do these proportions vary between different kinds of groups with different kinds of activity and resources? What do groups do if they want to influence political decisions? What do they do if they are not initially successful? What groups are typically successful? On these questions the urban politics literature is exceedingly thin, although one of the very few pieces of empirical research concludes that "the limited extent of organizational participation in major community decisions raises serious questions about this element in the pluralist equation ... We conclude tentatively that the role of voluntary organizations in ensuring pluralist forms of political decision-making has been somewhat overstated."[20]

Lack of evidence cannot show that the pluralists are wrong, only that neither they nor anybody else has produced evidence adequate to assess their claims. And yet there are some data by which to judge the theory, for although little is known about the political characteristics and activity of a wide range of citizen organizations, a great deal is known about the people who join them. The work is well known and its major conclusions need only brief summary. It shows that joiners are predominantly the better educated and the middle and upper class strata, that a relatively high proportion of manual workers belong to no voluntary organization at all, that a small proportion of people belong to a relatively large number of organizations and that these people are even more predominantly middle and upper class, that the activists and office holders in these associations are also drawn disproportionately from the upper social strata, and that business interests are especially well represented in the ranks of citizen associations.[21] In other words, it seems that a small and rather exclusively middle and upper class stage army runs a large number of organizations and, therefore, that insofar as they exercise any political influence, it is exercised not by a wide diversity of different sorts of people but by a narrow range of them.

Moreover, we also know that some sections of society are rather weakly organized, some scarcely organized at all, and that even some of those which do cohere into formal associations sometimes find it very difficult or impossible to penetrate the corridors of power.[22] Consequently, what at first sight seems to be a pluralist society with a vast array of different sorts of organizations and activists turns out, so far as one can judge from the rather limited evidence, to consist very largely of a rather lopsided range of middle and upper class organizations which are typically run by an even more restricted range of individuals drawn from the higher strata. The private centers of power turn out to represent not a whole range of social interests drawn from the four corners of modern urban society, but a much smaller fragment of that society. Indeed, the most recent and complete evidence suggests that the link between political participation and social status is stronger in the United States than in other countries for comparable data exist.[23] The pressure group world is a middle class world, and since, as we have seen, it is privately organized pressure groups which seem to carry most weight and influence in the urban policy, it is middle class pressure groups which normally win the day on any given issue. Weak and ineffective government, in the American case at least, appears to be a prescription for rule by the upper social strata. Each and every group and individual is formally free to participate in the pluralist political arena, but that is the same as saying that each and every individual is free to dine at an expensive restaurant every night of the week.

### Organized Business and Non-Government

This system of weak and ineffective public authorities combined with strong middle class private interests contains within itself the seeds of its own preservation. Since the formal powers of urban government to pursue distributive or redistributive public policies is severely curtailed and since the informal operation of the political system is directed by its mainly middle class elites away from these sorts of policies, so the ability of governments to produce a wide range of public goods and services is strictly limited. Consequently there is little incentive for the large mass of the population to participate in local politics. Those with the greatest short-run incentive to participate are those who gain most from weak governments which are unable or unwilling to control and regulate private interests. Among these, business interests and perhaps some trade unions are the most obvious, and it is these which organize themselves to preserve the status quo. Other social groups might gain considerably from changing the whole nature of urban government, but in the short run at least, the "exit" strategy is more rational.[24] Thus one has a self-preserving system in which the functional ineffectiveness of urban government is not conducive to widespread or intensive participation which, in its turn, is conducive to the preservation of a functionally ineffective system.[25] In Oakland, a not untypical council-manager and nonpartisan city, Jeffrey Pressman finds "a fundamental obstacle to mayoral leadership is the nature of the political environment itself. For this environment is characterized by a lack of interest in the electoral process and an absence of political parties and groups. It often appears as if politics in Oakland does not exist."[26] With so little input, it is not surprising that there is so little output.

Public officials who lack power and authority are bound to feel exposed and are likely, therefore, to look around for public support. The system in which they find themselves tends to militate against the delivery of public goods and services which appeal to the most numerous social strata, and in any case, these sections of urban society are typically the least capable of providing organized and effective support. Officials are likely, therefore, to look for support to the middle and upper class strata which are relatively well organized and which have an interest in the non-delivery of public goods and services. The logic of the situation thus drives politicians into the arms of the upper social strata, the most cohesive and best organized of which are often business interests that have a vested interest in the non-delivery of public goods and services. When combined with the belief, mentioned earlier, that the private sector is 'better' than the public, this produces a special affinity between politics and business such that the two are often indistinguishable. Edward Banfield sums it up in two sentences: "Politics in the American city has been serious business—that is, the politician has been a sort of businessman, and the businessman a sort of politician. Obviously this would have been impossible if power had been centralized."[27]

The strong influence of upper social strata over urban political systems, if not their actual control of them, shows itself in a large number of ways, three of which are especially important. They are the fragmentation of the formal structure of metropolitan government, the institutions of reformed government, and the ideology which justifies the whole system and which has been labelled "the public-regarding" or "unitary ethos." I have discussed some of the political, social and economic consequences of fragmented government in a previous paper.[28] It is worth quoting another article on the same theme because the main thrust of the arguments in both dovetail so well. Arguing the benefits of approaching the metropolitan complex as a system of social stratification, Richard Child Hill writes as follows: "Political incorporation by class and status is an important institutional mechanism for creating and perpetuating inequality among residents in metropolitan communities in the United States . . . a decentralized, fragmented metropolitan government facilitates the maintenance of perpetuation of class and status group privilege. . . . The political incorporation and municipal segregation of classes and status groups in the metropolis tend to divorce fiscal resources from public needs and serve to create and perpetuate inequality among urban residents in the United States. . . . Thus inequality in the distribution of fiscal resources among municipal governments occupies an increasingly important role in the urban stratification system."[29] Whether fragmented government was created with the conscious intention of creating and reinforcing an urban stratification system is neither here nor there; the point is that those at the top of the system gain very considerably from fragmentation of the political structure.

The second aspect of middle and upper class influence in the urban political system shows itself in the institutions of reformed government. There is some evidence to show that these institutions were set up mainly by business interests with the clear and explicit purpose of maximizing their own power. In an article which has become a classic in its field, Samuel P. Hays writes: "Available evidence indicates that the source of support for reform in municipal government did not come from the lower or middle classes, but from the upper class. The leading business groups in each city and professional men closely allied with them initiated and dominated municipal movements. . . . While reformers maintained that their movement rested on a wave of popular demands, called their gatherings of business and professional leaders "mass meetings," described their reforms as "part of a world-wide trend toward popular government," and proclaimed an ideology of popular upheaval against a selfish few, they were in practice shaping the structure of municipal governments so that political power would no longer be broadly distributed, but would in fact be more centralized in the hands of a relatively small segment of the population . . . there is little evidence that the ideology represented a faith in a purely democratic system of decision-making . . . It was used to destroy the political institutions of the lower classes and the political power which those institutions gave rise to. . . ."[30] There now exist several well documented accounts of how reform movements, spearheaded by business groups and institutions, created forms of urban government which were designed to serve the upper strata's own interests.[31] The reform movement aimed at creating government of businessmen, by businessmen, for businessmen, and in this it was largely successful.

### The Public-Regarding Ethos as a
### Private-Regarding Ideology

All this reads rather oddly when it is contrasted with the "public-regarding ethos" on which the reform movement was built and which is said to pervade much of modern American politics. According to Banfield and Wilson, "there are few if any large cities which have not adopted important parts of [the reform program]," the goals of which "are parts of the larger whole that we have described as the Anglo-Saxon protestant middle-class ethos—a view of the world which sees politics as a means of moralizing life and which attaches great importance to the individual's obligation to "serve" the public."[32] The dominant characteristics of the public-regarding, or as it is later dubbed, the "unitary ethos," are a cooperative search for the interests of the whole, an individual obligation to participate disinterestedly in public affairs, the desirability of rule by the best qualified (i.e. experts), and of honest, impartial and efficient government.[33] Banfield and Wilson's theory and their empirical work have been commented upon and criticized elsewhere and there is no need to cover the same ground again.[34] However, the main grounds of criticism of the public-regarding ethos seem to have been missed in all the published American work, namely that the ethos represents neither more nor less than a partisan and sectional ideology dressed up in the rhetoric of the public good. The difference between an "ethos," as Banfield and Wilson use the term, and an ideology is not altogether clear, but even to use the term ideology in this context is to let the cat out of the bag. In fact, the "ethos" has a homely ring about it to the ears of British political scientists who recognize in it the familiar phrases typically used by rather unsophisticated, backwoods Conservatives when they sternly lecture their public meetings about the need "to pull together for the public good," to "forget narrow, self-interest and work for the interests of the whole," to avoid "wasteful, spendthrift, and inefficient government," and "to have faith in those in high places who are best qualified by education and worldly experience to direct governmental affairs."

There is nothing in any way remarkable in a self-interested upper class ideology masquerading as the apotheosis of the public good, but is remarkable that such a palpable piece of political doubletalk as this should have survived so long in the United States without a direct political challenge. However, before going any further, this interpretation of the public-regarding ethos must be substantiated with argument and evidence, and since the proof of the pudding is always in the eating, the ethos must be judged by the flavor of its products. According to Banfield and Wilson, "The logically implied (but not always achieved) institutional expressions of this ethos were at-large representation, nonpartisanship, a strong executive (especially the council-manager form), master planning, and the strict and impartial enforcement of laws."[35] Two expressions of the ethos may be dealt with very quickly. In the first place, master planning is conspicuous by its absence from the urban scene, and this is partly because the reform movement, with its free-enterprise aims of minimizing the cost and scope of government activity, was flatly against 'government interference' in the business affairs of property and land development.[36] Also the autonomy of middle and upper class suburbs plus the number of special districts, which met reform goals of taking some services "out of politics," make it impossible even to think about comprehensive planning. The public rhetoric of the ethos seems to be basically at odds with its actual performance. But the rhetoric of the "strict and impartial enforcement of laws" was not at all empty, and it had two important aspects: first, the reformers were no doubt genuinely concerned about corruption even if this issue did happen to be an excellent stick with which the reformers could beat their political enemies; second, if the institutions of reformed government had the effect of helping to concentrate local power in the hands of local businessmen, then there was everything to be said from the business point of view of eliminating corruption and substituting in its stead the "legitimate" identification of business and politics. Why should businessmen want or need corruption when they themselves ran city government? Lastly, it ought to be said that the phrase "the strict and impartial enforcement of laws" is uncomfortably close to the Nixon-Agnew school of law and order—that is: law for them and order for us.

This leaves at-large elections, nonpartisanship, and council-manager government as the major political institutions by which we may judge the consequences of the public-regarding ethos. As Wolfinger and Field, among others, show, there is indeed a recognizable public-regarding syndrome involving the council-manager plan, at-large elections and nonpartisanship.[37] But what are the effects of this syndrome on urban politics? Summarizing a considerable amount of research, Dye states that nonpartisanship reduces the turnout of labor, low income, ethnic and Democratic voters while increasing the electoral influence of well educated, high income, WASPs. It also increases the influence of civic associations and of the press (which usually endorse high status WASP candidates), contributes to the election of incumbent councilmen, particularly when combined with at-large elections, tends to reduce the accountability of public officials, and encourages the avoidance of local issues in election campaigns.[38]

Williams and Adrian also pick out three major effects of at-large elections. They increase the handicap of candidates who appeal to working class and other low turnout groups, they tend to increase the costs of election campaigns and they increase the probability of candidates being drawn from the higher social strata.[39] In practice, at-large and nonpartisan elections tend to reinforce conservatism, to restrict the recruitment of public officials to the wealthier sections of society, to increase the lack of accountability of elected officials to the public, and generally to place a series of obstacles in the path of working-class political involvement.[40] As Lineberry and Fowler argue, reformed institutions maximize the power of the middle class and make public policy less responsive to the demands arising out of social conflicts in the population.[41] Wilson and Banfield also argue that the public-regarding ethos involves rule by experts; Marilyn Gittel points out the decision-making confined to professionals limits policy alternatives as well as public participation.[42]

All this is damning evidence in itself, but there is still more to suggest that the public-regarding ethos is not all that is seems. If the ethos is to live up to its name, one would expect cities with reformed institutions and/or a high proportion of upper and upper middle class white, Anglo-Saxon protestants who are typically the carriers of the ethos to have a high rate of public expenditure on public-regarding government activities. Unfortunately for the theory, most research shows the opposite to be the case. Aiken and Alford find that their indicators of public-regarding cultures correlate negatively with urban renewal and public housing programs and conclude that the ethos theory fares badly against their data.[43] Lineberry and Fowler find that reformed cities generally spend and tax less than unreformed cities.[44] Dye finds that suburbs (which have better educated, higher class and wealthier populations) spend less on all municipal services except education, choose to do without many services, or else use the services paid for by the taxpayers in the central cities.[45] Similarly, Masotti and Bowen find that communities with a high socioeconomic status spend relatively little on welfare, police, fire, employee retirement funds, housing and urban renewal and parks.[46] Banfield and Wilson regard homeowners as the best test cases for their theory; Kee finds central cities with a high proportion of homeowners to be more reluctant to pay property tax for the provision of public services.[47] Eulau and Eyestone find high resource cities to have poorly developed city policies.[48] Research in general finds that the high status WASPish suburbs invariably spend less public money on most services with the single and significant exception of education.[49] Hahn's Canadian research suggests that the public-regarding ethos is associated with strong moralizing and conformist attitudes, with positive feelings for private enterprise, and with a desire to restrict the entry into politics of groups which might take an attentive or independent political stance.[50]

Not all the work reported in the previous paragraphs constitutes a direct or exactly appropriate test of the ethos theory but all of it has a bearing upon it and insofar as it shows that reformed structures, or communities with a high proportion of ethos carriers are reluctant to spend public money or to provide public services for themselves, never mind anybody else, the research offers cold comfort for the ethos theory. In fact, the history and character of the reform movement, the effect of reformed institutions on urban political life, and the actual behavior—as opposed to the expressed attitudes and public statements—of people who are supposed to adhere to the public-regarding ethos, all add up to the same conclusion—that the public-regarding ethos is a rather nasty wolf in threadbare sheep's clothing. The public-regarding ethos is, in fact, an intensely self-regarding ideology. It may appeal to a genuinely public-regarding style of politics—that is, to a rational-legal, universalistic, corruptionless and efficient form of government—but the substance and content of the ideology is unmistakable. The lack of any strong left wing or even vaguely socialist movement in the United States means that right-wing movements find it relatively easy to perpetuate the notion that they are public-regarding.

### Urban Housing—the Graveyard of Good Intentions

It remains to show some of the consequences of urban political systems in the United States for the distribution of goods and services between different sections of the population. This is an enormous and complex task in itself, and at this late stage, this paper can only skim the surface with an illustration rather than present systematic evidence for the case which has been argued. Housing has been chosen as an illustration partly because it is mainly the responsibility of local government (although it also involves a complex set of relationships among all levels of government), partly because conflict over urban space and location is arguably a main, or even the main, issue in urban politics, and partly because housing has attracted more energy, time, money and controversy than almost any other urban issue in the post-war period.[51] How has the urban political system of the United States handled housing as a political issue?

After a long, careful and detailed examination of the postwar housing records of the United Kingdom, Sweden, West Germany and the United States, Paul F. Wendt writes: "Housing policies and programs in Sweden, West Germany and the United Kingdom were successful in directing public and private investment toward improving the housing standard of low-income groups of the population. Programs in the United States have relied upon high production rates of new housing and the filtering down process to improve general housing standards. Programs for direct improvement of the housing status of low-income and other special groups have, for various reasons, exhibited a number of shortcomings and have been, on the whole, relatively insignificant."[52] Clawson and Hall reach much the same conclusion in their comparison of the housing performance of Britain and the United States. They find that high income groups in both countries have probably gained most from housing and planning policies, but in Britain the very large public housing program has done a great deal to improve the lot of low-income urban populations. "In Britain," they write, "the existence of a large program of subsidized public sector house building for rent has ameliorated the position of this groups far more effectively than in the United States."[53] It seems that the redistributive housing policies of social justice in the United States have been almost totally ineffective. While American housing standards have undoubtedly improved in the past fifty years, the improvement has not been attributable to public sector housing. It is not difficult to see why this is so.

The implementation of any kind of planning and housing policy in the United States needs, at the very least, the tacit compliance of private interests in the building, real estate, banking and property development businesses. The enormous power of the businessmen's veto is shown with customary detail and precision by Robert Dahl in his account of urban redevelopment in New Haven. Dahl starts his account by showing that a series of prosperous businessmen have been leading figures in New Haven's city planning ever since the early Seventeenth Century and that Economic Notables still play a crucial role.[54] Heads of large firms made up 60 percent of the Board of Finance in the 1950–55 period. and smaller independent businessmen made up over 20 per cent.[55] In contrast, clerical and working class participation on the Board has increased only slightly since 1875.[56] More important for urban redevelopment, Economic Notables were over-represented on the Citizens Action Committee by a ratio of no less than 55:1 and made up at least thirteen of the 24 members of its executive committee. Dahl mentions three bankers, a businessman-Democrat, four of the city's most prominent manufacturers, the president of an investment firm, the chairman of a leading power company, the manager of a large chain store, the president of a construction company, and a partner in a leading law firm.[57] In addition, Mayor Richard Lee himself had strong business connections, having filled an office in the Junior Chamber of Commerce and having received contributions from many Economic Notables during his third and fourth campaigns.[58]

In crude numerical terms, then businessmen filled many important positions in the urban redevelopment field and were crushingly over-represented by comparison with other social and economic groups. This sort of head counting does not get us far unless it can also be shown that businessmen were also powerful in proportion to their numbers in the politics of urban redevelopment. Dahl's analysis suggests that they were powerful in three closely related ways. First, notables, developers and retailers initiated 20 percent of the successful redevelopment proposals, and while they also suffered 37 percent of the defeats, they had an overall success to defeat ratio of 3:2.[59] Second, and more important, Economic Notables formed a powerful veto group. Dahl states that their support was a necessary but not a sufficient condition for successful renewal plans,[60] a point well supported by the fact that at least four of Mayor Lee's seven defeats on urban renewal were inflicted by businessmen, and by the statement that the First National Bank could, if it wished, have made downtown redevelopment impossible.[61] Third, and most important of all, the Citizens Action Committee not only served as "a powerful selling agency," which "decapitated the opposition," and whose "importance. . .in assuring the acceptability for the redevelopment program can hardly be overestimated," but it also served as an important early-warning system for 'unacceptable' policies.[62] As usual, Dahl tells the story better than anybody else could. "Thus, properly used, the CAC was a mechanism not for *settling* disputes but for *avoiding* them altogether. . .in fact, the very existence of the CAC and the seemingly ritualistic process of justifying all proposals to its members meant that members of the administration shaped their proposals according to what they expected would receive the full support of the CAC and therefore of the political stratum. . . . If none of the administration's proposals on redevelopment and renewal were ever opposed by the CAC, the explanation probably lies less in the Mayor's skill in the arts of persuasion than in his capacity for judging with considerable precision what the existing beliefs and commitments of the men on the CAC would compel them to agree to if a proposal were presented in the proper way, time, and place."[63]

In other words, Mayor Lee and the public officials of the city would propose only what the big-business dominated CAC would dispose. And what would they agree to dispose? Once again, Dahl answers the question: "Their [the Economic Notables'] essential strategy is a familiar aspect of American politics; to gain services and benefits from government and as far as possible to displace the costs from themselves to others."[64] The strategy, of course, is common to almost all social groups, at all times and in all places and is not justified by its familiarity in American politics; but what is specially American is the fact that businessmen seem to be in a particularly strong political position to work the strategy successfully. Unfortunately Dahl's story is cut short before the results of the strategy can be recounted, but he does state the logic of urban renewal program very clearly—because of federal largess and local skill, urban renewal cost the city virtually nothing while the only people to suffer were "a handful of small businessmen and several hundred slum dwellers without much political influence."[65] In fact the few hundred turn out to have been at least fifteen thousand, for it has been estimated that more than five thousand families were displaced, the federal government footing the bill for $113 million, and the businessmen getting their downtown area redeveloped not merely at greatly reduced cost but with increased profits for themselves.[66]

This general interpretation of the New Haven study is shared by another writer, Peter Morriss, who after analyzing Dahl's methodology and evidence in some detail concludes that "nowhere in *Who Governs?* does Dahl give an instance of a business interest being defeated on a matter which could be considered of the remotest concern to business, and yet Dahl collects considerable evidence to show that business interests were powerful in the area of urban redevelopment. The hypothesis that New Haven is dominated by a business elite remains unrefuted."[67]

New Haven's experience of urban renewal and housing problems is in no way unique among American cities where big business has invariably played a crucial role. Wendt points out that Federal programs have relied almost entirely on private building and that the failure of the low-rent public housing program to make a greater contribution to the housing supply is partly attributable to influential real estate and construction industry groups opposing direct federal subsidies for housing.[68] Hartman points out that local housing authorities are overwhelmingly composed of upper income whites and are heavily weighted to those in business, real estate and insurance.[69] Friedland gives examples of the power of business interests in the development of urban renewal and model cities programs.[70]

Given this strong business interest and influence, the outcome of most housing and urban renewal programs is not surprising, not to say predictable. Between 1949 and 1957 urban renewal resulted in a net loss of very nearly eighty thousand housing units, especially low income housing, with consequent increases in rent for the poor.[71] Relatively few of those displaced have been rehoused, and many have been forced to move some distance from their work, thereby adding commuting costs to their rent increases.[72] Many of those who have been rehoused have simply been shifted to other slums, so giving grounds for the belief that 'urban renewal is people removal', the people in question being mainly low-income blacks. Meanwhile, middle class or luxury housing, or business accommodation is sometimes built, with public subsidies, on the land which becomes available.[73] Small businesses suffer as well as the poor, for their forced evacuation often drives them out of the market, while the downtown business district gets the lion's share of attention and resources.[74] Gans calculates that displaced residents receive one half of one percent of federal renewal funds, while businesses receive 1.5 percent of these funds.[75] Anderson calculates that up to 1961, low income housing claimed 0.8 percent of all construction costs, while commercial and industrial construction took 47 percent.[76]

The recent history of public housing in the United States has been described as "a graveyard of good intentions."[77] Only the good intentions are open to doubt.

## NOTES

1. L.J. Sharpe, "American Democracy Reconsidered: Part II and Conclusions," *British Journal of Political Science,* 3 (January, 1973), p. 135.

2. Quoted in Constance Smith and Anne Freedman, *Voluntary Associations* (Cambridge: Harvard University Press, 1972), p. 57.

3. Quoted in Robert A. Dahl, *Democracy in the United States: Promises and Performance,* 2nd ed. (Chicago: Rand McNally, 1972), pp. 74–5.

4. K. Newton, "Social Class, Political Structure, and Public Goods in American Urban Politics," *Urban Affairs Quarterly,* 11 (December, 1975), pp. 241–64.

5. Dahl, pp. 219–20.

6. Edward C. Banfield, *The City and the Revolutionary Tradition* (Washington, D.C.: American Enterprise Institute for Public Policy Research, 1974), pp. 1–6.

7. See for example, Charles M. Bonjean et al., eds., *Community Politics*

(New York: Free Press, 1971), pp. 45–55; Michael N. Danielson, *Metropolitan Politics* (Boston: Little, Brown, 1971), pp. 247–59.

8. Harold Kaplan, *Urban Political Systems* (New York: Columbia University Press, 1967), p. 32.

9. Oliver P. Williams and Charles R. Adrian, *Four Cities* (Philadelphia: University of Pennsylvania Press, 1963), pp. 292–3. See also Jeffrey Pressman, "Preconditions of Mayoral Leadership," *American Political Science Review*, 66 (June, 1972), pp. 511–24.

10. Wen H. Kuo, "Mayoral Influence in Urban Policy Making," *American Journal of Sociology*, 79 (November, 1973), pp. 620–38.

11. Matthew Holden, Jr., "The Politics of Urbanization" in Harlan Hahn, ed., *People and Politics in Urban Society* (Beverly Hills: Sage Publications, Inc., 1972), p. 586.

12. Banfield, p. 6. See also Robert L. Crain et al., *The Politics of Community Conflict* (Indianapolis: Bobbs Merrill, 1969), for an account of how weak political executives in American city government create a veto group and immobilist system.

13. Edward C. Banfield and James Q. Wilson, *City Politics* (Cambridge, Mass.: Harvard University Press and the M.I.T. Press, 1963), p. 31. If more evidence for the power of private organizations in urban political systems in the United States is required see Wallace S. Sayre and Herbert Kaufman, *Governing New York City* (New York: W.W. Norton, 1965), pp. 717–19; Alan A. Altschuler, *The City Planning Process* (New York: Cornell University Press, 1967), pp. 362–3; Roscoe C. Martin et al., *Decisions in Syracuse* (Garden City, New York: Doubleday, 1965), pp. 330–1.

14. Alexis de Tocqueville, *Democracy in America*, Volume II (New York: Vintage Books, 1956), p. 114. Although Toqueville is constantly invoked in writings on modern American voluntary organizations, those which he found in America in the 1830s were very different from the ones which exist now. For some important remarks upon Tocqueville's role as the patron saint of voluntary organizations in modern America see George Kateb, "Some Remarks on Tocqueville's View of Voluntary Organizations," in J. Roland Pennock and John W. Chapman, eds., *Voluntary Associations* (New York: Atherton Press, 1969), pp. 138–44.

15. James Bryce, *The American Commonwealth*, Volume II, 4 ed., (New York: Macmillan, 1910), p. 281.

16. Quoted in Smith and Freedman, p. 15.

17. Theodore Lowi, "The Public Philosophy: Interest-Group Liberalism," *American Political Science Review*, 61 (March, 1967), p. 22.

18. I have supported these assertions with argument and evidence drawn from a study of over four thousand formally organized voluntary associations which appear in Birmingham, England in *Second City Politics: Democratic Processes and Decision-Making in Birmingham* (Oxford: The Clarendon Press, 1976), chapters 3 and 4.

19. Smith and Freedman, p. 196.

20. Robert Presthus, *Men at the Top* (New York: Oxford University Press, 1964), pp. 271, 281.

21. See for example, Gabriel A. Almond and Sidney Verba, *The Civic*

*Culture* (Boston: Little, Brown, 1965), pp. 248–9, 258–9; William Kornhauser, *The Politics of Mass Society* (London: Routledge and Kegan Paul, 1960), pp. 70–1; Murray Hausknecht, *The Joiners* (New York: Bedminister Press, 1962); Robert E. Lane, *Political Life* (New York: Free Press, 1961), pp. 74–79, 220–234; Lester W. Milbrath, *Political Participation* (Chicago: Rand McNally, 1965), pp. 114–28; T.B. Bottomore, "Social Stratification in Voluntary Associations," in David V. Glass, ed., *Social Mobility in Britain* (London: Routledge and Kegan Paul, 1954), p. 374; Tom Brennan, *Reshaping a City* (Glasglow: Grant, 1959); Raymond N. Morris, "British and American Research on Voluntary Associations: A Comparison," *Sociological Inquiry*, 35 (Spring, 1965), pp. 191–6; E.E. Schattsneider, *The Semi-Sovereign People* (New York: Holt, Rinehart and Winston, 1960), pp. 29–35.

22. Schattsneider's classic statement about the pluralist heaven is supported by a wide range of more recent empirical studies including Michael Parenti, "Power and Pluralism: The View from the Bottom," *Journal of Politics*, 32 (August, 1970), pp. 501–30; V.O. Key, *Parties, Politics and Pressure Groups*, 4th ed. (New York: Thomas Y. Crowell, 1958), p. 150; A.J. Bornfriend, "Political Parties and Pressure Groups," *Proceedings of the Academy of Political Science*, 29 (no. 4, 1969), pp. 64–5; Michael Lipsky and Margaret Levi, "Community Organization as a Political Resource," in Harlan Hahn, ed., *People and Politics in Urban Society* (Beverly Hills: Sage Publications Inc., 1972), pp. 175–99; Harold L. Wolman and Norman C. Thomas, "Black Interests, Black Groups, and Black Influence in the Federal Policy Process: The Case of Housing and Education," *Journal of Politics*, 32 (November, 1970), pp. 875–97.

23. Sidney Verba and Norman H. Nie, *Participation in America: Political Democracy and Social Equality* (New York: Harper and Row, 1972), pp. 339–40.

24. See John M. Orbell and Toru Uno, "A Theory of Neighborhood Problem Solving: Political Action vs. Residential Mobility," *American Political Science Review*, 66 (June, 1972), pp. 471–89.

25. For an account of functional effectiveness in urban government in the United States see Sharpe, pp. 130–144.

26. Pressman, p. 513. Pressman's picture of a political vacuum in Oakland contrasts oddly with the more normal picture of urban politics as teeming with shouting and jostling actors and groups.

27. Banfield, p. 7.

28. Newton, "Social Class."

29. Richard Child Hill, "Separate and Unequal: Governmental Inequality in the Metropolis," *American Political Science Review*, 68 (December, 1974), pp. 1557–68.

30. Samuel P. Hays, "The Politics of Reform in Municipal Government in the Progressive Era," reprinted in Daniel N. Gordon, ed., *Social Change and Urban Politics* (Englewood Cliffs, New Jersey: Prentice-Hall, 1973), pp. 110–11, 124, 125. See also the same author's "The Changing Political Structure of the City in Industrial America," *Journal of Urban History*, 1 (November, 1974), pp. 6–38.

31. See for example, Lee Sloan, " 'Good Government' and the Politics of Race," *Social Problems*, 17 (Fall, 1969), pp. 161–75; Edward C. Hayes, *Power*

*Structure and Urban Policy: Who Rules in Oakland?* (New York: McGraw-Hill 1972), pp. 3–23; W.W. Charters, "Social Class Analysis and the Control of Public Education," *Harvard Educational Review,* 23 (Fall, 1953), pp. 268–83; James Weinstein, *The Corporate Ideal in the Liberal State* (Boston: The Beacon Press, 1969, pp. 92–116; James Weinstein, *The Decline of Socialism in America* (New York: Vintage Books, 1967), chapter 2.

32. Banfield and Wilson, *City Politics,* pp. 148, 139.

33. James Q. Wilson and Edward C. Banfield, "Political Ethos Revisited," *American Political Science Review,* 55 (December, 1971), p. 1048.

34. Lynn Foster, "Dimensions of 'Urban Unease' in Ten Cities," *Urban Affairs Quarterly,* 10 (December, 1974), pp. 194–5; and the letter by Abraham H. Miller and Stephen E. Bennett, *American Political Science Review,* 68 (September, 1974), p. 1268, pick out flaws in the survey design and methodology, in addition to which it is worth pointing out that 78 percent of the respondents were male. The sample does not seem to be a good basis on which to offer generalizations about American society or even about homeowners in Boston in 1966–7. In addition the results of the survey are really remarkably poor support for the ethos theory. A correlation of 0.135 (significant at .01, but nevertheless substantively trivial) is offered as evidence that the ethos shows a strain towards consistency, and even this is a correlation between only two out of three of the supposedly consistent dimensions of the ethos. From a sample of 1,059 the authors produce either 121 or 123 people who conform to the ethos theory. The doubt about the total number arises from the fact that on p. 1057 they report that 24 people combine all three dimensions of the individualist ethos, while on p. 1058, table 2, they report the figure as 26. These very poor results are produced not so much by faulty methodology as by a theory which treats the public-regarding ethos as if it really were public-regarding in some important respects and which, as a result, fails to find more than a small handful of people who behave as the theory says they should.

35. Wilson and Banfield, p. 1048.

36. Banfield and Wilson, *City Politics,* pp. 190, 195, 202–3. In addition, Robert L. Lineberry, "Community Structure and Planning Commitment: A Note on the Correlates of Agency Expenditures," *Social Science Quarterly,* 48 (December, 1969), p. 727, finds that his reform index correlates only slightly but, nevertheless, negatively with planning expenditure.

37. Raymond E. Wolfinger and John Osgood Field, "Political Ethos and the Structure of City Government," *American Political Science Review,* 60 (June, 1966), pp. 306–26.

38. Thomas R. Dye, *Politics in States and Communities* (Englewood Cliffs, New Jersey: Prentice-Hall, 1969), pp. 276–8.

39. Oliver P. Williams and Charles R. Adrian, "The Insulation of Politics under a Nonpartisan Ballot," *American Political Science Review,* 53 (December, 1959), pp. 152–63.

40. Charles R. Adrian, "Some General Characteristics of Nonpartisan Elections," *American Political Science Review,* 46 (September, 1952), pp. 766–76.

41. Robert L. Lineberry and Edmund P. Fowler, "Reformism and Public

Policies in American Cities," *American Political Science Review*, 61 (September, 1967), pp. 712, 714, 716.

42. Marilyn Gittell, "Professionalism and Public Participation in Educational Policy-Making: New York City, a Case Study," *Public Administration Review*, 27 (September, 1967), pp. 259–61.

43. Michael Aiken and Robert R. Alford, "Community Structure and Innovation: The Case of Public Housing," *American Political Science Review*, 64 (September, 1970), pp. 851–2; Michael Aiken and Robert R. Alford, "Community Structure and Innovation: The Case of Urban Renewal," *American Sociological Review*, 35 (August, 1970), pp. 653–5.

44. Lineberry and Fowler, pp. 707–14.

45. Thomas R. Dye, "City-Suburban Social Distance and Public Policy," reprinted in Jay S. Goodman, ed., *Perspectives on Urban Politics* (Boston: Allyn and Bacon, 1970), pp. 363–73.

46. Louis H. Masotti and Don. R. Bowen, "Communities and Budgets: The Sociology of Municipal Expenditures," *Urban Affairs Quarterly*, 1 (December, 1965), pp. 39–58.

47. Woo Sik Kee, "Central City Expenditures and Metropolitan Areas," *National Tax Journal*, 18 (December, 1965), pp. 337–53.

48. Heinz Eulau and Robert Eyestone, "Policy Maps of City Councils and Policy Outcomes: A Development Analysis," *American Political Science Review*, 62 (March, 1968), p. 133.

49. See for example, Harvey E. Brazer, "Some Fiscal Implications of Metropolitanism," in Benjamin Chinitz, ed., *City and Suburb* (Englewood Cliffs, New Jersey: Prentice Hall, 1964), pp. 136–9; Kevin R. Cox, *Conflict, Power and Politics in the City* (New York: McGraw-Hill, 1973), pp. 30–48. One source finds that council-manager cities spend more than nonmanager cities, but the author does not attempt to control for wealth, and so concludes that cities with more money spend more. See Edgar L. Sherbenou, "Class, Participation, and the Council-Manager Plan," reprinted in Gordon, ed., *Social Change and Urban Politics*, pp. 132–3. The Advisory Commission on Intergovernmental Relations reported in 1967 that the local taxes of central cities averaged 7.6 percent of personal income, while those outside the central city took 5.6 percent; quoted in Anthony Downs, *Opening up the Suburbs* (New Haven: Yale University Press, 1973), p. 39.

50. Harlan Hahn, "Ethos and Social Class: Referenda in Canadian Cities," *Polity*, 11 (Spring, 1970), pp. 295–315.

51. See Oliver P. Williams, *Metropolitan Political Analysis* (New York: The Free Press, 1971), pp. 12–14.

52. Paul F. Wendt, *Housing Policy–The Search for Solutions* (Berkeley: University of California Press, 1962), p. 269.

53. Marion Clawson and Peter Hall, *Planning and Urban Growth: An Anglo-American Comparison* (Baltimore: Johns Hopkins University Press, 1973), p. 194.

54. Robert A. Dahl, *Who Governs?* (New Haven: Yale University Press, 1961), pp. 115–16.

55. Ibid., p. 82.

56. Ibid, pp. 82–3.

57. Ibid., pp. 72–4, 131. Dahl does not, however, discuss (except for a fleeting mention on p. 247) the crucial role played in New Haven's urban renewal by Roger L. Stevens, a New York property developer. Stevens' part in the whole history of events is recounted by Allan R. Talbot, *The Mayor's Game* (New York: Praeger, 1970), pp. 117–35.

58. Dahl, p. 118.

59. Ibid., p. 125, table 10.3.

60. Ibid., pp. 115, 138.

61. Ibid., pp. 124–5.

62. Ibid., pp. 131, 133.

63. Ibid., pp. 136–7. Talbot, p. 65, states that Mayor Lee "continued to characterize it [the CAC] as a strong, unified group *that represented business and supported his program.*" (My emphasis.)

64. Dahl, p. 83.

65. Ibid., pp. 244, 117.

66. The figures are taken from Talbot, pp. 159, 171. Talbot's financial statistics appear to be reliable but his displacement figures are not. On p. xviii of the introduction to the paperback edition of his book he states that the urban renewal project tore down roughly five thousand housing units. A conservative estimate of four people per unit yields a total of 20,000 displaced people. On p. 171 he gives a figure of five thousand families. A conservative estimate of three people per family yields a total of fifteen thousand displaced people.

67. Peter Morriss, "Power in New Haven: a Reassessment of *Who Governs?*" *British Journal of Political Science,* 2 (October, 1972), p. 464.

68. Wendt, p. 193.

69. Chester W. Hartman, "The Politics of Housing," reprinted in Allan Shank, ed., *Political Power and the Urban Crisis* (Boston: Holbrook Press, 1969), pp. 442–3.

70. Roger Friedland, "Corporations and Urban Renewal: Conditions, Consequences and Participation," University of Wisconsin-Madison, Department of Sociology, mimeo, November, 1973.

71. Matthew Edel, "Planning, Market, or Warfare?—Recent Land Use Conflict in American Cities," in Matthew Edel and Jerome Rothenberg, eds., *Readings in Urban Economics* (New York: Macmillan, 1972), p. 146; James Q. Wilson, "Planning and Politics: Citizen Participation in Urban Renewal," reprinted in Downes, ed., p. 178; Scott Greer, *Urban Renewal and American Cities* (Indianapolis: Bobbs Merrill, 1965), p. 166; Hayes, p. 79–85.

72. Robert L. Lineberry and Ira Sharkansky, *Urban Politics and Public Policy* (New York: Harper and Row, 1971), p. 340.

73. Herbert Gans, "The Failure of Urban Renewal," *Commentary,* 39 (April, 1965), pp. 29–37. See also the discussion which follows among George M. Raymond, Malcolm D. Rivkin and Gans in *Commentary,* 39 (July, 1965), pp. 72–80.

74. Lineberry and Sharkansky, p. 341; Bernard J. Frieden, "Toward Equality of Urban Opportunity," reprinted in H. Wentworth Eldridge, ed., *Taming Megalopolis,* Volume 1 (Garden City: Doubleday, 1967), pp. 518–22; Raymond

Vernon, "The Myth and Reality of Our Urban Problems," in Chinitz, ed., pp. 103–6.

75. Gans, *Commentary,* July, 1965, p. 78.

76. Martin Anderson, *The Federal Bulldozer* (Cambridge, Mass.: M.I.T. Press, 1965), p. 244. Anderson's figures and argument have been strongly criticized by Robert Groberg, "Urban Renewal Realistically Reappraised," *Law and Contemporary Problems,* 30 (Winter, 1965), pp. 212–29.

77. Nathan Glazer, "Housing Problems and Housing Policies," in H.R. Mahood and Edward L. Angus, eds., *Urban Politics and Problems* (New York: Charles Scribner's Sons, 1969), p. 286.

Part Two

# New Actors in Urban Politics

Chapter Three

# Political Turbulence and Administrative Authority in the Schools

FREDERICK M. WIRT

### The Basic Theme

A continuing and basic problem in the governance of American schools has been the tension between the community's necessity to have a leadership that can lead and be trusted and that same community's desire to have its will carried out by that leadership. American public education, since its inception with Horace Mann's heresy, with what Raymond Fosdick termed the extraordinary possibilities of ordinary people, has sought responsiveness to public needs. The altering focus of American civic education over a century shows this.[1] So does the continuous search for instruments to ensure public responsiveness—from party control of schools through the Progressives' model of corporate centralization to the contemporary call for "community control." The history of big city schools shows the truth of Paul's adjuration that "There is nothing new under the sun," for there is an intriguing repetition in school issues over the last century.[2] Smaller school systems exhibit tensions between "bureaucracy vs. participation," superintendents dependent on Southern community power structures, and variations in principals' political styles.[3] In large part, I read both this repetition and variety as reflections of the classic political tension between the leaders and the led, in this case over the issue of having school policy work the way each wishes.

Assuming that this leader-led tension underlies the current urban school conflict, I wish to argue that this tension mobilizes different "core constituencies" of the school. "Core" indicates that these groups are separated here for analytical purposes, although not mutually exclusive in experience.   Each group

An original version of this chapter was presented at the David W. Minar Memorial Conference on Problems in the Politics and Governance of the Learning Community, Northwestern University, 1974.

creates special tensions for the school's political authority exercised by the board and administrators. Each core constituency, in turn, manifests its tension in a special issue which challenges the leadership over reallocation of school resources. These issues and their core constituencies are:

Parents—shared or community control/advisory input/decentralization, or whatever term is current.
Students—rights about governance, expression, dress, behavior, etc.
Teachers—organization for collective bargaining, hereafter shortened to "teacher power."
Taxpayers—reform of local financing by some larger assumption of costs by the state.
Minorities—the issue generated by the *Brown* decision which encompasses desegregation and integration.

While controversy over such issues vary from city to city, they move in response to natural forces. That is, local school conflict is shaped by forces both outside and inside the district. The absence of walls around the city—and the school district—lays them open to public and private influences from those external, multiple centers of decision-making which characterize American national life.[4] New concepts about how society should be conducted or life enjoyed, the episodic eruption of national events which crystalize local hopes and fears about school matters, the transmission by national media of such thought and action into every urban crevice—all are major extra-community stimuli of school conflict. When such conflict mobilizes new groups, when national currents are at work, and when the rancor and clamor swells, we have a level of conflict better termed "turbulence."

Moreover, each conflict is affected by local conditions. These are intervening contextual factors, i.e., the variation in community resources for policy outputs which has so fascinated political science recently. To date, such research has concluded that policy variation is mostly a function of a place's size and wealth. But a second intervening factor differentiating this political turbulence is the interaction of these sets of school demands, the least noticed and least studied quality of school politics today.

Here, then, is the complex of disaggregated inputs which impinge today upon school authorities. These inputs may be seen conceptually—and in real life—as demands upon the school board, when demands rise to the level of turbulence. That board, in turn, focuses these demands upon the administrators—the superintendent, central office and principals. That impact also varies with the mosaic of issues and communities. Too, administrators are increasingly constrained by forces outside the district, such as the state and federal government, court orders, statutes or regulations. As a result of this turbulence, there has occurred a dilution or transformation of administrative authority, as the last section of the paper will demonstrate. More significant, administrators' professionally-given norm of autonomy is undergoing change in the face of either local demands or those from outside authorities.

Some sense of this matrix of turbulence focusing upon school authorities may be seen in summary form in Figure 3–1.

**Figure 3-1.** Paradigm of Turbulent School Politics

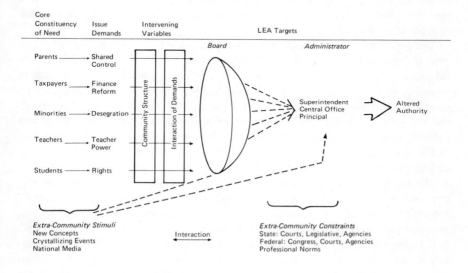

## The Currents of Turbulence:
### Constituencies and Issues

**Parents and Shared Control.** The concept of a lay share of school power emerged anew in the late 1960s. But clearly, this is *not* the first time that Americans have sought to control their schools directly and closely. After all, such close contact is characteristic today of the myriad of small town districts, both rural and suburban. Indeed, for the most of our history, school structure has been immensely decentralized; many more school districts existed before their consolidation in the middle quarters of this century. Too, big city schools were governed by numerous ward boards before the Progressives were successful in their centralization; in Philadelphia in 1905 there were 43 elected boards with 599 members.[5]

But this pattern altered, first with big city centralization and then with rural consolidation, thereby yielding fewer boards consisting of fewer representatives dealing with larger numbers of students and voters. As a result, where there had been over 127,000 districts in 1931, there were only about 35,000 as the 1960s opened and 16,000 by the early 1970s.[6] "Consequently," as James Guthrie has calculated, "where a school board member once represented about 200 people, today each board member must speak for approximately 3,000 constituents."[7]

So it was that the triumph of the organizational value of efficiency, achieved through centralization and bureaucracy, attenuated the linkages between leadership and constituents. That seemed acceptable in the pre-World War II decades, when schooling laid minimum claims on district resources and professionals benefited by their self-generated publicity about education as the sovereign key to the kingdom of success. Moreover, in the two decades after that war, this weakened linkage (as voting studies showed), seemed equally acceptable in the rush for schooling for all.[8]

But sometime during the late 1950s the professionals' aura began to fade. The *Brown* decision in 1954 held up to national view for the first time the disgraceful failure of Southern educators with their black students. Other complaints emerged that, regardless of race, Johnny couldn't read or speak languages or count to the base 10, and that the Russians were somehow "out-performing" our school system. The last discontent generated a vast injection of local and federal funds into schools—the National Defense Education Act in the late 1950s, university support in the early 1960s, and finally in 1965 the Elementary and Secondary Education Act.

But the more voters contributed, the more complaints emerged that somehow the bureaucracy of education was not sensitive to parental preferences in schooling their children. Social scientists joined in with analyses of the monolithic—i.e., unresponsive—nature of the administration of schooling, with New York City's 110 Livingston Street regarded as the prototype, not an exception.[9] Suburbanites objected that administrators were insensitive to demands for either richer or for plainer curricula, whether in affluent Scarsdale or working-class Maple Heights, Ohio. Inside the central city, particularly in the newly mobilized black communities, central offices and site principals were increasingly pilloried for their insensitivity, easily labelled "racism." In all, across a surprisingly wide gamut of life-styles, parents-as-voters came to criticize the lack of linkages with school district decision-making. The reasons differed with locale and status, but clearly the old participatory impulse had increased.

In an effort to deal with this impulse, the Ford Foundation stimulated experimentation in New York and elsewhere in "community control," which brought opposition from newly toughening teacher unions and developed finally into a set of 30 partially decentralized districts. But elsewhere this effort to build linkages between parents and school leaders took diverse courses.[10] Sometimes the sharing involved only citizen advice without guarantee it would be accepted, whether such councils were optional or required under federal programs. Sometimes it took the form of full constituency involvement in planning, including decision making and implementation—although the incidence here was small and dependent upon the vagaries of administrators' styles.[11] But one conclusion was everywhere evident—no parent constituency got full control over the sources, amounts and uses of funds for school programs.[12]

Only one state, Florida in 1973, has legislated some decentralization and accountability for all schools. Here the school site is conceived to be the main management unit for education. At each site, an elected parents' advisory council picks the principal with district board approval, advises him on staff selections, curriculum and discipline, and shares with him—and publicizes—fiscal accountability for the school's operations. While the phase-in was to be drawn out, with each district starting only with one school, a number of district boards mandated all the reforms for all schools in the first year.[13]

But in Florida, as elsewhere, district and state authorities set mandates and minimums of services which lay groups cannot contravene, and in most districts across the nation little parental participation continues to be the norm, especially in the big cities. As it is, Gallup reported in 1972 that only about one in three parents with children in public schools had attempted the minimum participatory task—attending a school meeting to review the school's purposes and operations.[14] The effect of this issue upon administrative authority will be seen later.

**Taxpayers and Financial Reform.** Demands for control of schools have not been restricted to parents concerned with what schools were doing to their children; over the last ten years taxpayers have also increasingly challenged school financing. A spate of litigation has developed from the fusion of the Ford Foundation and university scholars in law and educational finance which the United States Supreme Court's 1973 decision in the *Rodriguez* case narrowly prevented being elevated into a Constitutional principle. But these reform efforts have continued, now focused upon the state legislatures, after abortive attempts at change through the Supreme Court and statewide referenda.[15]

Such pressures to redistribute schooling resources accompany pressures to have the state take on a higher share of local school costs. Since 1900 that state share has grown, stabilizing at around 40 percent after World War II (a figure concealing numerous small shifts up and down), and by 1970 it was still at that level.[16] As if frustrated here in seeking relief, taxpayers' support for local financing fell off. The years 1964–1965 were the peak for support of local bond and tax issues; thereafter began the phenomenon of multiple trips to the public well to pass a single issue.[17] The refusal of most legislatures in the 1960s to accede to local pressures for tax relief seemed to cause venting of taxpayer frustration in the form of large majorities voting "no!" By 1972, Gallup reported that 56 percent opposed raising local taxes for this purpose, but 55 percent favored an increase in state taxes to pay school costs and reduce property taxes.[18]

War and inflation, in company with new research on school finance inequities, by 1970 combined to move the states to modify taxes. The score today is mixed, as befits the mosaic of American federalism. But a recent tabulation of the progress of this reform shows surprising progress in a short time, as Table 3–1 reveals. With one exception, Nevada in 1967, the dates for the thirteen "major changes" are 1973 and 1974, involving just the kind of equalizing schemes reformers had sought. Not all the reformer's dreams have known this dramatic success, however. The highly publicized voucher plan of Milton Friedman and Christopher Jencks has yet to have a full testing in even one school district (an experiment in Alum Rock, California, does not provide private school choices), much less being adopted state-wide.

The speed with which the issue of financial reform was raised, debated, litigated and adopted among the 50 states tells us much about the deep voter dissatisfaction at their increasingly heavy burden, particularly as the inflation of the Vietnam War took hold after 1965. But an unexamined aspect of such reform is its consequences for administrative authority, to be explored later.

**Table 3–1. School Finance Reform among 50 States as of May 1974***

|  | *Number of States* |
| --- | --- |
| Court Cases (mostly pending or on appeal) | 26 |
| Tax Studies | 10 |
| School Finance Study Commissions | 18 |
| Property Tax Relief Programs (mandatory, permissive, "circuit breaker," elderly homeowners, homestead exemptions, etc.) | 50 |
| Property Tax Reforms: Farm Land Use | 34 |
| Property Tax Reforms: Assessment | 15 |
| School Finance Reform Programs: |  |
| None | 18 |
| Pending | 7 |
| Passed | 25 |
| "Major Change" = 13 | |

*Source: Education Commission of the States, *School Finance at a Glance* (Denver: 1974).

**Racial Minorities and Desegregation.** The core constituency of racial minorities, so intimately involved in school desegregation, has in mind two purposes. These groups first seek a status goal, the recognition that the Constitution's commitment to equal protection of the law applied to them also, despite centuries of prejudice and discrimination. As such, then, desegregation is but one aspect of what I have elsewhere termed the "politics of deference," the central struggle of ethnic politics in America to gain respect for one's importance and value as individuals and as a group.[19] The second goal of minorities in school desegregation is material, namely, the reallocation of school resources to improve the life chances of their children. As such, then, desegregation is but one aspect of renewed concern for redistributive justice sparked in the last decade by challenges to the standards of urban service provided to America's poor of whatever race.

In this school effort almost nothing has been done without external pressure upon the local district. Everywhere the forces of court orders, and, in the South prior to Nixon's Administration, the threat of fund cutoffs to segregating schools have achieved whatever has been done.[20] Local protests alone brought little change in encrusted racial conditions, despite the nationwide publicity.[21]

Much physical desegregation has taken place in the South; now the politics of the pre-busing phase has yielded to the essentially educational problems that transpire thereafter. Certainly much more has taken place in that region than anyone—including Southerners—expected ten or even five years ago. Between 1962 and 1972, the South desegregated while the North intensified its segregation. In the South, the percentage of blacks attending schools with some whites rose from 1 percent to 91 percent, while 46 percent of the blacks attended predominantly white schools. In the North, however, fewer than 29 percent of the blacks attended such schools, while a substantial majority of black students in border state and Northern schools attended schools with 80 percent black enrollment; the figure in the South was only 30 percent. In Chicago and Philadelphia, only 3 and 7.4 percent, respectively, of black students attended predominantly white schools, to highlight the essentially urban concentration of this minority.[22]

The account in the North is of another world, where courts have moved slowly and the Nixon and Ford Administrations have sought to do little.[23] But where there has been litigation, there has also been a spate of district judges ordering desegration. Every fall for a few years past and more yet to come the opening of Northern schools has seen some big city in turmoil over beginning this task; in 1974 there were Denver, Boston and Baltimore. Wherever such turmoil transpires there is a formal, almost inescapable, drama that must needs unfold, each stage to be followed regardless of locale. Slowly across the Northern school system there are developing new mandates of desegregation with obvious impact upon local school authorities. The refusal by the Supreme Court in *Bradley v. Milliken* in mid–1974 to use metropolitan desegregation for dealing with the problem does not halt the spread of desegregation orders to central city districts. It is in this relative handful of districts, not much more than 100, with their large populations of black and brown minorities, that desegregation is now constrained by the Court's 5–4 decision. What this means for administrators will be noted shortly.

**Students and Their Rights.** The core constituencies sketched to this point are based outside the school walls, but two others operate inside them, i.e., students and teachers.[24] However, both have known the same remarkably brief, recent period when new concepts have suddenly flowered to provide new powers formerly dominated by administrators. Considering their relative defenselessness, the students have made strides which are particularly dramatic against the long background of the law's indifference to them.

For most of our history, the authority of the administrator over the student's life at school was almost complete. Legislatures provided the state departments of education with broad authority which the departments translated into highly permissive grants to local boards which in turn passed their daily implementation to the schoolmen. The federal constitution and statutes had no place here, for the idea of student rights rooted in these sources simply did not exist. In this era of *laissez-faire,* the administrator's response to any student even politely questioning why he had to dress, walk, eat, speak and otherwise act in the prescribed manner was much like that of writer Ring Lardner when his children questioned him: " 'Shut up,' I explained."

It now seems quaint to note major landmark decisions, because so much has changed so quickly. Thus New York in 1874 backed local school authorities when a nine-year-old's mother objected to the requirements about her daughter's hair. In 1923 the Arkansas Supreme Court upheld school bans against talcum powder and "transparent hosiery," and in 1931 North Dakota courts supported school prohibitions against heel taps on shoes. Courts left such matters almost entirely in administrators' hands unless the plaintiff could show they were "arbitrary, capricious or unreasonable"; claims that schoolmens' actions were unwise or inexpedient were ignored as irrelevant to the law.

All that has changed drastically and in just a few years. While the dust has not yet settled, it is clear that courts will now entertain other challenges to treatment of students. As one review of the field notes, "While a fairly uncritical acceptance of educators' views on the connection between a regulation and a legitimate school goal is still the rule, the recent cases indicate an increasing tendency to scrutinize facts and to give something more than cursory hearing to student claims."[25] That is particularly the case when the claim rests on grounds of free speech or press, of religion or of discrimination. As John Hogan has summarized in his magisterial review of new education law, "Whereas formerly the party attacking the statute, educational practice or school rule carried the burden, now, where a First Amendment or a Fourteenth Amendment right is alleged to have infringed, the school authorities must carry the burden of proving that the 'intrusion by the state is in furtherance of a legitimate state interest.' "[26]

The seminal United States Court decision in this field, which typified subsequent thinking by other courts, came in 1969 in the *Tinker* case. Des Moines students wearing black armbands to protest the Vietnam war were suspended, even though they were passive and created no disruption. The Court's opinion noted that where a basic Constitutional right, like that of free speech under the First Amendment, was being exercised, and there was no evidence that the student action interfered with school purposes or disrupted schooling, no punishment could be levied.[27] As later cases showed, such an exercise *could* create disruptions and be prohibited. Southern schools could not restrict the wearing of civil rights buttons if nondisruptive, but could do so if they caused disturbances.[28]

In a few years this principle, and those of due process and equal protection of the laws, have irradiated many traditional school practices. Only a brief listing of judicial restraint of once conventional disciplinary rules and management decisions is possible here, but recall that these emerged only since 1969. They include prohibitions against: censorship of student publications; use of athletic symbols, Confederate flags and school names; hair length; lack of procedures for suspension and expulsion;* corporal punishment; use of bulletin boards; use of achievement or aptitude tests; rules for athletic eligibility; preference for male rather than female sports programs, etc. The question of hair length may have generated the most widespread furor, but there is as yet no clear-cut decision. The Supreme Court has refused to review hair cases as minor matters. Different courts have both permitted and prohibited rules in this matter; one court permitted Utah Indians any hair length, so long as it was braided, while another forbade it for Pawnees.

There is no survey available of the national extent of these changes. Some court decisions have been limited to states or appellate regions, and few legislatures wander into this thicket. Some districts seemed untouched by any of these changes, but others, like those of urban California, have provided students with detailed statements of their rights.[29] Other challenges to traditional administrative autonomy loom ahead, however. Litigation is underway over (and a national citizens committee is publicizing) the use of students for educational or social science surveys.[30]

One thing is certain, though. We are a long way from Lardner's approach to student's queries when publications exist like that by Kathy Boudin and others, *The Bust Book: What To Do Till the Lawyer Comes.*[31]

**Teachers and Organizational Power.** The other core constituency challenging traditional administrative authority from inside the school are those teachers who were once widely seen as submissive. It would be hard today to find a city superintendent or principal who would so regard them, for a sea-change has transpired among teachers in the past ten years. Part of this stems from changes in American education itself and part from teachers' perceptions of themselves. But here, as with other groups, things will never be the same again.

Guthrie and Craig have pointed out that teachers achieved a potential for power partly because education became big business.[32] Because more parents wanted their children to have more schooling after World War II, and because

---

*In early 1975 the Supreme Court nullified school administrators' authority to suspend or expel students without notice and hearing.

there were more children to be educated, Americans spent more on education, and that meant more teachers were needed. Thus, as a proportion of the GNP, school expenditures rose during the period 1949 to 1970 from about 3.5 to 8.0 percent. Where we spent only $2 billion in 1940, we spend $50 billion in 1970, and the United States Office of Education estimates it will be over $100 billion in 1980. Riding this injection of massive funds into the schools, teachers also grew in number, from just over one million in 1940 to almost three million in 1971 and possibly to 3.5 million in 1980. They are now one million fewer in number than farmers, but are substantially greater than teamsters, auto workers, steel workers and doctors. Not surprisingly, too, their income rose; between 1952 and 1968 it increased by over 125 percent, while personal income and employee average earnings rose nationally by only about 94 percent. Their salaries passed the average earnings of industrial workers some time back, and the gap increased even more during the 1960s.

But this improvement in income was not caused simply by riding the economic boom of the postwar years. Some part of it must be attributed to teachers' increasingly conscious effort to organize for collective bargaining about salary and other matters. The cause and effect relationship is ambiguous, however. Did bargaining legislation and subsequent organization precede or follow teachers' dissatisfactions? Were boards and legislatures frightened into voluntary improvements in reaction against successful teacher strikes elsewhere? What were the costs incurred for such new power?

There is no question, however, of the growth of teachers in affiliations that have become more insistent on improving working conditions. This insistence was seen in the toughening up of the larger National Education Association, once passive on these issues, or the rise of the smaller but more militant American Federation of Teachers. The interaction between these two had led to signs of eventual merger. National merger efforts have failed recently, but in mid-1972, the state equivalents of the NEA and AFT in New York State did merge, creating the largest group of state employees in the nation; in early 1974 the two groups merged in Florida.

This organizational growth has been paralleled by the rise of the strike. Despite widely prevalent state laws against public employees' use of this tactic, some form of strike—"withholding of labor"—has developed as the main instrument for securing teachers' benefits in recent years. Between 1955 and 1965 there were only 35 strikes in all, but during the one year of 1967–1968 there were 114, and the next year 131. Coincidental or not, during this first period of strike action, 1966–68, the number of signed contracts increased by almost one-half.[33]

This success has not been without its attendant problems for teachers. As teachers participate increasingly in the reallocation of resources in the local, state and national political systems, they lose some of their aura of the "apolitical." It was this mythical quality which enabled them for so long to claim a large share of resources without contending with other claimants. Now, in the minds of state legislatures and city councils (where school budgets are sometimes reviewed), teachers are but one more pressure group whose claim to special treatment must be balanced off against others' claims. It follows that other pressure groups will increasingly combine against teachers' claims and thus draw them even more into open political conflict. There may also be some decrease in the status of teachers if they are seen as being just as "political," with all the opprobrium that term signifies in American culture.

As a consequence of these costs of success, some backlash effect has been found among teachers. Membership in a Los Angeles teacher group dropped off after a 1970 strike whose stigma made it difficult to enroll new members. Even that most publicized advocate of the strike, Albert Shanker, head of the New York AFT at the time, said, "Strikes may no longer be effective because of public resentment and because of the financial pressure on school boards. Now that they [teachers] have made big gains, the public reaction is likely to be 'what do they want now?' "[34]

Yet the growth in teacher power, which may have reached a zenith in New York City and Los Angeles by 1970, spreads differentially to other corners of the national education system. From the big cities, where the AFT has been most active, the movement has spread to suburbs, although rarely to small towns outside the metropolis. Sometimes the movement skips these places and blankets them in under state laws providing for negotiation of teacher salaries. However, these laws vary in their elaborateness and intensity of requirement. Some make it optional for the board to negotiate and others make it mandatory; some limit negotiation to a few issues and others provide wider scope. Whatever their form, however, they change the traditional interaction between teacher and administrator, adding yet another constraint to the authority which officials once knew.

### Extra-Community Stimuli

No constituency acts independently, for the turbulence of school politics is also affected by "extra-community stimuli." This may be the most important factor in contemporary local politics, whether they deal with schools, highrise buildings, welfare, ethnic conflict, roads or other public policies.[35]

There are three broad stimuli which affect these school constituencies. First, the state of the economy has great consequences both for the size of school resources and for their allocation. Many administrators, particularly the older superintendents, have witnessed two extremes of our national economy—bust and boom. The Great Depression of the 1930s clearly shrank all school budgets, thereby preventing the emergence of new programs and cutting others. Under such constraints from a public sorely pressed, the school boards could listen to few if any claims of core constituencies except the taxpayer.[36]

But more recently an enormous prosperity and subsequent recession penetrated probably every school district in the nation. In the resurgence of public support for schools, beginning with the post-Sputnik fervor and ending in the late 1960s as a direct consequence of the Vietnam War, a local politics of booming expenditures is visible. With ever-expanding resources available, many claimants for new programs and new benefits could be satisfied by boards and administrators. As this brief era ended federal money also entered the local scene to support claims of parents of the poor and minorities for compensatory education. At the present time the recession and inflation of the Nixon years have penetrated local districts, with constraining effects upon the core constituencies. All of these periods demonstrate the reality of the truism that ours is an interdependent economy.

Another extra-community stimulus is the power of new concepts, particularly those centered on social change. Every change concept mentioned earlier for core constituencies illustrates this process. Education also seems particularly subject to faddishness in curricular matters, as in new math, language instruction, ethnic studies, career education, etc. Certainly the new concept of "evaluation," given a powerful initiative by Title I of the 1965 ESEA, has penetrated many elements of school activity.

Spawned by some scholarly "scribbler," funded by foundations, transmitted by schoolmen's meetings and journals, researched and certified by schools of education, reform ideas sweep in recurring tides throught the American school system. Some are transitory, e.g., Nixon's "Right to Read" program, but others leave behind a permanent deposit upon schools, as with desegregation in the South. Behind them all, however small or large, lies someone's notion of the preferable, the efficient, the humane, the inexpensive and the just in matters of schooling.

Another class of extramural stimuli is those highly publicized, crystallizing events which quickly become visible to core constitutencies, dramatically generate new demands upon local school authorities and thereby add even more to the turbulence of school politics. A successful statewide teachers strike in Oklahoma and Florida; a precedent-shattering judicial decision in the *Tinker, Brown* and *Serrano* cases; a clash over community control in New York City—all illustrate the kind of event which the larger nation cannot ignore. Economic booms or busts are of this type, too, but of such enormous, pervasive effect that they deserve separate consideration.

These extramural events are not totally separate from extramural concepts, for each of the examples noted above emerged from a full-blown conception about change in the allocation of those resources and values which schools can distribute. But a concept lacks both life and influence when it is merely circulated among scholars, until an event embodying it crystallizes national attention and transmits consideration to the total school system. Of course, a concept can have an effect without the crystallizing event; the dissemination of sex education programs by school administrators illustrates this boring-from-within process of change.[37] But the combination of concept and event, by their mutual interaction, creates a more powerful stimulus for change among the core constituencies which now make local school politics so turbulent.

### Administrative Responses to
### School Turbulence

As in any political system, the pressures for change focus upon authoritative bodies, in this case the school boards and the administrators. This paper treats only administrative authority, which has been the focus of so much criticism for frustrating democratic inputs into school policy. The account of school board authority can be noted in brief, though. Whether it is a broad survey, as by the Carnegie Commission, or an in-depth analysis by social scientists, observers of these boards find them increasingly impotent. Harmon Zeigler and M. Kent Jennings' recent study shows there is some variation in this weakness, but their results are not much different from the Commission conclusion:

> It must be plain from all that has gone before that in three major aspects, all vital to public education (integration, teacher power, and finances), the American school board has reached a point where what was merely inadequacy has come close to total helplessness, where decline and fall are no longer easily distinguished.[38]

My concern is rather with the consequences of turbulence for administrative authority. How has each of these newly politicized constituencies affected that authority?

The *parent-shared-control* factor overtly seeks to alter that authority. Note, however, that superintendent and principal have been affected differently. Typically, a decentralization reform (remember that no full community control exists) devolves decisions about allocations of resources and personnel to another professional who captains an elementary or secondary school. Even in the Florida plan noted earlier, or in New York City's highly publicized system of multiple districts, authority is still invested in publicly accountable agencies under state law, i.e., local boards and superintendents. That authority's operationalization is put in the hands of subordinate professionals who receive inputs, usually advisory and rarely compulsory, from school site parents. For the superintendent, this lay requirement seems like a diminution of his use of that authority, although it can also free him from management to engage in educational policy planning.

For the principals, however, the reform can mean an increased role in decision making, even though it also raises problems. The actual effects of parents upon the new-found authority of principals is highly various. In Chicago, one study found that while most parent councils were responsible in selecting principals (decisions ratified by higher authorities), in a few cases they evaded procedural safeguards for such professionals.[39] Administrators in New York, when exposed to lay channels, become more open to such influence.[40] However, Harry Summerfield has shown how this openness is more a function of administrators' style than of community requirements.[41] Among major cities, though, there is considerable variation in the influence of parents (although always less than predicted), depending upon local pressures.[42]

But there is no evidence that the pressure of shared control has either diminished all administrative authority or has increased all parental influence. All reports do agree, however, that when this issue generates a change in policy, both superintendent and principal begin to act in different ways. They exhibit increased sensitivity to lay concerns, new perceptions of what the school system is doing that has caused parental concern, and a willingness—albeit grudgingly at times—to accept the once heretical notion of lay participation in decisions about "professional" matters.

This does not mean that a mass conversion of spirit has taken place among the professionals. After all, there are reports from New York City that some lay district boards have become as bureaucratic as 110 Livingston Street ever was. Some caused parental appeals to the city's central board for justice, equity or plain help; these local boards had adopted their district superintendents' views. Certainly no administrator under decentralization has become an impotent instrument of the neighborhood; if he felt so, he usually left. Many have gained more resources to do their task, and most have adjusted in some degree to new ideas about their tasks.

Whether this lay influence persists depends upon a problem that plagues all reform, i.e., can lay organs find the sticking power to continue guarding their interests? There are persistent turnover problems in lay councils. A paid bureaucracy would be effective in providing protection and permanence if established, but seems unlikely now. Note that such educational ombudsmen would provide control not only for local parents but for superintendents and boards as well. For the latter, a continuing flow of reports on complaints and their resolution would be indicators of compliance below with policy authorized above. Even without this, however, the rigid monopoly of power centralized in schools, so criticized a decade ago, has been diluted. These changes are not small, and they contribute to the evolving model of administrative authority.

The pressure of the *taxpayer-finance reform* came at a time when superintendents had depleted their authority over raising revenue; principals never had any. The growing costs of education after World War II placed the superintendent in a key position to generate and direct the new flow of local revenue. While all states had some limits upon local revenue, up to those limits the school authorities had wide rein. This was particularly so for the superintendent, whose recommendations provided the prime information available to the lay boards for their decisions.[43] But growing costs finally met up with those limits in many places, engendering cuts in existing programs, thereby contributing to the finance reform effort.

But where state limits had been reached, superintendents had lost the power to administer finances. Even where some margin remained, school officials faced a growing voter opposition to more bonds and levies; new strategies had to be adopted such as repeated submission of the same finance measure to the voters, threats to cut back popular programs, etc. But after the mid–1960s, referendum voters listened less to their school authorities and more to their pocketbooks, a clear sign of the diminution of the former's authority. In the face of these rebuffs, wise superintendents could find a scapegoat in the legislature's failure to provide sufficient funds, thereby adding another force to the reform impulse.

Looking ahead, the effect of finance reform upon administrative authority depends upon the degree of controls accompanying the new monies.[44] If equalization measures bring more controls, they must dilute administrative authority, but if they come with few limitations then that authority could actually be increased. That is because new funds may not require the approval of local voters which is presently required. However much the state currently controls local schools—and it is quite varied in scope and intensity—most of it comes through regulatory powers, as in teacher and administrator credentialling. Little control is exercised through finances, as with Washington's categorical grants-in-aid. Most often, the state's financial control employs the devices of minimum, mandated expenditures in certain fields or maximums on tax efforts.

This reform can actually combine the taxpayer and parent constituencies; the Florida program was noted earlier, in which advisory councils prepare, oversee and publicize the school site budget. In California, there has developed a movement, especially in the suburbs, for superintendents to decentralize budgeting to the school site under control of the principal—but without a parental advisory council. Even without the latter, however, an extensive study of this development finds that the reform "had an effect upon decision outcomes. When new actors at the local school site [principal, teachers] were given the opportunity to develop budgetary priorities, they made differential decisions among schools and as compared to prior decisions made by the central office under a centralized budgetary system."[45] Hence, the eventual effect of finance reform of local authority depends upon whether state law is written to ensure either that "control follows the dollar" or that the existing decentralization of control is retained. That outcome, in turn, is a function of the highly various political cultures of the American states, in some places highly centralized and elsewhere highly decentralized.[46]

When we turn to the *minorities-desegregation* contribution to school turbulence, the surrounding emotionalism makes agreement difficult about its effect on anything, much less on administrative authority. But it is certain that the major purpose of this change has been to redirect school districts' allocations of resources, that is, to change those decisions which authorities had been making about minority education. In the process, numerous reports have shown that the change affects not merely this group but all others who minister to the schooling needs of children.

The administrative reaction to this external thrust has made a difference in its success. Robert Crain's longitudinal analysis of 555 Southern schools found not merely different reactions by administrators but different schooling results directly traceable to those reactions.[47] More recently, Gary Orfield, surveying that experience to determine what is needed for desegregation success, found among other criteria that "principals play a crucial role in the adaptation of a school, both in setting a social climate and in providing educational leadership." What eventuates under desegregation depends upon whether the administrator is seized by a self-fulfilling or self-denying prophecy. If he thinks desegregation can "work," he develops a staff of like-minded teachers, incorporates planning by constituencies both inside and outside the school site, and encourages children and staff alike that it can be done.[48]

One unintended consequence of desegregation for administrators, however, has been the firing or demotion of black principals in the South. Official United States reports and complaints by administrator organizations attest to this outcome; some of those demoted take lesser administrative positions, some return to the classroom, and some leave schools altogether.[49] Here is evidence of the old Southern practice of double standards for the quality of black vs. white education; "national" standards were little observed for black teachers or administrators until court orders compelled elimination of dual schools to create a unitary system.[50] Then, application of "professional" standards suddenly achieved a massive demotion of these blacks, an outcome which federal courts have increasingly reversed.[51]

But even in the North, where blacks hold administrative positions somewhat closer to their proportions in the local population, they face community challenges which weaken them. Divisions within the black community itself focus upon the black principal or, more rarely, upon the superintendent who is held responsible for the failure of the schools to achieve much change in outcomes for black children. While litigation, and occasionally state or local school policy, may require an affirmative action program to increase minority administrators, those benefiting soon find themselves under attack and constrained by intra-ethnic frictions.

Hence, whether we focus upon the superintendent or principal it is clear that they have borne the brunt of the responsibility for managing the conflict attendant upon desegregation. North or South, black or white, administrators are caught between an obligation to obey the law—a high value in any professional group's norms—and large and unhappy segments of the white community. Often resentful of or unused to dealing with the new ethnic group, uncertain about the strategies to make desegregation work, lacking training from their certifying school of education, administrators across the nation are in different stages of accommodation to this enormous reform. Few think this reform has augmented their authority. All radiate concern for recent constraints from litigation or the electorate which leave them uncertain about their personal fate, much less their authority.

Increasingly they know that in middle and larger cities it takes two superintendents to desegregate.[52] For the community will "burn" the first one who initiates it or seeks faithfully to carry out court mandates; he bears the brunt of outraged whites even though he lacks any options to do otherwise. The superintendent who replaces him usually reverses little of this change but rather consolidates the first one's gains while more effectively smoothing white fears. In this desegregation policy requiring the highest capacity for conflict management, we can see most clearly a pattern of administrators bowing to outside forces which alter their autonomy. But we can also see, in the successes of some superintendents and principals in conflict management and educational improvement, that administrators react differently to such extramural forces. As with any group of potential leaders, some convert challenge into opportunity.

As an issue, *students' civil rights* have been like desegregation. Both were imposed from the outside primarily as a result of litigation, the first arising from a concern for freedom or expression and due process, the other from a concern for equality. But desegregation has been under way at least since 1954, but the students rights issue only since 1969, and as a result much less is known about the latter's effect on administrative authority. Its central thrust, of course, is to constrain that authority over the expression, dress, manners and morals of students. To date, the national extent of subsequent change is simply not known.

But there are some signs of response. One is seen in the advisories provided to teachers and administrators by their professional organizations. Their journals highlight recent developments in litigation, and their national offices develop written materials which can be used as guidelines for local action. For example, in 1970 the National Association of Secondary School Principals isolated ten aspects of student rights and devised "defensible positions" for administrators on each. These included rights in: freedom of expression, personal appearance, behavior codes, student property, extracurricular activities, discipline, student government, student press, right to petition and the use of drugs.[53] Each was centered in a discussion of the prevailing court opinions under the First and Fourteenth Amendments, and each discussed policies which administrators could appropriately take. Such professionals are far removed from those who, acting *in loco parentis*, once knew few limits on their definition of students' rights to justice or expression.

Legislatures in some cases have added to these constraints by following through on court decisions. When a federal court in 1970 found unconstitutional California's education code provisions on student expression, the legislature a year later repealed them and substituted others, thereby recognizing the introduction of the First Amendment to the campus. Students were given specific rights to use of bulletin boards, distribution of printed materials and petitions and the wearing of buttons, badges and other insignia. But these forms of expression were not permitted if obscene, libelous, slanderous or inciteful of student acts which were unlawful, if they violated lawful school regulations or if they disrupted orderly operation of the schools. While the exceptions take much away from the grants, the specific recognition of these grants' constitutionality is itself a new constraint on administrative authority. But again, the full extent of such constraints across the nation is not yet known.

The *teacher bargaining power* factor in current school turbulence has the same result for the dilution of authority as parents seeking shared power. That is, both involve the direct participation of a core constituency in decision making. But in both cases there is considerable ambiguity, because legally the responsibility lies with a board and its chief officer. Whatever direction this new teacher role may take, to date teachers have focused primarily upon improving themselves materially, not educationally.

This can be seen in a simple count of the provisions in 398 comprehensive agreements negotiated during 1966–1967, just as this movement broke into full stride. The items most sought (in the 90 percent range) were grievance procedure, salary schedule and salary increment. Little if any of these and other items dealt with the teaching function directly; the class size (sought in half the contracts) may deal as much with workload considerations as with educational reasons. Directly educational matters are much farther down this list, e.g., selection and distribution of textbooks (35 percent) and curriculum review (21 percent). In short, the teachers' search for power at this date had gone no farther than bread-and-butter issues.[54]

What have been the measurable consequences for the superintendent in such negotiations? His role obviously varies with the legal authority to negotiate, which is shared differently across the nation. In Figure 3–2 data are assembled on

**Figure 3–2.** Negotiators for the School Board

| Role of the Superintendent | Board members | Board members and superintendent | Board members and school administrators | Superintendent | School administrators |
|---|---|---|---|---|---|
| Negotiator with full authority | 0.5% | 2.5% | 1.5% | 11.9% Cal. Mich. Ohio | 5.4% |
| Negotiator with limited authority | 0.8% | 3.7% | 1.1% | 8.8% | 1.7% |
| Advisor to negotiators for the board | 5.8% | 3.3% | 1.4% | 0.5% | 2.5% |
| Advisor to negotiators for both the board and the teachers | 21.5% Conn. Ore. Ill. Wash. Mass. Wisc. N.J. U.S. N.Y. | 10.6% | 3.1% | 4.3% | 1.3% |
| Neutral resource person | 4.5% | 1.1% | 0.5% | 0.4% | 0.1% |
| Nonparticipant | 0.3% | 0.1% | 0.0% | 0.0% | 0.6% |

United States: patterns in negotiation (1493 responses) Each state name indicates the location of the modal response for that state. (Only the eleven states with more than 50 responses each are included.) The mode for the United States is indicated, also.

Source:  Jack Culbertson et al., *Preparing Educational Leaders for the Seventies* (Columbus, Ohio: University Council for Educational Administration, 1969), p. 139.

this variation among the 11 states which in 1968 reported more than 50 negotiations. In only about 22 percent of the agreements did the superintendent have full authority, whether on his own or acting for others. But in about 41 percent of the agreements he was an advisor for both board and teachers and in about 8 percent he was neutral or nonparticipant. This suggests that his power in this area may not have been as great as the model of administrative autonomy asserted or that it has been drastically reduced recently.

Several of these turbulent issues may interact in the future so as to cause the teacher constituency to look elsewhere to satisfy its goals. If the state role in financing local school costs increases, teachers may turn to the legislature for salary and other benefits; at the local level the game for them simply may not be worth the effort. Too, as the federal government becomes increasingly involved in desegregation, its funds will go to help in that change, making Washington, not the local system, the focus of teacher concerns about compensatory education. That has certainly been the case under ESEA and the more recent Emergency School Assistance Program for court-mandated schools.

Considerations such as these lie behind the recent observation of Guthrie and Craig that:

> ... as teachers achieve political strength and force boards to share their delegated authority, a power realignment begins to emerge. The aggressive tactics of teachers, particularly at the local level, have made it increasingly difficult for school boards to resolve value conflicts, and educational policy decisions are therefore being forced to higher and higher governmental levels. If this trend continues, one can envision educational policy being made at the federal level in annual negotiating sessions between the 'American Brotherhood of Educators' and the 'Secretary of Education.'[55]

The movement of teachers into organized labor, rather than their staying with the traditional client-centered professionalism, is probably inevitable if their demands for better income are to be heeded by boards and administrators. But it will mean that administrators have lost a major resource, the inducement of salary increases for those schools and teachers providing leadership for an entire system. Because it has been a long time since teachers have had salaries cut, we cannot say the administrator has lost the threat of such cuts. Down the road lies a course which should parallel organized labor in both the crafts and industrial unions. The role of the foreman and plant manager in the modern production unit is so circumscribed by union and governmental conditions that the notion of individual leadership has long disappeared. Whether there is a better working community as a result is strongly questioned at this time both by management and labor. Whether the future for teachers under similar conditions can produce an improved learning community is at least debatable.

We must not leave this world of limits upon administrative authority without brief mention of extra-community constraints. The federal role has been mentioned throughout as it emanates from litigation and statute. No one in education dealing with the world of Washington regulations and categorical programs in the last decade can deny the constrictions imposed—at the very least in terms of filling out forms. Clearly the courts have imposed new definitions of the rights of taxpayers, minorities, students and teachers. But even more compelling has been the longer-lived force of the state.

Because schools, like all governmental units, are instruments of state constitution and statute, American schools have grown under that direction. Moreover, this control has altered over the decades from being very general to being very specific.[56] The details of such control for all states were recently assembled for the first time by the National Institute of Education.[57] Even a scan of these details suggests the validity of the conceptual linkages of state control which Figure 3–3 lays out. As a detailing of the right side of Figure 3–1's paradigm laid out earlier, Figure 3–3 provides an impressionist sense of the world with which most superintendents have had to contend. Of course, some cling to these constraints as ways of life, in which "going by the book" is the only—and safest—professional norm. However, some manipulate these constraints at the margins

**Figure 3–3.** Constraints on Big-City School Boards' Control over Budget

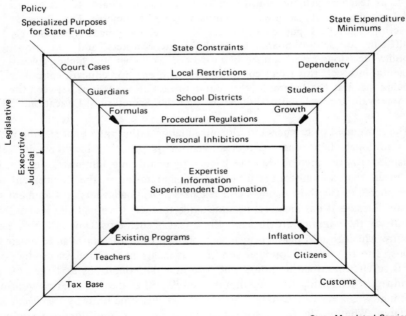

Source: Frederick M. Wirt and Michael W. Kirst, *The Political Web of American Schools* (Boston: Little, Brown, 1972), p. 82.

where they believe their own efforts can improve children's learning. But for all, these state requirements, constantly increasing, set the path by which their professional course proceeds. However, that course is itself undergoing change, as new definitions of professional roles are emerging.

### New and Old Models of Professionalism

At a rate not known for half a century, superintendents during the 1960s left or lost their jobs, particularly in big city schools, and herein lies one major sign of the consequences of the political turbulence this article sketches. Larry Cuban, studying the turnover of these officials during this century, found that:[58] during the 1960s, only two large cities kept their superintendents; during 1970–1973 in the 25 largest school systems, 23 new superintendents were appointed; the tenure in these 25 has dropped regularly, from 6–1/2 years in 1953 to 5–1/2 years in 1963 to just over 4 years in 1973 (it was 27 months in California in 1974);[59] the number of candidates for the biggest, ostensibly most attractive jobs is down sharply even while the salary and prerequisites have increased (in Pennsylvania, 50 applied for the Pittsburgh system with 75,000 students while 160 applied in York with its 8000). Suddenly, the most significant jobs in the profession of education administration are untenable.

Curiously, it was even more difficult during the 1910s, although the issues which could explain the turnover (e.g., consolidation) were not those of our day. In the judgment of experienced observers of the current scene, there is one similarity between the two periods which accounts for the turnover.[60] This is that the role model of the superintendent is in severe transition because of political challenge to the traditional model. Cuban believes that in the earlier period turnover was accounted for by the transition from the role of "teacher-scholar" to that of "administrative chief," from a head regularly called "professor" to one called "manager." And today, observers believe, the managerial role, which required considerable autonomy, centralization and responsiveness to technocratic norms of efficient management, is the central focus of attack by the constituencies discussed here. All the attributes of the rigid, inward-oriented, system-maintenance administrator are what the five issues traced earlier have in common in their criticisms.

This new role has been shaping since at least the *Brown* decision, when outraged Southern whites were faced with superintendents responsive to professional norms which emphasized obeying the law. I earlier noted how subsequent challenges, such as the competency of instruction for Johnny and other criticisms, brought the professional's autonomy into question. The new role is labeled "negotiator-statesman" by Cuban, but whatever the term the position now demands skills for which these leaders were poorly prepared. One review of their training concludes that "the literature contains no evidence of a generally accepted program for preparing superintendents to deal with social problems, and . . . most evidence indicates that current training programs are inadequate in this regard."[61] Superintendents in larger systems are more keenly aware of socio-cultural issues and ferment, however, and it follows, of the personal pressures accompanying them.[62]

Indeed, there are numerous signs that role expectations are changing, demanded not merely by these constituencies but by the profession itself. The reason is simple—survival. These constituencies demand some kind of sharing with the once independent chief, and their demands are everywhere rampant. Outside forces and authorities compel that these demands be heard; after adjusting for all the mosaic differences of the American school system, it is clear that the local and outside influences compel some acquiescence. Administrators may learn to adjust to some of them and still retain some autonomy, but they do so only when permitted by their constituencies. Therefore, "to get along they must go along" always the motto of those who survive in any system change.[63]

But in this new turbulence there are opportunities for dramatic educational leadership. Superintendents in Riverside, Pasadena, Berkeley and many Southern sites have found new ways of adapting to, indeed stimulating, currents of desegregation, shared control and student rights. In almost every desegregating system principals appear who make a difference to the education of minorities, who bring all constituencies into their planning and implementation to produce an educational environment that literally bubbles with the excitement of learning. These professionals may have thrived in this fashion even under the old model of administrative autonomy, but amidst such new events they are more significant as models of the future administrator.

In one sense, effective education leadership has always involved skillful balancing of impulses in the school environment. Under the model which prevailed until recently, that skill could be exercised with a minimum of oversight by others, except the influence of professional norms. The need for money, the desire for parental interest, the problem of educating the disadvantaged, the calls for justice and freedom by students and the preferences of teachers—all existed before the recent turbulence, and all administrators learned to work with them. What is new, of course, is that the balancing of these forces no longer takes place without some outside referent. In broadest terms, these constituencies are a modern version of the American people's historical and endemic fear of unchecked political power. This secular version of original sin has finally touched school administrators, moving them far more than their traditional rhetoric about "responsibility" to "the community" in a "democratic" nation. Those words took on much fuller meaning in the past ten to fifteen years, and education administration will never be the same again.

Those who cannot adapt, like the superintendents in the big cities, will leave as "burned out cases" after a few years. Those who replace them for longer periods will come from the cadre of superintendents who were "burnt" in smaller cities, themselves principals who earlier learned how to thrive under this turbulence. Currently, in training the next generation of superintendents, the schools of education seem to be doing a less than adequate job of working with the new model. Meanwhile, those currently on the firing line find their earlier graduate training to be of limited value, as they try hastily to catch up by intensive seminars and frequent conferences. A few schools of education are exceptions here, particularly those seeking to apply concepts of social science to understanding the administrator's new role.[64]

At the end of this period, that new role will center strongly around the function of persuasion. This art lies at the heart of all political decision-making, whether it be done by president of the nation or of the bank, or by superintendent, principal or board member. But persuasion is much more than some expressive skill obtained from majoring in Speech. Rather, it is the recognition of the true interests of those in contention before the political system of the schools, the search for the potential common ground on which coalitions of interests can be formed and the ability to cause others to see that common pursuit of mutual interest.

As the best of the old model types were, so will the best of this evolving model type be—a political leader in the best sense of the word. They will work among the competing demands for always limited resources in search of the agreement among constituencies about what they do want presently and—more important—what they will want in the future. Politicians are always with us, of course, providing constituencies with their current desires. But those who can achieve agreement about what will be desired are always hard to find and train. Ironically, one of the continuing needs of democracies is to find the second type, for they are political *leaders,* who are bound inexorably to the fate of their constituencies.

### Theories of Change in School Policy

This review of the new political turbulence of American schools has stressed the rise of constituencies, charged by American ideology to control those who control the allocation of resources. At the end, it is important to return to our first theme, that this resurgence is but one aspect of the continuing tension between leadership and citizens in a democratic polity. Were our measures of social and political life larger and harder, we might plot the secular rhythms of this tension, from popular acquiescence and leadership dominance to popular pressure and leadership acquiescence.

If this theme is an old one, it has also been particularly a part of the urban scene. There has always been a greater potential for a more lively school politics in the bigger cities, rather than in small town and rural America, because of a greater mix of life-styles and the attendant conflict over what schools should provide children to be found in the urban scene.[65] The impulse toward reform in American schools has sprung mostly from the city, not the countryside. The latter has preferred to maintain its homogeneous preferences about schools—and about most other aspects of life.

Thus, each of the reform issues discussed here—desegregation, finance reform, student rights, teacher power, parental input to decision making—came from the cities or the states with large urban populations. The *Brown* case, after all, had Topeka and other cities as the defendants twenty years ago; the *Tinker* case arose in Des Moines, and the urban states of New York and California have led in state-wide innovations for students; finance reform was spearheaded in California, Michigan, Florida (95 percent urban), and other states of this size; the concept of community control arose in New York City (smaller places and rural schools have always had it); and teacher power stems from the power of New York and California teachers with an early statewide strike arising in Florida.

The tension between leadership and citizens, then, is overlaid by the status differentials of the American people which generate school conflict between districts and within them. The status bases of this conflict create differing ideas about whom the school should respond to, who should pay its costs and what it should teach. Professional educators' ideas about such matters tend to be accepted, sometimes for long periods, as long as they do not severely contradict constituents' ideas of responsiveness, cost and service. In this respect, then, school administrators are in much the same relationship to their constituents as the elected official or those administering other kinds of urban services.

But contradictions are bound to arise in this policy system, as in any other. One explanation for this alteration is a modified devil theory—insensitive bureaucrats, playing their own closed game called "professionalism" which really distributes hard as well as symbolic rewards, ignore their constituents' demands when their sources are powerless. The powerless are teachers, parents, students, minorities and—with some modifications—taxpayers. This explanation is most clearly seen in the Ford Foundation efforts to have community control adopted in New York City and elsewhere. But the explanation fails to explain a vital facet of these times—what accounts for the changed attitude and new behavior of the constituents? Too, it does not countenance growing evidence, such as this survey of such studies points out, that administrators do change, like any official in a democratic system, when groups organize and push their demands.

Another explanation is more a theory of social and political change than the devil theory (which argues there is no change). This assumes the interdependence of parts of the nation, such that they all respond to national conditions as they change. Such conditions would be: shock at the engineering advances of the Russian Sputnik effort of the late 1950s; widespread publicity by educators that schools needed more money, as in the early 1960s; the inflationary impact of a war or the deflationary impact of a depression; the development of a national pressure group of teachers whose composition changed to include more men more aggressive about putting demands upon school boards, etc. Alterations of the national scene have reverberations among all local areas, albeit at a differential rate. In such cases, the conventional wisdom and accepted authority of local school systems become targets of challenge by school constituents who are affected adversely, i.e., those who are caught between the prevailing local conditions and the emergent new conditions with their ideas about changing existing allocations of resources.

This explanation is more satisfactory because it encompasses more of seemingly disparate reforms, but it sets up the problem of infinite regress, namely, what or who caused the change in national conditions which have impact locally? In a paper of this size that larger question cannot be answered, merely raised. This explanation has another strength, though, in that it permits a historical dimension to be explored. For it suggests that underlying the continuing tension among leaders and citizens over time have been national forces, some reflective of an international order, whose alterations generate new possibilities and threats for the existing structure of resources.

Here again, schools are a mirror not merely of some local happenstances. Rather, they reflect a national system in all its social, economic and political networks, a system which alters over time in response to events outside its borders, to the mistakes of its leadership and to new preferences of its citizens. The five issues newly politicized and discussed here reflect, in all but the case of parental inputs, another facet of that national system. This is the tendency to centralize decision making somewhere beyond local units. We have noted the enlarged role of state governments over schools. But note, too, that federal courts and a federal Congress have also contributed to new rights of students and minorities without quite accepting the concept of schooling as a constitutionally protected right—although failing to do so only by a very narrow margin in the 1973 *Rodriguez* decision.

That schools mirror America—surely not their exclusive role—reveals growing uniformity and also variety. And in that variety the urban schools stand forth most prominently, whether in the suburban or central city sectors. The variety of suburban schools reflects their familiar diversity in suburban life styles. But core city schools in most places still also display variety: good and bad schools, technical and commercial schools, schools with little and those with much parental participation, those with exciting and those with dull administrators and teachers, etc. In short, because so many Americans now live in cities, particularly in metropolitan areas, these places and their schools must necessarily reflect the variety of the American people. That variety means, at its heart, differences in life styles which generate differences in preferences about public policy and the authority of their officials—even about how they should be elected. This explanation seems to offer a richer analytical framework which explains what has happened to school officials in recent years.

As a theory, then, it predicts that the recent school turbulence will diminish when constituencies are increasingly less active. This implies a future state when a match will exist between popular inputs and authorities' actions (the optimistic prediction) or when citizens give up trying to change the actions of authorities (the pessimistic prediction). But if the past is any guide, such popular upswellings in the history of education have always left behind a new policy system and new roles for authorities. Indeed, each of the reforms noted in this chapter rebelled against ideas which, in their time, had been themselves new challenges to prevailing wisdom. There seems no reason to judge that our future will be any different.

## NOTES

1. Gladys A. Wiggin, *Education and Nationalism* (New York: McGraw-Hill, 1962).

2. Joseph M. Cronin, *The Control of Urban Schools* (New York: The Free Press, 1973); Michael B. Katz, ed., *School Reform: Past and Present* (Boston: Little, Brown, 1971); and Diane Ravitch, *The Great School Wars: New York City* (New York: Basic Books, 1974).

3. Robert R. Alford, *Bureaucracy and Participation* (Chicago: Rand McNally, 1969); Ralph Kimbrough, *Political Power and Educational Decision Making* (Chicago: Rand McNally, 1964); Harry L. Summerfield, *The Neighborhood-based Politics of Education* (Columbus, Ohio: Merrill, 1971).

4. Norton Long, *The Unwalled City* (New York: Basic Books, 1972), and Frederick M. Wirt, *Power in the City* (Berkeley: University of California Press, 1974).

5. Frederick M. Wirt and Michael Kirst, *The Political Web of American Schools* (Boston: Little, Brown, 1972), p. 7; republished as *The Political and Social Foundations of American Schools* (Berkeley: McCutchan, 1975).

6. Edgar Fuller and Jim B. Pearson, *Education in the States: Nationwide Development Since 1900* (Washington: National Education Assn., 1969), p. 12.

7. James W. Guthrie, "Public Control of Public Schools: Can We Get It Back?" *Public Affairs Report,* 15 (June, 1974), p. 2.

8. Richard F. Carter and John Sutthoff, *Communities and Their Schools* (Stanford: Institute for Communication Research, 1960).

9. David Rogers, *110 Livingston Street* (New York: Random House, 1968).

10. George R. LaNoue and Bruce L.R. Smith, *The Politics of School Decentralization* (Lexington, Mass.: D.C. Heath, 1973).

11. Summerfield, *The Neighborhood-based Politics of Education.*

12. See the variety displayed by 32 large systems in 1969 in Education Research Service, "Decentralization and Community Involvement: A Status Report" (Washington: National Education Assn.), Circular No. 7, November, 1969. See also Albert P. Cardarelli, "Decentralization and Community Control: A National Survey of the Public School System in the United States" (Washington: American Federation of Teachers, May, 1970), which reports that only 9 of 55 big city systems had decentralization; these were large student population and more than 25 percent black.

13. Guthrie, pp. 4–5, reports on the Florida experience.

14. LaNoue and Smith, chapter 9; and George H. Gallup, "Fourth Annual

Gallup Poll of Public Attitudes Toward Education," *Phi Delta Kappan,* 54 (September, 1972), p. 38.

15. See the in-progress work of Donna Shalala, Columbia University, on the latter, and of Michael Kirst, Stanford University, on the former.

16. R.L. Johns, "State Financing of Elementary and Secondary Education," in Fuller and Pearson, p. 180.

17. Wirt and Kirst, pp. 138–41, provide national data on bond support.

18. Gallup, pp. 35–36.

19. Wirt, Part V, explores this politics of deference among the "arrived" and "arriving" minorities.

20. See every report of the U.S. Commission on Civil Rights. A theoretical basis for this outcome is found in T. Bentley Edwards and Frederick M. Wirt, *School Desegregation in the North* (San Francisco: Chandler, 1967), chapters 1, 13.

21. Robert Crain et al., *Political Strategies in Northern Desegregation* (Lexington, Mass.: D.C. Heath, 1973).

22. Gary Orfield, "Federal Policy, Local Power and Metropolitan Segregation," paper presented to the American Political Science Assn. convention, 1974, p. 3. For the latest demographic analysis, see Reynolds Farley, "Residential Segregation and Its Implications for School Integration," *Law and Contemporary Problems*, 34 (Winter, 1975), pp. 164–93.

23. A detailed analysis of this judgment is found in *Justice Delayed and Denied: HEW and Northern School Desegregation* (Washington: Center for National Policy Review, September 1974).

24. This section draws heavily upon John C. Hogan, *The Schools, the Courts, and the Public Interest* (Lexington, Mass.: D.C. Heath, 1974).

25. Note, "Public Secondary Education: Judicial Protection of Student Individuality," *Southern California Law Review,* 42 (1969), p. 130, cited in Hogan, p. 83.

26. Hogan, p. 79.

27. *Tinker v. Des Moines Independent Community School District,* 393 U.S. 503 (1969).

28. *Burnside v. Byars,* 363 F. 2d 744 (5th Cir. 1966), and *Blackwell v. Issaquena County Board of Education,* 363 F. 2d 749 (5th Cir. 1966).

29. For an example of new California city system rules, see Hogan, chapter 5.

30. National Committee for Citizens in Education, Columbia, Md.

31. Katharine Boudin et al., *The Bust Book: What To Do Till the Lawyer Comes* (New York: Grove Press, 1970.)

32. Following data cited from James W. Guthrie and Patricia A. Craig, *Teachers and Politics* (Bloomington, Ind.: Phi Delta Kappa Educational Foundation, 1973), pp. 9, 12, 13. For evolution of teacher power see also Jack Culbertson et al., *Preparing Educational Leaders for the Seventies* (Columbus, Ohio: University Council for Educational Administration, 1969), chapter 7.

33. Guthrie and Craig, pp. 12–13.

34. Ibid., p. 26.

35. This theme is illuminated in my writings cited earlier, as well as in *The Politics of Southern Equality* (Chicago: Aldine, 1970).

36. Studies may exist of the local politics under such conditions of economic bust which would demonstrate this observation, but its validation rests more upon the personal accounts of elder administrators whom I have interviewed over several years.

37. Neil Milner and James Hottois, *The Sex Education Controversy* (Lexington, Mass.: D.C. Heath, 1975).

38. Robert Bendiner, *The Politics of Schools* (New York: Harper and Row, 1969), p. 165; Harmon Zeigler and M. Kent Jennings, *Governing American Schools* (North Scituate, Mass.: Duxbury, 1974).

39. Mark M. Krug, "Chicago: The Principals' Predicament," *Phi Delta Kappan*, 56 (September, 1974), pp. 43–45.

40. Dale Mann, *The Politics of Administrative Representation* (Lexington, Mass.: D.C. Heath, 1976).

41. Summerfield, *The Neighborhood-based Politics of Education.*

42. LaNoue and Smith, *The Politics of School Decentralization.*

43. The process is described elsewhere in Norman D. Kerr, "The School Board as an Agency of Legitimation," *Sociology of Education,* 38 (1964), pp. 34–59.

44. Explored for suburbia in Frederick M. Wirt, "Financial and Desegregation Reform in Suburbia," in Louis Masotti and Jeffrey Hadden, eds., *The Urbanization of the Suburbs* (Beverly Hills, Ca.: Sage, 1973), chapter 14.

45. First report of this long range study is found in Patricia A. Craig, "Determinants and Effects of School-Site Management Reform in California Public Schools," paper presented to the American Political Science Assn. convention, September, 1974.

46. Six of these state cultures are examined in depth in Joel Berke and Michael Kirst, eds., *Federal Aid to Education: Who Benefits? Who Governs?* (Lexington, Mass.: D.C. Heath, 1973).

47. Robert L. Crain et al., *Southern Schools: An Evaluation of the Effects of the Emergency School Assistance Program and of School Desegregation* (Chicago: National Opinion Research Center, 1973).

48. Gary Orfield, "How to Make Desegregation Work: The Adaptation of Schools to their Newly-Integrated Student Bodies," *Law and Contemporary Problems*, 34 (Spring, 1975), pp. 314–40.

49. See source cited in note 22; for testimony and reports, see U.S. Senate, Select Committee on Equal Education Opportunity, *Hearings Part 10: Displacement and Present Status of Black School Principals in Desegregated School Districts* (Washington: U.S. Govt. Printing Office, 1971).

50. De Lars Funches, "The Superintendent's Expectations of the Negro High School Principal in Mississippi," *Journal of Experimental Education,* 34 (1965), pp. 73–77, reports a survey of 121 principals and 86 superintendents on 30 professional practices, on most of which they were deficient.

51. For a review of five cases since 1971 attacking teacher examinations, see Hogan, pp. 126–30. Most decisions have been critical of their use as not being demonstrably job-related and hence discriminatory in effect.

52. One California study found that small districts with few blacks desegregated without problems see; Eldon L. Wegner and Jane R. Mercer, "Dynamics of the Desegregation Process: Politics, Policies, and Community Characteristics as Factors in Change," in Frederick M. Wirt, ed., *The Polity of the School: New Research in Educational Politics* (Lexington, Mass.: D.C. Heath, 1975), chapter 8.

53. Hogan, p. 83.

54. Culbertson et al., p. 138.

55. Guthrie and Craig, pp. 22–23.

56. Fuller and Pearson, in every chapter document this dramatic change.

57. Lawyers' Committee for Civil Rights under Law, *A Study of State Legal Standards for the Provisions of Public Education* (Washington: National Institute of Education, 1974), and state-by-state reports.

58. Larry Cuban, "Urban Superintendents: Vulnerable Experts," *Phi Delta Kappan,* (December 1974), pp. 279–82; this is based on Cuban's dissertation, School of Education, Stanford University, 1974.

59. Conversation with Dr. Herbert Salinger, School of Education, Univeristy of California, Berkeley.

60. This section benefited from the collective judgments of senior members of the School of Education, University of California, Berkeley, including Dean Merle Borrowman, Theodore Reller, James Guthrie and Herbert Salinger.

61. Robin H. Farquhar and Philip K. Piele, *Preparing Educational Leaders: A Review of Recent Literature* (Columbus, Ohio: University Council for Educational Administration, 1972), pp. 6–7.

62. Robert T. Stout, *New Approaches to Recruitment and Selection of Educational Administrators* (Columbus, Ohio: University Council for Educational Administration, 1973), p. 9; see p. 9 ff. for studies of contemporary superintendents.

63. This motto, originally offered by Speaker Sam Rayburn in advising new Congressmen on how to succeed, is usually viewed as a system maintenance rule. But it also is appropriate for survivors in time of system change.

64. For a full treatment of this subject, see Jack Culbertson et al., *Social Science Content for Preparing Educational Leaders* (Columbus, Ohio: Merrill, 1973).

65. This distinction is explored at length in Frederick Wirt, "Social Diversity and Board Responsiveness in Urban Schools," in Peter Cistone, ed., *Understanding School Boards: Problems and Prospects* (Lexington, Mass.: D.C. Heath, 1976).

Chapter Four

# The Press and the
# New Urban Politics

**E. TERRENCE JONES**

During the past decade, social scientists in general—and political scientists in particular—have become much more concerned with the effects that changes in governmental structures and policies have on the everyday lives of the typical citizen. In Eastonian terms, a greater share of today's research is devoted to outputs and impacts and a lesser portion to inputs and conversion processes; moreover, much of the work done on the latter topics takes great care to discuss the findings' implications for outputs and impacts. Put another way, yesterday's dependent variable has become today's independent variable and, one suspects, today's dependent variable will become tomorrow's independent variable. In urban research, one can trace a movement from the environment's effect on governmental structure[1] to governmental structures' effect on policy outputs[2] to outputs' impact on outcomes.[3]

Pursuing this research trend, the next question is in what ways do outcomes—the consequences that governmental goods and services have for various categories of citizens—affect the early stages of the next round of the policy-making process? As more is known about outcomes, how will this information be fed back into the input and conversion portions of the policy process? In trying to answer this type of question, we are closing the Eastonian circle of inputs-conversion-outputs-impacts-feedback and thereby transforming a schema which has been most frequently used statically into one which can and should be applied dynamically.[4] And, as we increasingly look at the urban policy process as a never-ending cycle, it becomes especially important to examine the linkage between one cycle and the next—the point at which information about the outcomes of yesterday's policy is fed back (or, more precisely in a temporal sense, fed forward) as part of the input into the making of tomorrow's policy.

This essay is a prolegomena to such an examination of the links (if any) between the results of one policy and the making of another, with special attention paid to the present and future role played by the press in this linkage process. The remaining discussion will cover (1) two other intellectual movements compatible with the increasing amount of research on policy outcomes; (2) the implications such intellectual trends have for suggesting reforms for improving urban governance; (3) possible mechanisms for transmitting information about policy outcomes and social conditions; (4) the likelihood that major metropolitan newspapers might assume a much broader role in providing systematic information about policy outcomes and social conditions in the metropolitan areas which they serve; and (5) the possibility of viewing the urban policy process as a game, man as a gameplayer, and the press as a scorekeeper.

### Compatible Intellectual Currents

The increased emphasis on outcomes in urban research can be viewed as part of a larger intellectual trend having two principal components: (1) the condition of the individual person is the ultimate measure of any public policy, and (2) man is capable of consciously improving the quality of life. In addition to outcome analyses, two types of work—the one highly empirical, the other quite abstract and speculative—are in the mainstream of this trend.

The empirical work has been labelled the "social indicators" movement. Although, like most new phrases, "social indicators" has been applied to a wide variety of studies, one very common concern is with "quantitative data that serve as indexes to socially important conditions."[5] The mid-1960 pleas for more measurement of social conditions have been plentifully, albeit imperfectly, answered by several groups. The United States government made an early response with *Toward a Social Report*[6] and, after a lag of several years, followed up with a more extensive volume entitled *Social Indicators 1973;*[7] federal officials plan another edition for 1976 publication. At the local level, the most work has been done by the Urban Institute.[8] Finally, with strong funding encouragement by the Russell Sage Foundation, scholars have responded with books,[9] journals (*Social Indicators Research*), and newsletters (*Social Indicators Newsletter*). In brief, the measurement of social conditions has become a common item on both governmental and academic research agendas.

Preceding and accompanying the sharp jump in empirical studies of policy outcomes and social conditions have been several speculative discussions of man's capacity to control his own social destiny. Major contributors to this genre include Karl Deutsch, Amitai Etzioni and Daniel Bell.[10] All three men emphasize consciousness (man as actor rather than man as acted upon), cybernetics (self-steering organizations), and the critical part that information about goal-attainment plays in any ongoing social system. This last point—the centrality of knowledge in controlling future change—is especially pertinent to this discussion. Research on policy outcomes and social conditions is generating much more knowledge about to what extent, how and why the actions taken by various communities are or are not improving the human condition of their inhabitants. How, if at all, will this larger body of information affect those communities' capacity to steer toward a better life?

### Scholarly Research and Urban Policy Advice

The past decade has been a sobering experience for those who thought that social science had advanced to the stage where it could tell policy officials how to design and execute programs which would accomplish their objectives with minimal unintended negative consequences. After the heady days of the early 1960s when social scientists became more frequent occupants of federal government posts and when at least one apparently successful policy (Revenue Act of 1964) was applied, the record changed to a series of failures. Vietnam, the War on Poverty, the federal anticrime programs, and the various economic phases are among the more notable disasters. Although some social scientists console themselves with the rationalization that the ideas are still valid and that it was only inept execution or the selfish desire to reap short-term political gains which led to failure, good public policy recommendations should anticipate and incorporate implementation.

Within the confines of urban research—especially that conducted by political scientists—the question of what influence such efforts had on public policy formation was large irrelevant during the 1960s since studies on power structures, determinants of governmental form and expenditures, and decision-making processes had few direct implications for formulating policy suggestions. The earlier reform-oriented tradition—replete with suggestings for redesigning governmental forms—was still being heard from in some quarters;[11] but this movement's advice has largely been ignored and, even when followed, no significant relationship between changes in governmental form and changes in citizens' lives seems to have developed.

The greater 1970s attention by urban scholars to policy outcomes and social conditions, however, brings the question of relevance back into prominence. Such efforts have great potential for assessing the impact of past policies, recognizing systematically the nature of the present environment, and influencing the development of future policies. But given disillusionment among both scholars and policy officials resulting from the widespread failures of recent social science advice, one suspects that many academics are exceedingly reluctant to move from research results to policy recommendations.

How, then, might these new efforts actually affect ongoing urban policymaking? One answer can be based on Moynihan's suggestion, found in his postmortem of the Office of Economic Opportunity, that "the role of social science lies not in the formulation of social policy, but in the measurement of its results."[12] Currently, one suspects, policies have a beginning, a middle and an end, but that each policy is in many ways an entity unto itself so that the end of one policy has little to do with the beginning of any others. In addition, social scientists, it seems, rarely know enough to say that, if one begins in such-and-such a way, then the ending will be thus-and-so. Social science, however, has developed sufficient methodological sophistication to measure such things as policy outcomes and social conditions. One would then hope that as we learn more about which policies do and do not work and about who is or is not well off, that such knowledge would be used to improve future policymaking so that the end of one policy *would* have some influence on the beginning of the next policy and that policy makers would learn from their mistakes and their successes.

For such knowledge to be used, however, at least three things must happen: (1) someone must generate the knowledge, (2) someone must disseminate the knowledge so that policymakers learn about it, and (3) there must be incentives for policymakers to employ the knowledge. As has already been noted, the knowledge is being produced. What now needs to be discussed is the dissemination process and the incentives policymakers might have for paying more attention to results.

### Disseminating Knowledge: Major Alternatives

If urban policymakers are to receive knowledge about policy outcomes and social conditions in such a way as to encourage them to act on the basis of such information, social scientists can potentially use one or more of three channels: direct communication with policy officials, the educational system and the mass media.[13] Of these, the mass media—particularly the press—seems to be the best possibility. Before saying why, let us examine the weaknesses of the other two communication mechanisms.

Since, in a great many cases, policy outcome and social indicator research will reflect unfavorably on incumbent officials, communications that all is not well with Policy X or Citizen-Type Y must be more public than an academic whispering in an official's ear. Although the official will most often listen politely, there will be little incentive for him to act if the information is known only by him and the academic. Nor is it likely that an incumbent official can be frequently moved to act by having the academic whisper the information to that official's challenger. Such a strategy can only work in competitive urban governments at times close to an election with challengers who will use the information both in the election campaign and, if elected, after assuming office. This combination of circumstances simply does not occur that often. Sole or prime reliance on private academic-official communications also deprives the public from obtaining the information, a matter of much normative importance in a democracy.

Along with the mass media, the educational system is the major societal institution involved in transmitting information to large segments of the population. Given the fact that academics dominate the curricular aspects of higher education, one assumes that, if policy outcome and social indicators research is more than a passing intellectual fad, then such knowledge will become an increasing part of postsecondary training in the social sciences. On the other hand, history's disciplinary monopoly over elementary and secondary social studies education makes one much less optimistic that these curricula will soon incorporate new knowledge about policy outcomes and social indicators.[14] Moreover, the educational system has other weaknesses as a transmitter of policy-relevant information. The recipients of the information are relatively minor participants in the political process, thereby creating a long lag between individuals' receiving any information and being likely to act politically on the basis of that information. There is more emphasis on past facts than on contemporary information, and—quite appropriately—there is more concern with teaching people how to process information than there is with simply passing on facts.

Although academics have much less control over mass media content than they do over curricular subject matter, the mass media—unlike the educational system—are aimed primarily at adults, pass information on quickly, concentrate more on current happenings than on past events and focus almost exclusively on transmitting information rather than on teaching how to process it. In the short run, if policy outcome and social indicators research are going to have a major impact on policy officials' behavior, their results must be increasingly reported in the mass media. Among the mass media, the press seems the best initial choice for taking the lead in disseminating this new knowledge. *Inter alia,* the physical characteristics and communication style of the electronic media greatly limit their ability to convey quantitative data or complex reasoned arguments.[15] Hence, the remainder of this discussion will focus exclusively on the press. Nevertheless, the electronic media also merit a similar examination since a substantial segment of urban populations—especially the poor—rely on them as the primary source of local news.[16] For now, however, the two key questions are what is the press's current performance in reporting policy outcomes and social conditions and what is the press's potential for improving this performance?

### The Metropolitan Press

This review of the press's present performance in, and future potential for, providing clear and reasonably complete coverage of policy outcomes and social conditions for metropolitan areas is divided into four parts: (1) criteria for evaluating current press content; (2) the major ways in which current content fails to meet the criteria; (3) instances where current coverage does come close to fulfilling the criteria; and (4) the implications that regularities in the press's organizational structure and behavior have for its present and future ability to describe policy outcomes and social conditions. The evidence for what follows is a combination of critical reading of a large number of major metropolitan newspapers, ongoing discussions with about twenty St. Louis journalists and other studies of the mass media.

**Content Criteria.** Without attempting to construct anything approximating a comprehensive set of criteria for evaluating press coverage of outcomes and conditions, here are several factors which would be a part of such a set.

To begin with, those aspects of the human condition which are common to most normative schemes would be covered regularly. This list of important conditions would include health, public safety, employment, income, wealth, education, housing, physical environment, transportation, leisure and taxes. Ideally, reports on each condition should, at a minimum, have the following characteristics.

First, multiple measures should be used for each condition, with a special effort made to incorporate both objective (e.g., infant mortality rate) and subjective (e.g., survey responses to "How healthy do you feel?") indicators. Second, adequate information should be provided about the reliability and validity of each measuring device. Third, both longitudinal and cross-sectional comparisons should be made. Is this year's score better or worse than last year's? Is it better or worse than City X's or SMSA Y's? Fourth, the composite scores should be sensibly disaggregated. For example, scores should be reported for subgroups when either a subgroup's score is markedly different from the overall total (e.g., Subgroup R has a higher unemployment rate) or when a subgroup is subject to a different governmental jurisdiction for that policy area (e.g., crime rates should be disaggregated by police department). Fifth, the formulation, adoption, initiation, implementation and evaluation of major attempts to change social conditions should be covered, with special attention given to governmental policies. Sixth, when attempting to explain changes in, or the distribution of, scores, the press should use the best available social science explanations and should provide some assessment of the current strength of those explanations. Seventh, all information should be expressed in as understandable a manner as possible; in this regard, maximum use should be made of graphs and charts.

These criteria are admittedly ideal and no existing organization within a metropolitan area presently has the intellectual and economic resources necessary for fulfilling them. Nevertheless, the mass media—and especially the press—come closest to having the wherewithal to perform this function. They alone are experienced at conducting a daily monitoring of events in a metropolitan area.

In addition, the criteria can be interpreted as an attempt by one profession (social science) to impose some of its values (systematic measurement and careful evaluation of governmental policies) on another profession (journalism). Such an interpretation is legitimate, but it should not serve as an obstacle to a critique of press practices. Social scientists should not be bashful about the progress that has been made in social measurement and policy evaluation in the postwar period and, since journalists frequently claim to be chroniclers (i.e., measurers), it seems eminently fair to apply measurement standards to their work.

**Press Coverage: Major Weaknesses.** Taking the above criteria *seriatim,* it is apparent that current press coverage fails to meet each standard in one or more major ways. First, among the list of some of the more important dimensions of the quality of life, some aspects are given a great deal of attention, some a modest amount of coverage, and a few are virtually ignored. Public safety and employment are reported on the most, the lack of either receiving the bulk of the coverage. There are few editions without one or more stories on violent crime, fatal traffic accidents or damaging fires. Changes in metropolitan unemployment rates and layoff/hiring announcements (including help wanted classified advertisements) are also regular items. For most newspapers, income and taxes are next in amount of coverage, at least insofar as the reports tell readers something about how people are faring. Stories on per capita income, number of persons receiving benefits under one or another governmental program, number of families below some poverty level, and the dollar impact of existing and proposed taxes on different income and property classifications do appear from time to time although coverage of these matters is far from routine.

As for the remaining topics, the accounts are sporadic and, more often than not, there is minimal concentration of how well or poorly individuals are doing on each of these dimensions. There are health tips from physician columnists, but little about metropolitan mortality and morbidity. There are stories about the assets of a rich few, but little about the wealth of the great bulk of the population. There is a great deal of coverage of educational personnel, curricula, costs and politics, but little about increases or decreases in learning. There are stories about new housing developments and urban renewal projects, but little systematic information about changes in the quality and quantity of the housing stock. There is much ado about extreme instance of air and water pollution, but little attention to day-to-day changes in the physical environment. Often there is detailed coverage of grandiose plans for new rapid transit systems, but little information about changes in journey-to-work patterns. There are many accounts about a wide variety of amusements (e.g., movies, sports events, symphonies), but virtually nothing about the extent to which various types of individuals' leisure needs and wants are being met.

Even when a condition is frequently covered, as is the case with public safety, imbalance exists in the types of events reported. For example, within the St. Louis Standard Metropolitan Statistical Area, the ration of reported forcible rapes to reported murders for 1971 and 1972 was 2.5:1 (i.e., for every one murder, there were 2.5 rapes), whereas the ratio of *St. Louis Globe-Democrat* and *St. Louis Post-Dispatch* column inches devoted to rapes as compared to murders for the same two years was 1:11 (i.e., there was one column inch on rape for every eleven column inches on murder). More broadly, for the same time span, the ratio of reported crimes against persons (murder, forcible rape, robbery, aggravated assault) to reported crimes against property (burglary, grand larceny, auto theft) was 1:5.5 whereas the comparable column inch ration was 9:1. In sum, certain types of crimes against persons are covered much more than others, and crimes against persons are reported on more frequently and in greater detail than crimes against property. Thus, although typically there are a few articles each year summarizing the latest FBI *Uniform Crime Report* data, the far more frequent daily coverage of crime is decidely skewed.

In addition to setting forth what kinds of conditions should be covered, the criteria presented above specified how each dimension should be discussed. The first criterion was that multiple measures—some objective, some subjective—should be used. Only rarely is this done. Most commonly, one measure (e.g., unemployment rate) serves as a proxy for a broad concept (e.g., economic standing). Representative subjective measures for metropolitan populations are rarely found; instead, either an especially poignant example or an unspecified group of people become substitutes for public reaction.

Second, only infrequently is information provided about the reliability and validity of measures. Each of the two areas covered most—public safety and unemployment—provide good examples. The numerous reliability and validity problems of the FBI's *Uniform Crime Report* are generally mentioned in articles only when some public official wishes to minimize the importance of an increase in the crime rate or as a brief sentence toward the end of the article.[17] The sampling error and definitional problems of principal economic indexes are almost never mentioned in metropolitan press accounts, thereby limiting a reader's ability to interpret properly measures like the unemployment rate, cost of living and per capita income.[18]

Third, when newspapers do report social conditions, few meaningful longitudinal or cross-sectional comparisons are made. The typical over-time comparison is with the preceding one or two time periods, thus making it impossible to distinguish among trend, cyclical and other variation. In drawing cross-sectional analogies, little attention is given to whether it is reasonable to compare the several cities of metropolitan areas. Quite commonly, for example, a city with historically restricted boundaries (e.g., Baltimore or St. Louis) is compared with a city with almost unlimited annexation authority (e.g., Houston or Phoenix).

Fourth, the press's performance in describing how social conditions and policy outcomes apply to various groups is mixed. During the past decade it has become quite common for blacks to be singled out for special attention. Thus, crime reports frequently mention the number of black victims or black offenders, and economic stories give the black unemployment rate or black per capita income. Some consideration is also given to differentiating among age groups, especially the very young and the very old. Nevertheless, the above distinctions are not always made and many appropriate disaggregations (e.g., the differential impact that cost-of-living increases have at various income levels) are rarely mentioned.

Fifth, press coverage of governmental attempts to alter social conditions is almost exclusively confined to the formulation, adoption and initiation phases of the policy process. Much is said about new proposals and legislative and executive debates, discussions and compromises—frequently with a whose-political-career-is-being-helped-or-hurt motif. Much is also written about policy initiation, aided by the drum-beating of governmental public relations specialists. But little is written about how, or even whether, a program was implemented or evaluated. Readers are often told that Federal Program Q will contribute umpteen million dollars to SMSA Y and that local officials plan to spend the funds thus and so, but unless blatant scandals occur, seldom is there any follow up on whatever happened to Federal Program Q.

Sixth, the press is reluctant to offer explicit explanations for social conditions and policy outcomes. Even though the notion that "the facts speak for themselves" is passé among philosophers of science and most social scientists, it apparently still thrives among many journalists. Since, however, it is almost impossible to avoid some explanatory or interpretive statements in a great many stories, implicit explanations and partial interpretations abound. Typically, these efforts take one of two forms. The first practice is to obtain quotes from a few individuals associated with the activity as to why things are this or that way. Such attempted explanations are limited by being offered only by those participating in the policy area, by being frequently truncated by newspaper style conventions (multi-paragraph quotations are discouraged), and by being placed in the article with little or no effort to articulate the degree of fit between the explanation and the available evidence. The second explanatory style chosen by most reporters is to interpret officials' actions in terms of personal goals (e.g., reelection, election to some new office, individual desire to achieve some objective). Attempts to account for phenomena in broader terms are rarely found in the press.

Seventh, although clear writing is highly valued among journalists and hence found more often in newspapers than, say, in academic expositions, two other journalistic practices impair the press's ability to do a better job of transmitting condition and outcome information. The first of these practices is the reverse-pyramid structure which places a compact summary of the story's main points (who-what-where-when-why) first and relegates qualifying comments (such as measurement reliability and an explanation's more subtle elements) to the end of the article. As a result, these qualifiers—essential to a sophisticated understanding of the material— are at best separated from the referent statements and at worst lopped off the end because of space requirements. The second limitation is the underutilization of charts and graphs by the press. Few newspapers are staffed to provide graphic aids on short notice.

**Press Coverage: Some Strengths.** Although the preceding recitation of press sins against the canons of social science might provide the grist for an *a priori* case for damnation, a close reading of newspaper coverage reveals some strengths as well as certain other causes for concluding that the press can come much closer to meeting the above criteria.

The first strength is that scattered here and there are instances where the criteria have been honored rather than breached. Sometimes, more than one measure is mentioned (*Uniform Crime Report* and victimization survey data), reliability information is provided (sampling error and confidence levels in public opinion articles), longitudinal comparisons are made (metropolitan unemployment series for the past decade), measures are disaggregated (impact of proposed sales tax increase on families earning $3000 or less), policy outcomes are reported (reading scores in elementary schools), social science explanations are described (the 1966 study on educational opportunity by Coleman and his associates) and information is related both in words and in graphs. That these cases where the criteria are met are far outnumbered by instances where the criteria are not fulfilled should not hide the fact that examples of adequate coverage can be identified.

The second strength are well-done special articles and series which can be found from time to time in many newspapers. For example, before the distribution of educational resources had become a prominent topic for public debate, both the *Boston Herald* and the *Chicago Sun-Times* presented articles on the matter for their respective metropolitan areas.[19] The *New York Times* has done several articles on police protection and public safety, with perhaps the most notable being a two-part series comparing the distribution of police resources and crime in New York City.[20] More recently, the *Washington Post* did a series on citizen reactions to and evaluations of a long list of topics, including most of those given earlier as key aspects of the human condition.[21] The articles were based on a Washington metropolitan area sample survey conducted by the Bureau of Social Science Research.

The principal difficulty with these special articles is that, no matter how well done, they are not part of any newspaper's routine coverage. Hence, assuming that repetitive accounts are typically needed to produce noticeable changes in readers' perception or officials' behavior, particular series are not likely to have long-lasting effects on changing the nature of policymaking process. (Such articles may, of course, often result in officials' resignations, adjustments in one year's budget or symbolic gestures.) Moreover, such articles are not likely to form the core of a knowledge-based change in the linkage between today's social conditions and policy outcomes and tomorrow's policy formulations.

Although coverage of outcomes and conditions is not part of the routine in the news sections, other portions of the newspaper come much closer to providing systematic information on outcomes or conditions or both. The best performance is generally turned in by the sports section. Each day, during the appropriate season, a reader can readily discover how his or her metropolitan area team is faring in comparison with all other metropolitan squads. To aid the reader, most newspapers place the standings in the same format and in approximately the same location each and every day. Longitudinal comparisons are frequently made as to whether a team is doing better or worse than some preceding or base (i.e., last pennant-winning) year. The subtleties of the measurement process are usually pointed out, such as when readers are cautioned not to be overoptimistic that their team is in first place since the locals have a tougher schedule remaining than do their closest competitors. Multiple measures are given for each athlete so as to maximize a reader's chances of assessing both the participants' performances and administrators' competencies; in basketball, for example, each game's box score displays the minutes played, field goals attempted, field goals made, free throws attempted, free throws made, assists, rebounds, personal fouls, technical fouls and total points for each player. Most new policies (e.g., player trades, starting lineup changes) are commonly assessed by the reporters, so that effects on conditions (e.g., team standing) can be judged. Indeed, from a social science perspective, the only major weakness in sports reporting is the uncritical acceptance of explanations for team and individual success or failure.[22] For example, one widely-held proposition is that friendly interpersonal relationships among all or nearly all team members (i.e., good team spirit) is a necessary although not a sufficient condition for success. This argument is still often put forth as gospel, with no attempt to explain how, if it is true, the Oakland A's—a team where the owner publicly chastises the manager and players, where many players show little public respect for the manager, and where verbal and physical disputes occur frequently among the players—have won the last three World Series championships. For the most part, though, if sports were covered in much the same manner as metropolitan governance, readers would be forced to rely primarily on participants' comments as to how they performed rather than having some external measures of player and team competence.

Financial and weather matters are also described more systematically and with greater attention to measurement quality than are social conditions and policy outcomes. The Tuesday through Saturday editions give substantial data on financial conditions in a large number of markets, and the Sunday paper provides a weekly summary. Longitudinal comparison are commonly made, and multiple measures are used. Explanatory statements about changes in financial conditions (e.g., common stock price indexes) are decidedly *ex post facto* and continue to be accepted without question in most financial stories. Weather information is displayed in both a cross-sectional and a longitudinal setting, multiple measures are used (e.g., temperature and wind-chill factor), modest use is made of graphs and explanations having some predictive capacity are put forth with the proper probabilistic qualifications (e.g., the chance of precipitation in the next twenty-four hours is twenty percent).

In sum, this review of the weaknesses and strengths of the press indicates that, in the main, coverage of metropolitan social conditions and policy outcomes generally fails to meet social science criteria. Selected examples, however, show that the criteria have occasionally been fulfilled, and the continuing performance of other portions of the newspaper—most notably the sports section—reveals that routine attention to conditions and outcomes can be accommodated within a newspaper's ongoing activity.

**Organizational Considerations.** It is a truism to state that any organization develops routines which greatly influence the kind of output it produces. In the case of the press, the nature the organization, including journalists' professional socialization, can and does have a decided impact on what and how phenomena are reported. Without engaging in an exhaustive enumeration of organizational factors and their implications, this section will discuss two aspects having a direct bearing on metropolitan-level coverage: reporters' strategies for searching out and identifying news and newspapers' receptivity to change.

Confronted with a near infinity of things to describe, it is not surprising that journalists have developed criteria for determining what is and what is not news. As Sigal notes,

> Conventions perform for the reporter the function that rules of evidence do for the scientist: they are his epistemological premises, the criteria accepted in the field for assessing validity, the argumentation for defending his findings. Unlike those rules of evidence, however, conventions are rarely subject to conscious scrutiny by newsmen; they are just the way things are done around the newsroom.[23]

Five conventions which directly affect the coverage of social conditions and policy outcomes—conventions having much to do with the press's failure to fulfill the criteria discussed earlier—are the restrictive definition of public affairs, heavy reliance on persons as sources of information, emphasis on the unique, the need to relate any story to some recent event and the concentration of criminal wrongdoing by public officials in investigative reporting.

The press is much more likely to regard certain topics as public affairs or governmental matters than other subjects, and newspapers cover certain areas of governmental activity much more intensively than others. Topics which are more readily understood (e.g., personal disputes between officials) are more likely to be reported than are topics having highly technical aspects (e.g., enforcing pollution control standards), and concrete stories (e.g., a new award system for outstanding police officers) are more likely to be covered than are abstract ones (e.g., a change in a police department's crime measurement procedures). Moreover, journalists concentrate their governmental coverage almost exclusively on the elected executive and legislative officials, thereby telling their readers a good deal about policy formulation and adoption but very little about policy implementation and evaluation. Such a focus on mayors and councils occurs even in suburban coverage, although—using Williams and Adrian's typology— most suburban municipalities view their role as providing life's amenities or as maintaining traditional services rather than as arbitrating among conflicting interests.[24] Even when nothing of much relevance to the general citizenry is happening at council meetings—a common situation in most suburbs—readers are still provided with a reasonably detailed account of the legislative business. At the same time, however, there are very few stories on the quality and quantity of public goods and services in suburbia.

In great measure, reporters rely on persons—especially high-level officials—as their primary sources of information. As Dunn notes in his study of capital reporters in Wisconsin, "the newsman normally gathers information in four ways: (1) covering meetings, (2) attending press conferences, (3) examining handouts or press releases, and (4) talking with sources."[25] This dependence on spoken comments from top officials has three implications. First, it tends to produce news which overemphasizes certain personalities, largely neglects many more typical officials, and virtually ignores middle and lower-level governmental personnel even though the last group might know the most about policy outcomes. Second, such a reliance means that the archival records go unused in describing outcomes and conditions, consequently lowering the quantity and the quality of news containing systematic description. Third, many reporters develop such a need for information provided by certain persons that, in order to prevent their informational supplies from being drastically reduced, they take care not to offend their sources.

The press's desire to relate the unique is well known to any casual reader. Most have heard the cliché that dog biting man is not news but man biting dog is. As one journalism textbook puts it,

Since, however, a newspaper's capacity for printing news compels it to be selective, an editor needs some kind of guidelines or benchmark for estimating what will interest his readers. What he does, therefore, is to look for the presence in each event of certain elements which he believes to be interesting. Although he thinks of a story as being about some subject matter, such as crime, labor, or death, he also looks for an additional dimension which makes the event different from similar events of its class. Sometimes this element is odd, eccentric, or bizarre, but most often it is merely unusual.[26]

The impact of such a standard on systematic coverage of outcomes and conditions is obvious. To the extent that reporters are rewarded for finding the unique, there will be less news about the typical.

According to journalistic convention, a story is only news if it can be directly related or pegged to an event which occurred in the very recent past or will happen in the very near future. A story on changes in robbery rates, for example, would probably be held back until it could be pegged to some specific robbery. The supposed rationale for the pegging convention is to prevent the press from manufacturing its own news and to reinforce the notion that the press only reflects what is currently happening in the world it covers. It is doubtful whether pegging does that much to help accomplish its avowed purpose, and it also has the effect of deterring regular (e.g., weekly) coverage of conditions and outcomes. Since such coverage (assuming it occurs) must be pegged and since the pegs do not happen at predictable intervals, the coverage of systematic information loses its regular character because it is being wagged by an episodic tail.

Over the past decade, there has been a noticeable increase in investigative reporting; a rising number of newspapers are releasing one or more reporters from day-to-day deadline responsibilities to do an in-depth analysis on some topic. Since such stories are the stuff of which Pulitzer Prizes and the like are made, most journalists eagerly seek out investigative assignments. To date, however, very few of these efforts have produced analyses of policy outcomes or social conditions. Instead, the modal report has dealt with corruption among governmental officials—who paid whom to get what. The material and professional rewards reaped by *Washington Post* reporters Carl Bernstein and Bob Woodward in the Watergate Affair have and will serve as an additional incentive for aspiring young reporters to find still another government official taking money from the wrong place. Although, of course, there is much virtue in identifying corrupt politicians, the implicit message encoded in present investigative reporting—don't worry about how your actions affect citizen lives if your procedures are honest—is discomforting.

Overall, then, many of the press's faults enumerated earlier can be seen as the partial product of the way reporters define what is news. If there is to be improved coverage of social conditions and policy outcomes, then reporters must have a broader definition of public affairs, make more use of the written record, place less emphasis on idiosyncratic matters, be less concerned about pegging stories and begin to regard ineffectiveness worthy of as much attention as corruption.

Can the press change? Can it improve its performance in covering outcomes and conditions? One can find both optimistic and pessimistic straws in the wind. Pessimistically, several analysts have come away from their studies of the press with strong impressions that the press is a conservative institution. Sigal, for instance, concludes:

> Changes in news conceptions are likely to be glacial. Habits of mind resist change. If inertia is characteristic of individual belief, it is all the more so for organizational routines. Establishing new procedures takes time, a scarce resource for newsmen with daily deadlines to meet. Uncertainty about the nature of news compounds the difficulty. If no one knows what

news is, newsmen attain at least a measure of security from their reliance on the same channels and sources and on common values. Uncertainty makes any change in routines and conventions a scary prospect.[27]

Practically all close observers of the press comment on its imitative character. Although this great similarity in press practice among metropolitan newspapers can be viewed as supportive of change (i.e., once an innovation catches on, it is likely to be diffused rapidly), in the short run such homogeneity can smother any attempts to be different. Hence, the press's mediocre record in meeting social science criteria and the underlying journalistic conventions together with the institution's tendency to resist change do not, in combination, support a conclusion that the press's coverage of social conditions and policy outcomes is inevitably on the rise.

Nevertheless, it is also possible to find reasons to sustain a conclusion that a rise is quite possible. First, there are several voices within the journalism profession arguing for greater use of social science explanations and methodologies. Although, to my knowledge, none of these arguments has explicitly incorporated policy outcome and social condition research, such concerns are implicitly anticipated. The most detailed support for social science is found in Philip Meyer's *Precision Journalism*. The author, a Knight newspaper correspondent, states:

> The social sciences can help us in two ways: their findings in many fields provide a continuing check on the conventional wisdom. We can save ourselves some trouble, some inaccuracy, and some lost opportunities by merely paying attention to what the social scientists are doing and finding out. More importantly and of more direct practical value, we can follow their example by abandoning the philosopher's armchair, giving up the notion that a few facts and common sense will make any problem yield, and make the new high-powered research techniques our own.[28]

Another example of a movement to increase social science knowledge among journalists is the three-week seminar on statistics and experimental methods held at Northwestern University for some twenty plus journalists in the summer of 1974.

A second reason for thinking that the press might expand its coverage of conditions and outcomes lies in the great importance many members of the press place on being objective. Based on his intensive study of one metropolitan newspaper, Argyris describes this need:

> Newspapers are crucial for a healthy democracy; they are protected by the Constitution of the United States and they are manned by human beings whose behavior is rarely examined from within or from without. This

implies that newspaper people are human, and are expected to be super-human. Perhaps it is saddling newspaper people with the requirement that they be both human and superhuman that helps to make them so de-fensive. . . . The need to externalize one's weaknesses and deny their existence may be partly a defense against the feelings of enormous responsibility placed on the reporter. The disillusionment that the young reporters may feel when they discover that their emperors have no clothes on may be partly caused by the fact that as reporters for a great newspaper they are emperors—and they know better than anyone else how naked they are. . . . Perhaps this is also one of the causes for the emotionality and polarization around the issue of objective versus subjective reporting. The defenders of subjective reporting note that all news reporting is based on subjective observations, and is complicated by the need to condense reality into a small space without distorting its meaning. With all due deference to the difficulties involved, this task is faced by all human beings. . . . Few of us, however, have these built-in characteristics of human fallibility protected by the Constitution of the United States. The anxiety about being objective, under these conditions, would understandably be high, especially among brighter and better educated people.[29]

One of the principal virtues of an additional emphasis on systematic coverage of conditions and outcomes is that such an approach has a greater claim on objectivity (more precisely, intersubjectivity) than do present press practices. Thus, although some aspects of a new approach run counter to current operating procedures, at least in one respect this new type of reporting would buttress a longstanding journalistic value.

Third, based on my discussions with reporters and some comments offered by other analysts,[30] one gains the impression that many newspersons want to exert an independent influence on the policy process and that they are currently dissatisfied with their present ability to make a difference. Several have cynically noted that exposés of corruption seem only to damage the careers of a few and that the political system continues to produce the same outcomes as before. In many respects, this reaction is similar to that expressed by many political scientists in what is now called the postbehavioral revolution. Just as, in the mid–1960s, an increasing number of political and other social scientists began to ask "so what" to studies of the process, so too, in the mid–1970s, a growing number of journalists appear to be asking "so what" to the way the process is covered. Put more crassly, if someone wished to preach a sermon to reporters that more systematic attention to social conditions and policy outcomes might ultimately make a difference in policy quality, one suspects that there are many journalists ripe for conversion.

### Concluding Comments

The preceding discussion has been conducted at two levels. The first of these is an argument that (1) information about social conditions and policy outcomes is growing at an increasing rate; (2) such knowledge has great potential for influencing the making of succeeding policies; (3) the feedback mechanisms which might convey this knowledge and how officials might or might not receive, interpret and be affected by this information have received insufficient study; (4) the mass media—particularly the press—are perhaps the most important feedback channel and thus are a prime candidate for detailed analysis; (5) an extensive (but nonsystematic) monitoring of the press's current performance reveals many weaknesses and a few strengths in covering social conditions and policy outcomes, thereby lessening any possible immediate effects such knowledge might have on policy makers; and (6) a review of some of the press's organizational routines can identify both factors deterring and encouraging improved coverage of outcomes and conditions.

The second level of discussion is speculative and reformist; it is directed at improving—according to social science criteria—the mass media's coverage of metropolitan public affairs as an end in itself and as a lever for influencing officials to alter policies more rapidly and in such a way that their actions have a greater chance of bettering the human condition. What follows are a few additional comments about such a reform.

If we set as a goal a metropolitan area with a strong results orientation, a clear focus on man as the measure, balanced one hopes by an appreciation of the democratic process, then what might be done to move toward such a situation? Among the principal items on any list of proposals would be the regular production of high quality knowledge of social conditions and policy outcomes, disseminated to all through the mass media and utilized by officials responsible for policymaking.

The knowledge is being generated. If those doing the research want their results to improve urban policymaking, the best initial change strategy might be to work to reform mass media reporting practices rather than to attempt to influence directly the behavior of public officials. Why? Journalists resemble social scientists more than they do governmental officials; reporters, despite the organizational inertia discussed earlier, are probably more open to idea-based arguments and are more willing to present material critical of an existing regime. In addition, there is a substantial multiplying effect associated with newspersons: influencing a few journalists will change public discourse on urban policymaking more than will convincing a few officials and, if media coverage affects officials, then the policy makers will ultimately be reached anyway. Because of the imitative nature of reporting practices, changes in coverage are apt to become part of the media's standard operating procedure in a metropolitan area.

But will better media coverage change policymaking patterns? One way it might is by making metropolitan governance more of a game in order to have more incentives (economic and noneconomic) for improving performance. As several scholars have already suggested, much of life can readily be viewed as a game.[31] If urban man does play games—deadly serious games—it thereby follows that one way of changing the course of urban events is to alter some or all of the rules of one or more games, with two very important rules being who keeps score and how the score is calculated.

At present, however, insofar as the mass media currently reflect the urban world, only two sectors—financial and sports—are described in game terms and only the latter explicitly so. Yet, no matter how silly it might sound at first hearing (e.g., in last month's infant mortality contest, the score was New York 21, Cleveland 19), there might be much to be gained by having the mass media extend this perspective to the coverage of metropolitan affairs, thereby making the media—especially the press—the chief scorekeeper in the metropolitan policymaking game. But such an extension of the game metaphor will only improve the policymaking process if there is a competent scoring system—reliable and valid indicators of the human condition and capable evaluations of policy outcomes—and if the mass media adopt such a system in their metropolitan coverage.

## NOTES

1. John H. Kessel, "Governmental Structure and Political Environment: A Statistical Note about American Cities," *American Political Science Review,* 56 (September, 1962), pp. 615–620.

2. Robert L. Lineberry and Edmund P. Fowler, "Reformism and Public Policies in American Cities," *American Political Science Review,* 61 (September, 1967), pp. 701–716.

3. Frank Levy, Arnold J. Meltsner and Aaron Wildavsky, *Urban Outcomes* (Berkeley: University of California Press, 1974).

4. David Easton, *A Systems Analysis of Political Life* (New York: John Wiley, 1965).

5. Albert D. Biderman, "Social Indicators and Goals," in Raymond Bauer, ed., *Social Indicators* (Cambridge, Mass.: MIT Press, 1966), p. 69.

6. U.S. Department of Health, Education, and Welfare, *Toward a Social Report* (Washington: Government Printing Office, 1969).

7. U.S. Office of Management and Budget, *Social Indicators 1973* (Washington: Government Printing Office, 1974).

8. See for example, Michael J. Flax, *A Study in Comparative Urban Indicators* (Washington: The Urban Institute, 1972).

9. Two major volumes are Eleanor B. Sheldon and Wilbert E. Moore, eds., *Indicators of Social Change* (New York: Russell Sage, 1968); and Angus Campbell and Philip E. Converse, eds., *The Human Meaning of Social Change* (New York: Russell Sage, 1972).

10. Karl Deutsch, *The Nerves of Government* (New York: Free Press, 1963); Amitai Etzioni, *The Active Society* (New York: Free Press, 1968); and Daniel Bell, *The Coming of Post-Industrial Society* (New York: Basic Books, 1973). These two movements are linked more than intellectually, since Bell had much

to do with promoting social indicators research; see Bell, "The Idea of a Social Report," *The Public Interest,* 15 (Spring, 1969), pp. 72–84.

11. For example, Committee for Economic Development, *Reshaping Government in Metropolitan Areas* (New York: Committee for Economic Development, 1970).

12. Daniel P. Moynihan, *Maximum Feasible Misunderstanding* (New York: Free Press, 1970), p. 193.

13. An additional communication channel which will not be discussed in this essay is professional journals, newsletters and associations; for an excellent analysis of this topic, see Jack L. Walker, "The Diffusion of Knowledge and Policy Change: Toward a Theory of Agenda Setting," paper presented at the 1974 Annual Meeting of the American Political Science Association.

14. In making such statements about the diffusion of social science research results in the educational process, one is struck by the dearth of systematic studies on the topic.

15. Marshall McLuhan, *Understanding Media* (New York: McGraw-Hill, 1964).

16. Leslie W. Sargent and Guido H. Stempell, "Poverty, Alienation, and Mass Media Use," *Journalism Quarterly,* 45 (Summer, 1968), pp. 324–326; Thomas H. Allen, "Mass Media Use Patterns in a Negro Ghetto," *Journalism Quarterly,* 47 (Spring, 1968), pp. 525–527; Carl E. Block, "Communicating with the Urban Poor: An Exploratory Inquiry," *Journalism Quarterly,* 47 (Spring, 1970), pp. 3–11.

17. Recent examples of crime measurement critiques are David Seidman and Michael Couzens, "Getting the Crime Rate Down: Political Pressure and Crime Reporting," *Law and Society Review,* 8 (Spring, 1974), pp. 457–493; and Wesley G. Skogan, "The Validity of Official Crime Statistics: An Empirical Investigation," *Social Science Quarterly,* 55 (June, 1974), pp. 25–38.

18. See for instance, Oskar Morgenstern, *On the Accuracy of Economic Observations* (Princeton, N.J.: Princeton University Press, 1963).

19. The authors of the *Boston Herald* series were William J. McCarthy and Ronald Kessler; the writers of the *Chicago Sun-Times* articles were Christopher Chandler and Joel Havemann. The *Herald* series appeared on the following 1966 dates: February 27 and 28; March 1, 2, 3, 4 and 6; and April 10, 11 and 12. The *Sun-Times* articles were published on June 1–4, 1969.

20. The dates of the two *New York Times* articles, written by David Burnham, were February 14 and 15, 1972.

21. The *Washington Post* articles, authored by Jay Matthews, appeared on the following 1974 dates: February 21; March 6, 12, 17, 24 and 28; April 6, 7 and 30; and May 1, 3, 8, 9, 13, 14, 15, 19, 20, 21 and 24.

22. The *New York Times'* Leonard Koppett, also a regular columnist for *The Sporting News,* is a major exception to this statement.

23. Leon V. Sigal, *Reporters and Officials* (Lexington, Mass.: D.C. Heath, 1973), p. 3.

24. Oliver P. Williams and Charles R. Adrian, *Four Cities* (Philadelphia: University of Pennsylvania Press, 1963).

25. Delmer D. Dunn, *Public Officials and the Press* (Reading, Mass.: Addison-Wesley, 1969), p. 37.

26. Chilton R. Bush, *Newswriting and Reporting Public Affairs* (Philadelphia: Chilton Books, 1970), pp. 33–34.

27. Sigal, p. 19.

28. Philip Meyer, *Precision Journalism* (Bloomington: Indiana University Press, 1973), p. 13.

29. Chris Argyris, *Behind the Front Page* (San Francisco: Jossey-Bass, 1974), pp. 253–255.

30. Ibid., pp. 50–51; and Dunn, pp. 12–16.

31. Johan Huizinga, *Homo Ludens* (Boston: Beacon Press, 1950); and Norton Long, "The Local Community as an Ecology of Games," *American Journal of Sociology*, 64 (November, 1958), pp. 251–261.

Chapter Five

# Limitations of Black Urban Power:
# The Case of Black Mayors

MICHAEL PRESTON

The new black politics is in search for what many blacks currently believe to be the only game in town. That game is the search for political power. The thrust that began in the 1960s, rather than receding, has intensified. This trend is exemplified by Mervyn Dymally, the newly elected Lieutenant Governor of California. Dymally was recently quoted as saying: "Politics is now the cutting edge of the civil rights movement."[1] This belief is shared by other black elected officials throughout the country, and whether one shares this belief or not, it is a fact that electoral politics is currently the dominant game in the black search for equality.

There are several emergent patterns which suggest that the reservoir of political energy among blacks is still very high. First, the Congressional Black Caucus has grown from nine members in 1969 to eighteen members in 1975 (sixteen members and one non-voting delegate from D.C. in the House and one Senator).[2] This represents the highest total in United States history. Black congressmen are different from their white brethren in that black congressmen are considered by most blacks to be "congressmen-at-large." They speak, both individually and collectively, for blacks nation wide.

Second, and perhaps the more interesting political development is the new focus on *state* politics. The 1974 election produced two new black Lieutenant Governors (in California and Colorado); a Secretary of State in Michigan; and a State Treasurer in Connecticut. This group joins Wilson Riles, who was reelected Superintendent of Public Instruction in California. The emergence of black elected officials statewide is a relatively new pattern. Aside from Senator Brooke's election as Attorney General of Massachusetts and Gerald Lamb's election as State Treasurer of Connecticut, few blacks survived statewide elections in the preceding ten year period.[3]

The 1974 elections also produced some new black *state legislators*. Some of these include: Robert Holmes, Atlanta; Joseph Rhodes, Pittsburgh; and Antonio L. Harrison, Birmingham. The impetus behind the election of black senators from the South has been the Voting Rights Act of 1965. Civil rights observers and others have hailed the Voting Rights Act as the most successful law enacted during the period of the "Great Society." The results in the eleven southern states show that blacks elected to state legislatures increased from 60 in 1965 to 94 in 1975. When the Voting Rights Act was passed in 1965 there were fewer than 100 black elected office holders in these states; today there are over 900 blacks holding office in the South. And if we include blacks in Southern state legislatures, there are, according to the Joint Center for Political Studies, 3003 black elected officials nationwide.[4] While these figures represent substantial progress they also indicate how much remains to be done.

The optimism that flows from these increases, when put in perspective, shows that black elected officials hold less than one percent of the 79,000 public offices throughout the South. On the national level, where blacks are 12 percent of the population, their 3003 black elected officials represents approximately six-tenths of one percent of the elected officials in the nation.

Third, the emergence of blacks in the urban political arena is the most significant political development in recent years. The symbol of the new black urban politics is the black mayor. Today there are 26 medium and large cities with black mayors. Some of these include: Berkeley and Compton, California; College Park, Maryland; Ann Arbor and Grand Rapids, Michigan (President Ford's home town); Chapel Hill, North Carolina; Boulder, Colorado; New Brunswick and Newark, New Jersey; Gary, Indiana; and Atlanta, Georgia. In addition, three of the nation's largest cities have recently elected black mayors—Los Angeles, Detroit and Washington, D.C. In the last year alone the number of black mayors rose from 83 to 108—an increase of 30 percent.[5] And while most of these mayors come from small rural communities in the South, an increasing number of blacks are becoming mayors in large and medium size cities in the North.[6]

Black mayors, then, have become the "hub" of the new black urban politics. Their election signals something else—the gradual institutionalization of black political power in the urban arena.

The election of black mayors in cities where blacks are a distinct minority dispels the argument that black candidates can win only where blacks are already a majority.[7] The recent election of two black Lieutenant Governors and several other black statewide officials also helps to counter this argument. Contrary to popular belief, most of the cities with black mayors do not have predominantly black populations. In the majority of these cities (17 out of 26) blacks are a distinct minority.[8] In fact, in only three of these cities could blacks have elected mayors without white support: Compton, California; East St. Louis, Illinois; and Washington, D.C.[9]

It is important to note that the new focus on electoral politics represents a new strategy for blacks and has some important policy implications: (1) electoral politics can be used to improve the social and economic positions of black Americans; and (2) blacks currently seem to believe that more can be gained from working within the system than from without. In other words, blacks have come to believe that "political power" is better than "street power." And whether they will continue to believe that "politics is the new cutting edge of the civil rights movement" may well depend less on what black politicians say, but more on what they are able to produce.

What does the new emphasis on institutional leadership mean? First it means that some of the flair with which blacks pressed their demands will be missing. A focus on institutional leaders is less dramatic than a focus on one charismatic leader. Less drama means less media attention. Second, the shift to a more diffuse leadership has also lead to a shift away from a preoccupation with presidential politics as the key to protecting and advancing black political rights. This decline in presidential reliance is a belief that the recent civil rights laws have moved the arena from the national to the state and local levels. It has also been clear for some time that neither the Nixon nor Ford administrations are receptive to advancing black rights. In fact, President Ford has let it be known that his domestic policies are very similar to those of George Wallace.[10] There is little wonder, then, that black interest in presidential politics is on the decline.

Third, given the decline of interest in presidential politics by blacks and the diffusion of new black elected officials at the state and local levels, blacks have come to expect more from their black elected officials. The view taken by this paper is that if the high expectations of blacks are not to be dashed on the rocks of despair, a more realistic assessment of the limitations on black urban power is needed. That is to say simply that black mayors are limited in what they can do to improve the plight of their black constituency. But before we look at the limitations on the new urban politics, we must first understand how politics became the new cutting edge of black urban politics.

The maturation of black urban politics must be viewed as part of the more general development of black political activity. Indeed, it is probably more to the point to say that to understand the maturation of black urban politics, one needs to also understand two basic factors: (1) the unique historical background of blacks in America; and (2) the use by blacks of a theoretical framework which has its roots in the beginning of the early 19th Century. The new thrust for urban power by blacks roughly parallels the search for power by other immigrant groups.

Daniel N. Gordon, for example, describes how in the early 19th Centruy masses of propertyless people became politically active and established the ward system of elections and the direct election of mayors. He asserts that ward-elected city councilmen spoke for their local areas. He goes on to suggest that changes in municipal government produced a system within which immigrants could later obtain political power.[11] The point here is that newly politicized immigrant groups challenged old values of participation and sought to broaden them to include their own values.

The challenge by blacks to urban authority structures, then, is not new. In fact, V.O. Key, Jr., in his classic, *Politics, Parties and Pressure Groups,* observed that, "To carve out a place for itself in the politico-social order, a new group may have to fight for reorientation of many of the values of the old order."[12] This is what past immigrant groups have done, and it is precisely the same tactic that is now being attempted by new groups—mainly blacks. Black urban politics takes its theoretical orientation from the more general political experience of other immigrant groups, but its roots are based on its own historical past.

One way to conceptualize that past is to look at the phases through which black politics has passed. These phases are: (1) politics of protest; (2) politics of participation; and (3) politics of reform.[13] A brief review of these phases will set the stage for the final phase, which is the basis for the new urban politics. This phase is best described as the politics of governance.

### Politics of Protest

Protest politics has been, for blacks, the dominant politics over the last 100 years. Its actions were aimed at correcting certain blatant racial injustices in the political system. The basic targets, according to Hamilton, were *de jure* segregation in education, housing, employment, the military and public accommodations, as well as inequitable teachers' salaries, all white juries, acts of lynching, voter registration denials, and so on.[14] The strategies adopted to protest these inequalities varied from elitist-oriented legal suits to direct mass action. And while race was the focus, the basic appeal was moral. The politics of protest appealed to the morality of Americans and sought white allies to help secure these rights. Two results were the Civil Rights Act of 1964 and the Voting Rights Act of 1965.

The politics of protest resulted in some legal victories, but left the basic structure of government intact. As Kenneth Clark notes, the politics of protest was a conservative politics.[15] Stated differently, protest activity only asked for inclusion of the Negro in existing society and did not call for changes in the political and economic structure.

### Politics of Participation

The politics of participation has been (and in some cases still is) primarily focused on recognition. The rewards have been mostly symbolic, reminiscent of Wolfinger's description of ethnic politics.[16] Whether it was the Republican or the Democratic party, blacks have received little more than symbolic recognition—that is, the appointment of a few blacks to political office. In local politics blacks participated in political alliances with white groups but received limited benefits. In Atlanta in the 1940s the alliance was with the white middle-class business groups; in Chicago since the 1930s it has been with the Democratic political machine. What Edward Banfield has said about Hartfield of Atlanta can also be said about Daley in Chicago, i.e., blacks have received only minor rewards for their votes.[17]

The critical aspect of the politics of participation is that it is still in vogue. This type of politics relies on the numerical strength of the group to ascertain benefits. And its bargaining power, if it has any, depends on its political alliance with one or another group. Power is enhanced with financial resources; but for blacks the only resources they have is the ballot, and in most cases it has been used badly. For politics of participation to be effective, and this is still the dominant situation for blacks in this country, it must adhere to one dominant political principle: that those who do nothing for blacks should be rewarded in kind.

This principle should be used in national, state and local politics. That it has not been used effectively to date does not mean that poor judgment at one time needs to be continued. This principle, if applied properly, should lead politicians to anticipate swift retribution if they disregard black rights. If the deed is negative, the organized response at the next election should reflect the deed. Power, when limited mostly to the ballot, must be used judiciously to "reward friends and punish enemies" as labor was once urged to do by Samuel Gompers. To be sure, there are limits to this type of strategy. Votes cannot easily be swung from one party or candidate to another. Blacks, with their heavy commitment to the Democratic party, it may be argued, will not easily be moved. The strategy seems viable only in those nonpartisan cities where parties are absent.[18] While the argument is a good one, it may be missing the point. The black vote may not be swung easily, but it can be used just as effectively in some cases by not voting for the party's candidate. That, I believe, is partially what happened in the 1972 presidential election. A variant of this strategy has been used in Houston, Texas, for example, where running a black candidate who could not win had the effect of denying the vote to other undesirable candidates.

### Politics of Reform

This type of politics is characterized by an attempt to change *existing structural* arrangements that may impede the advancement of new groups.* It is similar to what Gordon reported about earlier immigrant groups.[19] This is the type of activity by blacks that one observed in the 1960s, a period which witnessed increasing demands in some cities for "community control" and/or political decentralization. Hamilton argues that "this demand stems from a de-

---

*It is here that I think Hamilton's categories break down. I believe that both for conceptual and analytical reasons, his politics of governance should be divided into two categories. Thus I have added the politics of reform and used the politics of governance to denote the current electoral emphasis. The politics of reform normally precede the move toward electoral politics. Where groups cannot dominate or control their communities, they seek ways to alter the structure to get more equitable rewards. This may be done by boycotting, demonstrating, or the use of other pressure type of activities.

sire on the part of those groups to restructure decision-making institutions in urban areas in order to maximize the ability of local residents to govern. . ."[20] What this phase suggests is that the politics of participation is a limited politics. It is limited by certain *structural arrangements* which prevent the black vote from being effective, ranging from centralized governmental structures to non-responsive bureaucratic institutions located in the black community.[21]

The resistance of these structures to change has led to what Alan Altshuler has called a "crisis of legitimacy."[22] For what came to be questioned was not just the *effectiveness* of these institutions, but their *legitimacy* as well. These institutions were seen as political institutions designed to oppress black people. And thus community control was urged as a means of political reform. The observation by David E. Apter underscores this point: "Politics is peculiar insofar as principles of legitimacy are normative first and structured second."[23] And Seymour Martin Lipset follows up the point by stating:

> . . . while effectiveness is primarily instrumental, legitimacy is evaluative. Groups regard a political system as legitimate or illegitimate according to the way in which its values fit with theirs.[24]

The politics of reform, then, was initiated by groups who sought to restructure the urban decision making process so that it would reflect their interests. *The question raised in the politics of reform is not whether community control or political decentralization is efficient or inefficient, but whether the institutions are meeting the needs of the people they are supposed to serve.* When the question is answered in the negative, as it has been by most blacks, then the quest will be for control or alterations of those institutions. In the final analysis, a politics of reform seeks to give excluded groups a feeling of efficacy and legitimacy. Unlike the politics of participation and politics of protest, it seeks a restructuring of the urban decision making process. Where it is numerically possible, blacks have now come to seek a more stable form of political activity—the politics of governance.

At some stage of the political process a group will attempt to exercise dominant power over a particular unit. This may be done in several ways: first, where numerical strength permits, groups may simply out vote other groups to win public office in already established structures; second, where the population is more evenly mixed, a group may form a coalition with other groups to win political office; and third, where a group is a distinct minority, they may win public office by showing the majority they have the competence to be an outstanding public official. The election of black officials in large and medium size cities adhere to the patterns discussed above.

Cities with black mayors are of several types. The *type A* city is one in which blacks are a majority (N = 3); *type B* cities have a more evenly mixed population

(N = 8); and *type C* cities are those where blacks are a distinct minority (N = 11). The schema in Table 5–1 describes the various types of voters in the twenty-three cities with black mayors.

In some of these cities, blacks have become the majority; in most, however, they are still the minority. All of the core cities, however, have large, black, poor populations. Herein lies the dilemma for black mayors: in most of these cities, black mayors cannot be elected without white support, but it is equally true that they depend heavily on the black vote. Thus as blacks move to the fourth phase—the politics of governance—black elected officials will be faced with not

**Table 5–1. Racial Mixture of Voters in Cities with Black Mayors***

| Cities | Voters % Blacks | Voters % White | |
|--------|--------|--------|--------|
| Type A | 50%+ | Under 50% | N =  3 |
| Type B | 30-50% | 50-70% | N =  8 |
| Type C | 0-30% | Over 30% | N = 11 |
| | | | N = 12 |

*The racial mixture of these cities raises significant empirical questions on the kinds of leadership styles exhibited by mayors in these cities. This will be explored in a later paper. Also see Table 5–2 for a list of these cities.

only the problems of reform, but with the need to effect substantive policy changes as well.

### Politics of Governance

The politics of governance is the new focus of the black urban politics. It is a pragmatic politics. As used here, the politics of governance, as distinguished from the politics of reform, means not only an alteration in structural form but also an attempt to control the decision-making process through the electoral system. In other words, the politics of governance seeks to institutionalize, where possible, the political power and values of the new group.

This new pragmatism is based on the assumption that the interests of black people can be enhanced and advanced with the acquisition of political power. Kwame N. Krumah put it this way: "Seek ye the political kingdom and all things shall be added unto you."[25] While this may be an exaggeration, it has, nevertheless, come to be accepted as folk wisdom by most black politicians today.

The pragmatic view holds that blacks have three alternatives to the present American political system: try to overthrow it, try to ignore it or try to control it or decide who does.[26] The first, according to Chuck Stone, is reckless romanticism. The second is an implicit acceptance of the oppressor's control over their lives. The third has become increasingly a realistic strategy for blacks to control major metropolitan centers, Southern counties, and congressional districts. That the pragmatic view has won out is seen in the increasing number of black elected officials, the most important of whom, from the standpoint of the politics of governance, are the black mayors. It is here that black urban politics draws its major strength; and it is here that most blacks today are resting their major hopes for a more egalitarian society.

### The Problems of Black Mayors in
### Large and Medium-Sized Cities

Black mayors are in general agreement that "politics is the new cutting edge of the civil rights movement." For example, Johnny Ford, the black mayor of Tuskegee has said, "In the late 1950s and 60s those marches were appropriate. We were trying to demonstrate that segregation was wrong. We appealed to the conscience of America. Now all those laws are on the books. . . . The question is, now that we are in the door, how do we take advantage of it?" Charles Evers, mayor of Fayette, Miss., has said, . . . "I think we are in phase three and four now . . . the doors are open . . . now we begin the economic and political phase of our struggle for equality and justice."[27]

One of the most popular black mayors is Maynard Jackson of Atlanta. He has stated that there are still community civil rights leaders, "but more and more of the black community is evolving to the point that it manifests its concerns and positions through the elected black officials rather than independent or black non-elected officials. . . ." Finally, Johnny Ford of Tuskegee sums the views of black mayors up this way: "The mayors have a particularly viable role because they are in a position to make decisions—day-to-day decisions—that affect people's houses and jobs. . . ."

It is clear, then, that some black mayors see their role as the new "cutting edge." To be sure, there are still civil rights organizations, but there is no longer a movement with widespread appeal. In fact, the black mayors arrived on the scene just as the civil rights movement declined. Electoral politics, not civil rights organization, seems to be winning the day.

But politics is not all glamour, for election to public office carries enormous responsibilities. The problems of cities with black mayors are in some cases significantly different from those of other cities of the same size. Analysis of 845 cities with a population of 25,000 or more led to the following conclusions:

1. As noted earlier and contrary to popular belief, most of the medium and large-size cities with black mayors are not predominantly black. In over half blacks are a distinct minority.
2. Those cities governed by blacks rank among the poorest, most overpopulated cities in the nation.
3. Many of these cities with black mayors are among those which suffered the largest loss of white population to the suburbs. Those losses occurred prior to the election of the black mayor.

4. These cities are among those with the oldest housing in the country, and many have experienced a sharp decline in their housing supply.
5. The capacity of these cities to raise revenues from their own taxes is among the lowest in the nation.
6. Contrary to popular belief, a sizable majority of these black mayors do not preside over weak mayor systems.[28]

In some cases, the black mayor's plight is like that of the gambler who knowingly plays against a marked deck because it is the only game in town. One assumes that he plays because he enjoys the challenge, or because electoral politics is where the "action is." Whatever the case, the mayors not only face problems, they frequently are limited in what they can do about them.

**Limits of Mayoral Power.** It has been argued that the quality and performance of mayoral leadership reflect how well resources are employed to mobilize politically effective *constituencies*, to seek out and maximize *fiscal assistance* and available programs from the federal government, and to overcome formal resistance from *executive authority* and municipal powers in dealing with urban problems.[29] More specifically, Jeffrey Pressman has argued that big city mayors require the following seven resources to exercise effective community leadership: (1) Sufficient financial and staff resources on the part of the city government; (2) city jurisdiction in social program areas—e.g., jobs, education, etc.; (3) mayor jurisdiction in these policy fields; (4) a salary for the mayor which will let him spend full time on the job; (5) sufficient staff support for the mayor—for policy planning, intergovernmenta. relations, etc., (6) ready vehicles for publicity, such as friendly newspapers or television stations; and (7) politically oriented groups, including a political party, which the mayor could mobilize to help him achieve particular goods.[30]

Given these preconditions of mayoral leadership, do black mayors in big and medium size cities have the necessary resources to exercise effective leadership? We might address this question by looking at the mayors' (1) personal leadership qualities and (2) statutory powers.

**A. The Black Mayor: Leadership Styles.** In some respects, black mayors differ from other mayors in that they normally lack party support, get few resources from powerful interest groups and are independent from political machines. They face other problems as well—that is, while they draw their support in most cities from a majority white voting population, the most needy in the city are black. These factors force black mayors to rely heavily on their personal leadership qualities.

Personal leadership styles are important to most politicians, but especially so for blacks. Black mayors depend heavily on their styles to get them elected or reelected. For the most part they *lack* most of the resources that Pressman specifies for big city leadership. On the other hand, they are active, innovative types who emphasize new programs and policies; they believe in governmental intervention to help solve social problems; but they frequently fail to achieve program objectives, either because they are dependent upon Washington for financial assistance or because the goals of social welfare policy may alienate crucial groups within their political constituencies.[31] As was noted earlier, black mayors are faced with three rather diverse situations: (1) a predominantly black electorate (this is true in only three cities); (2) a balanced mixture of black and white voters; and (3) a predominantly white voting-age population. And since the last two are the most representative, programs must appeal to a broad segment of the public. Black mayors, under these circumstances, must take a universalistic view. In doing so, they become in essence, cosmopolitan mayors.

Black mayors are also cosmopolitan for other reasons. First, urban problems are state problems. In many states, the cities are still under Dillon's rule. That means that the state governments have, if they choose to exercise it, unlimited power over local governments except where state constitutions provide the contrary. Another restraint on cities is the "one man, one vote" principle, which has meant, as Matthew Holden so aptly pointed out, an important increase in the suburbs' influence in state legislative politics. That is simply because seats follow people.[32]

One example of the potential influence that state legislatures can have on cities will suffice. In 1975 in Atlanta, Maynard Jackson began his second year as the city's first black mayor. As more whites have fled the inner core, Atlanta has gone from 38 percent black in 1960 to 55 percent black in 1975.[33] White business interests which until recently ran the city are unhappy; they assert that the downtown's robust economic health is being threatened by crime, poor schools, racial polarization and white flight. As a result, some members have talked to Governor George Busbee and members of the General Assembly about the need to study annexation and merger of services. Most of the people going to Capitol Hill have been white, but there is also a feeling in Atlanta's black community that something must be done to expand the tax base. The General Assembly has also been asked to study whether governmental efficiency in the metropolitan area could be improved through merger, of say, city and suburban water and police departments.

What does the mayor think? Mayor Jackson has acknowledged the need for an expanded tax base and cooperation of certain services and states that he would support "a certain enlargement, if it is done right." Right now these are only studies. Once these studies are completed, however, and if the legislature so chooses, consolidation or merger might be required. Being an urban mayor today means, for most black mayors, being cosmopolitan.

Second, urban problems are national problems. Most of the major decisions about health, education, housing and transportation, for example, are made in Washington. Black mayors must deal not only with a local constituency and state legislatures but also with the federal bureaucracy. When dealing with state legislatures and the federal bureaucracy, the black mayor must make the transition from a *cosmopolitan* mayor to a *diplomat.*

Diplomats are supposed to be able to negotiate with others. When, for example, black mayors are being threatened by a state legislature, they will have to become diplomats of the highest order if they are to protect their political base of power. On the other hand, as James Q. Wilson has pointed out, they will have to deal with an "audience" that is "different from their constituency."[34] By "audience" Wilson means those persons whose favorable attitudes and responses the mayor is most interested in, those persons from whom he received his most welcome applause and his most needed resources and opportunities. Constituency means those people who vote for him in elections. The new audience will become crucial for black mayors given the poor fiscal conditions of their cities. This audience consists of various agencies (mostly federal) that give grants directly to the cities; foundations, especially the Ford Foundation; the mass media—which give major access to the suburbs, the state and the nation. He also has his affluent—often liberal—suburban voters who must appraise his leadership abilities.

For black mayors this audience is crucial. From this audience come *power* and *resources* to meet the demands for services and to hire new staff; publicity comes from media exposure; from foundations comes expertise. If black mayors are not to become innovators without funds, they will have to become skillful diplomats in an arena that is crowded with other skillful political actors.

We should also be aware that black mayors are mostly independent from political machines or local ruling elites. They have little if any *party* support and must develop their own campaign organizations and financial support. Because of their independent posture, they have difficulty in transferring electoral coalitions into new public policies. Reforms are often blocked by a reluctant city council or a recalcitrant bureaucracy (e.g., Gary).

Independent black mayors have two other major problems: (1) black mayors are normally handicapped by not being able to influence the selection of state and congressional candidates. In some cities (e.g., Chicago) the mayor controls legislative and congressional delegates. These delegates protect the interest of the city of Chicago. (The black delegates from Chicago present a problem, they speak for city interests, not the for interests of black people.) For black mayors in those cities where control is weak or nonexistent, legislators need not be accountable to city interest; and (2) black mayors also lack control over county machines which may run elections, control courts, operate independent law enforcement departments, control prosecution, etc. County governments as in East St. Louis, for example, are an alternate form of maintenance of the old organizations displaced in cities by the election of black mayors.*

---

*These two points were brought to my attention by Phillip Monypenny, a colleague at the University of Illinois, Urbana.

In brief, the black mayors in large and medium-sized cities are often both independent and cosmopolitan in outlook. They have, however, not yet become capable diplomats. Mayor Jackson, for example, has not negotiated well with the business elite or state legislature, and Mayor Hatcher has had problems developing good intergovernmental relations with the state and federal bureaucracy. Consequently, some of the support they need is not forthcoming. Therein lies another major limit to mayoral power.

**B. Statutory Power of Black Mayors.** Other limits are structural or institutional, and most are embedded in local charters. City charters specify the methods by which a citizen becomes a mayor, the mayor's appointive authority, terms of office, and the form of government. They also specify the mayor's authority to veto ordinances and prepare the budget. Regardless of a mayor's personal virtues, such provisions may well determine the actual amount of authority a mayor has. To what extent, then, do these factors limit the black mayor's impact on city government in large and medium-sized cities? Are black mayors being elected to powerless positions by whites?

According to the *Joint Center for Political Studies,* ten of the 23 black mayors have charter authority and responsibilities to influence the course of their communities. The other thirteen black mayors have no such authority and must find power, if any, through personal talents or by being a member of the city council. These thirteen have no significant authority over appointments and budget control and no veto over ordinances and resolutions.[35]

The study also found three other significant factors relative to black mayors. First, the fact that over half of the black mayors are in weak statutory positions is significantly related to the size of the cities. Weak mayoral forms are common in cities with a population of 25,000 to 250,000 where 74 percent of black mayors serve. There is no evidence that white minorities are deliberately electing blacks to weak mayoral governments. Second, most black mayors are elected to four-year terms and most succeed themselves. Third, black mayors are elected by popular vote in communities which have a majority white voting age population. (See Table 5–2).

As for the forms of government, over half of the medium and large-sized cities have council-manager forms of government, not uncommon for cities in the 25,000 to 250,000 range. In fact, according to the International City Managers Association, nearly 56 percent of the cities of that size have this form of government.[36] Most of the larger cities where blacks are 45 percent or more of the population do not have city council forms—e.g., Atlanta, Gary, Newark, and Washington, D.C. (See Table 5–3). The *commission form* exists only in East St. Louis, and it is currently being changed to the *mayor-council* form. The mayor-council form is found in ten of the 23 cities with black mayors, and six have administrative officers appointed by the mayor.

The problem here is that each mayor-council city operates differently, and

**Table 5-2. Methods of Election, Voting-Age Population and Term of Office**

| City and state | Election by Popular Vote | Council Vote | Total voting age population Number | Percent black[a] | Term of office (years) |
|---|---|---|---|---|---|
| Prichard, Ala | x | | 24,549 | 46 | 4 |
| Berkeley, Cal. | x | | 93,022 | 20 | 4 |
| Compton, Cal. | x | | 42,517 | 65 | 4 |
| Los Angeles, Cal | x | | 1,966,855 | 16 | 4 |
| Boulder, Colo. | x | | 48,443 | * | 2 |
| Atlanta, Ga. | x | | 377,438 | 46 | 4 |
| East St. Louis, Ill. | x | | 41,848 | 63 | 4 |
| Gary, Ind. | x | | 107,425 | 48 | 4 |
| College Park, Md. | x | | 20,293 | 3 | 2 |
| Detroit, Mich. | x | | 1,017,608 | 37 | 4 |
| Grand Rapids, Mich. | x | | 130,727 | 9 | 4 |
| Highland Park, Mich. | x | | 23,897 | 46 | 4 |
| Inkster, Mich. | x | | 22,538 | 44 | 4 |
| Pontiac, Mich. | | x | 53,472 | 23 | 2 |
| Ypsilanti, Mich. | x | | 23,567 | 16 | 2 |
| East Orange, N.J. | x | | 55,898 | 46 | 4 |
| New Brunswick, N.J. | x | | 31,515 | 17 | 4 |
| Newark, N.J. | x | | 240,033 | 48 | 4 |
| Chapel Hill, N.C. | x | | 20,157 | 8 | 2 |
| Raleigh, N.C. | x | | 88,857 | 20 | 2 |
| Cincinnati, Ohio | | x | 312,055 | 24 | 2 |
| Dayton, Ohio | x | | 166,849 | 27 | 4 |
| Washington, D.C. | x | | 532,404 | 64 | 4 |

*Less than one percent
[a]Calculations based on data taken from U.S. Census of Population, 1970.
SOURCE: *Joint Center for Political Studies,* October, 1974, p. A2.

the power of mayors fluctuates accordingly. For example, control over the budget equals power. The mayors who are authorized to submit or veto budgets have more power than those who cannot. In Atlanta, the mayor controls the budget by serving on two bodies: the budget commission, which has four members (three are appointed by the mayor), and the appropriations committee, which consists of the mayor, three members of the council (appointed by the mayor), the chairman of the council's finance committee, the chief administrative officer and the director of finance. They prepare the budget, and the mayor submits it to the council. In Atlanta, then, the mayor has control over the budget. But in Washington, the mayor prepares a balanced budget for submission to the council and the Congress. The Congress retains "line item" approval of the total District budget. In New Jersey cities, budget items *cannot* be vetoed by the mayor. But in ten cities, black mayors have veto power.

In even fewer cities, mayors are limited in their appointive authority by civil service rules and departmental personnel systems. In Gary, for example, the

Table 5-3. Form of Government in Cities with Black Mayors

| Size class and City | Mayor-Council | Mayor-Council with chief admin. officer | Council-Manager | Commission |
|---|---|---|---|---|
| 25,000 – 49,999 | | | | |
| Prichard, Ala. | x | | | |
| College Park, Md. | | | x | |
| Highland Park, Mich. | x | | | |
| Inkster, Mich. | | | x | |
| Ypsilanti, Mich. | | | x | |
| New Brunswick, N.J. | | x | | |
| Chapel Hill, N.C. | | | x | |
| 50,000 – 99,999 | | | | |
| Compton, Cal. | | | x | |
| Boulder, Colo. | | | x | |
| E. St. Louis, Ill. | | | | x |
| Pontiac, Mich. | | | x | |
| East Orange, N.J. | x | | | |
| 100,000 – 249,999 | | | | |
| Berkeley, Cal. | | | x | |
| Gary, Ind. | | x | | |
| Grand Rapids, Mich. | | | x | |
| Raleigh, N.C. | | | x | |
| Dayton, Ohio | | | x | |
| 250,000 – 499,999 | | | | |
| Atlanta, Ga. | | x | | |
| Newark, N.J. | | x | | |
| Cincinnati, Ohio | | | x | |
| 500,000 – 999,999 | | | | |
| Washington, D.C. | | x | | |
| 1 million or more | | | | |
| Los Angeles, Cal. | | x | | |
| Detroit, Mich. | x | | | |

SOURCE: *Joint Center for Political Studies,* October 1974, p. A4.

police are run by a city commission; two members are appointed by the council and one by the mayor. Unless the mayor can obtain the consent of the other two members of the commission (in a recent case he could not) he cannot fire the police chief even if he desires to do so. In fact, it is not uncommon to find in most cities statutory provisions which govern the action of firemen, policemen and teachers. Some municipalities have rules governing all municipal employees. In the larger cities, ethnic claims restrict mayoral powers. The police, firemen, educators and sanitary workers are all well entrenched. A recent report prepared for the city council in Washington shows how deeply some groups are entrenched.

In Washington, D.C., a study by one member of the city council to assess the affirmative action and promotion opportunities for minorities found that:

1. In the police department, the chief and all eight of his deputy chiefs are white males, as are also 22 of the 24 inspectors, 45 of 49 captains, 160 of 186 lieutenants and 458 of 609 sergeants. Of 118 employees GS–9 and above, 68, or 75 percent, are white. Hardly any of the top police officers live in Washington—not the chief, none of his eight deputies, none of the 24 inspectors, only one of 409 captains and just 18 percent of 186 lieutenants.
2. In the fire department whites hold 1018—72 percent—of the 1410 GS–level jobs. Only 259 of these 1410 GS employees live in Washington.
3. Environmental Services, Corporation Counsel's office, Department of Highways and Traffic, Department of General Services, Office of Municipal Planning, Public Library, Motor Vehicles—all are much like the fire and police departments. Finally, the Personnel Department has 54 jobs GS–9 and above, with blacks holding 17 and women of all races just 14. Only 18 percent of the GS–12 and above employees live in the city. And this, the council member asserts, is headquarters command for municipal employment.[37]

The point made by this study may also apply to other cities with black mayors. Washington, D.C., a city that is almost 80 percent black, is, as Councilman Barry puts it, run by "an occupational army of white males."[38] The implication for affirmative action is clear—if black men and women are to get jobs with the city, a new assortment of jobs must be made available. If not, conflicts will ensue over the current ones. This point should not be lost on all the doomsayers of the "Great Society's" programs. For after all, if it did nothing else, it created new jobs in municipal governments which allowed for black employment without the necessity of having to directly challenge the old entrenched bureaucracies. Whether this was "good" or "bad" need not be argued here—what needs to be questioned is how black mayors will fare under these conditions.

The new black mayors have limited powers; like white mayors they become facilitators or housekeepers. Only about ten have substantial power over budgets and appointments, and even here they have limits. Black mayors govern cities where most voters are white and the needy are black. As a consequence, policies must be broad in scope and, of necessity, of limited value to poor blacks. Personality has its role, but statutory authority puts severe restrictions on its use. Without question, the election of black mayors is an important development in black urban politics. Yet, if one is to assess the present for future trends, it becomes an open question whether electoral "politics can or will continue to be the cutting edge of the civil rights movement." The implications are serious and deserve a final comment.

### Conclusions

The institutionalization of black urban politics is now a reality. Yet there is one fundamental fact about the accretion of political power that black politicans have yet to learn; that is, organization equals power. The point is important because those who seek and get power will not keep it for long if they do not have an organized political base. Political organization is not only necessary to win elections, it is also necessary to govern effectively. The assumption here is that election to political office is not an end result but *only* a means to achieve a more desired outcome. Political power cannot be used effectively when it is dependent solely upon the "charismatic traits" of the leader; rather the effective use of political power depends on organization. This discussion leads us to several problems about the nature of black urban politics.

**Endemic Problems:** There are two basic structural constraints on black politics. They are: (1) the structure of political power—i.e., black politics suffers from weak political organization at the *local level*; and (2) the structure of political power at the *national level* where group representation is also weak and effective national urban policy is dependent upon group bargaining power. To be effective, group bargaining power is dependent upon group organization. The pluralist nature of American politics implies that outcomes are determined *by* and gained *from* a position of organized strength. To bargain from a position of weakness is a virtual guarantee of neglect; at best, unorganized groups can expect few rewards.

The two points described above spell out significant endemic problems of black urban politics; hence they also describe some of the political realities of black politics.

*Problem one*—local organizational weakness—can possibly be controlled, if not surmounted. On the other hand, *problem two*—nature of organizational weakness—is more elusive. Blacks cannot hope to control the situation exclusively by their efforts; it requires *coalition politics*—among blacks and whites on a basis of common interest. The point made by members of the Congressional Black Caucus is pertinent here—they have pointed out that they have no permanent enemies, no permanent friends, just permanent interest. If these two problems represent "the nature of things" in American politics, then only structural changes can alter or eliminate the problems. In the meantime, however, what are the options?

**Option 1: Local Voter Mobilization.** Mayor Jackson of Atlanta has called for a national black strategy based on local voter mobilization. This seems to be one of the most effective means to deal with the problem of weak local political organization. Related tactics would include Chuck Stone's call for more participation in electoral politics (especially by black youth), voter registration drives in urban and rural areas and voting with the party that is likely to maximize the options of black voters. The point here is that the "politics of participation" must be preferred to the "politics of withdrawal," since the former has previously demonstrated its potentialities—e.g., Adam Clayton Powell's ability to help shepherd through sixty major pieces of legislation in six years, the war on poverty, the Congressional Black Caucus' efforts to protect black interests, etc.

Second, this strategy offers the possibility of moving from the local level to the development of a unified national political network which would allow blacks to make serious demands on the political system.

**Option 2: The Formation of a National Black Party.** Option two has been much discussed, but little systematic research seems to have been done. The success of this option will be determined by the success of option one—mainly the development of a unified national political network and a high level of participation. But in general and in the *immediate* sense, it is not profitable to expend considerable energies on this option for several reasons: (1) the structural characteristics of American politics deny the possibility of third parties, whose success historically has been limited. Historical and institutional forces do not lend themselves to third parties. In addition, America does not have a history of unbridgeable religious and cultural beliefs as do some other countries. Therefore, a two-party system rather than a multi-party system is likely to dominate for some time to come.

Hence, the position taken by Baraka, to join a new Pan-Africanist Party based on Marxism, is likely to prove unproductive at best and self-destructive at worst. This option seems to be a variant of the politics of withdrawal, except that it seeks to build a power base independent of the existing power holders, i.e., whites in general, but mainly the two parties and the powerful interest groups. Nothing would be more destructive given the nature of pluralist politics and the organizational weakness of blacks in America.

The discussion of the options above places much emphasis on: (1) the structure of power and the nature of politics in America; and (2) the significance of interest groups in American politics. These points need to be stressed because much of the writing on black politics ignores these two points or fails to stress their importance adequately. These are the kind of constraints that the new black urban politics must contend with. And it is for this reason that the analysis of the structural limits of black mayors is important.

### Implications, Possibilities and Problems of the New Urban Black Politics

Generally speaking, most articles on black politics (some explicitly and some implicitly) advocate more participation by blacks. Some possible reasons are:

1. The emergence of a new willingness of whites to commit their welfare to outstanding black candidates. Proof comes from the emergence of black mayors who have been elected in cities not having a predominantly black electorate, e.g., Los Angeles, Boulder, Grand Rapids, etc., and the election of two lieutenant governors in states where blacks are a distinct minority;

2. The argument made by some that the emergence of black mayors implies a higher level of political sophistication by black politicians.

This emergence has certain consequences for the new urban politics. First, it can possibly lift or instill a sense of pride in blacks about their community. Second, the emergence will inevitably raise the level of black expectations. Both consequences put black mayors on the spot. That is, black mayors are expected to deliver certain outcomes demanded by blacks; *but,* black mayors also face severe institutional constraints, and these will limit their ability to deliver on these demands. If they fail to deliver, the role of the black mayor will become more symbolic than substantive. The failure to deliver, moreover, might also have other serious consequences; blacks are liable to lose hope, become more frustrated and come to view the failure as substantial evidence of the futility of their plight. The result may be a resort to unorganized collective violence.

The rise of black mayors can thus become a two-edged sword; that is, it may become a temporary source of black pride on the one hand, *but* it may, on the other hand, also become a signal that the system does not work for blacks. The question thus becomes: *will the emergence of black mayorships be a political advantage to blacks or will it lead to increased political cynicism?* The question has its roots in the fact that while black mayors are emerging, *there is no corresponding change in the structural characteristics of city politics which by nature are painfully restrictive and often unresponsive.* The control of the bureaucracy by entrenched groups leaves many mayors open to "creative sabotage" by career bureaucrats. Thus, where the sword is dull on one edge, it is likely to cut only one way.

Finally, for black urban politics to reach its full potential, there needs to be a more systematic discussion of the following points:

(1) If the new urban politics is to succeed, there must be a simultaneous emergence of new organizational strength. That is, the emergence of new mayorships will have to be correlated with an increase in interest group activity. *It is naive to think that politics alone can be the new cutting edge*; black urban power will have to be supplemented and extended by *organizational power.* That means very simply that the NAACP and the Urban League will become (or should become) more important in the future, not less. These organizations have support in the black community and are invaluable in the struggle for equality. They are also stable and well organized. Given the nature of American politics and the dismal history of black Americans in this country, to rest one's hope on one strategy is politically indefensible and intellectually unacceptable. This point cannot be overstressed.

This is not to suggest that pressure tactics are to be abandoned. On the contrary, electoral politics and organizational interest draw most of their sustenance from the tactics used by pressure groups. Electoral politics never has been, nor is it likely to be in the future, the only way to achieve equality.

Consequently, politics not directly based on electoral power—welfare rights organizations, tenants unions, general obstructions directed to specific ends—are all likely to be as important in the future as they are today. What we are suggesting is that people, whose implicit cooperation is necessary to authorities doing their jobs, have power. Albeit, it is not as strong as other more stable institutionalized groups, but is is power nevertheless.

(2) The emergence of black mayorships offers yet another opportunity to the black community—that is the development and recruitment of new young blacks with administrative expertise. All mayors need their own men in key positions and the black mayor is no exception. That does not mean replacing all whites with blacks; it does mean recruiting competent blacks and developing their expertise. One of the major weaknesses of the black community is a lack of expertise. Where skilled personnel exist, they should be recruited. An effective recruitment process can help determine the distribution of power, the decisional process and the control over policy outputs. Control of the recruitment process is vital to the success of the new black urban politics. Think, for example, of the possibilities which might arise from a new urban politics which can take advantage of the emergence of black mayors, the emergence of new political sophistication, a reorganization of power capabilities of black interest groups and effective control of the recruitment process in urban politics.

(3) What is needed in the mass media's discussion of the plight of the cities is more *sustained* coverage and attention on problems confronting urban politics, rather than relying on occasional "special reports." Elsewhere in this volume E. Terrence Jones has made this point, though his concern was not specifically on the plight of black mayors.

If the above three tactics of the new urban politics require coalitions of blacks and whites, occasionally denying one party black support and giving it to another, denying it to both major parties or lending support to a third party, then that is what should be done (e.g., in New York politics, groups employ such tactics). This is the *politics of expediency,* whose objective is to maximize black options.

In the final analysis, whatever the tactics or strategy, one thing is certain: black mayors face severe limitations that will restrict what they can accomplish. Where this is understood by black citizens, black mayors will not be faced with unrealistic demands; where high expectations exist and performance is low, the growth of electoral politics as the new cutting edge will surely diminish.

What, then, can we conclude about the new black urban politics? If there is anything which can be asserted, it is that there is "no one best way." Instead, a general strategy is required which includes an arsenal of tactics, each to be used as the specific situation dictates. The dynamics of American politics compels such an approach, and the future protection of black Americans may well depend on it.

## NOTES

1. Quoted in the *New York Times,* November 7, 1974. Dymally is the first black to be elected Lieutenant Governor in the state's history.

2. The newest member of the Caucus is Harold Ford of Tennessee. Thus Ford became the third black congressman elected from the South. Both Barbara Jordan of Texas and Andrew Young of Georgia were reelected. It should also be noted that a white liberal congressman from California, Fortney Stark, has recently applied for caucus membership. His status has not yet been determined.

3. Other blacks have been elected to statewide positions but most of these are of low visibility.

4. National Roster of Black Elected Officials, Joint Center for Political Studies, 4 (1974), p. xiv. Latest figures released by the Center now show 3503 black elected officials in the nation.

5. Harrington J. Bryce, "Problems of Governing American Cities: The Case of Medium and Large Cities with Black Mayors," *Joint Center for Political Studies,* 1974. Also see "On Black Mayors," *New York Times,* April 19, 1975. This paper is an analysis of 23 of the 26 cities with black mayors. It excludes Waco, Texas, Gainesville, Florida; and Charlottesville, Virginia.

6. Cities of 25,000 or over are today the types of cities in which most Americans live.

7. See for example, the argument of Mack H. Jones, "Some Notes on Black Political Conditions in the U.S. South," paper, W.E.B. DuBois Conference, Department of Sociology, Atlanta University, October 3, 1974.

8. Bryce, p. A1.

9. Ibid.

10. Quoted in the *New York Times,* July 25, 1975.

11. Daniel N. Gordon, "Immigrants and Urban Governmental Forms in American Cities, 1933–1960," *American Journal of Sociology,* 74 (September, 1968), pp. 158–71. Also cited in Charles V. Hamilton, "Racial, Ethnic and Social Class: Politics and Administration," *Public Administration Review,* 32 (October, 1972), p. 638.

12. V.O. Key, Jr., *Politics, Parties and Pressure Groups* (New York: Thomas Y. Cromwell, 1964), p. 57.

13. Hamilton, pp. 640–45. I have added one category to the phases suggested by Hamilton and that is the politics of reform. I distinguish this from his politics of governance later in this paper.

14. Ibid., p. 640.

15. Cited in ibid., p. 641.

16. Raymond E. Wolfinger, "Some Consequences of Ethnic Politics," in Harman Zeigler and Kent Jennings, eds., *The Electoral Process* (Englewood Cliffs, N.J.: Prentice-Hall, 1966). See also Wolfinger, "The Development and Persistence of Ethnic Voting," *American Political Science Review,* 59 (December, 1965).

17. Edward C. Banfield, *Big City Politics* (New York: Random House, 1965). Politics in Chicago presents an excellent example of how political machines maintain power. For blacks, it offers the politics of recognition. That is, blacks

hold some highly visible offices in the city, in the state legislature and are represented in the Chicago congressional delegation. Second, the loyalty of the black masses is kept through high welfare payments (Chicago delegations consistently support higher appropriations of welfare payments against downstate and suburban interests), funds for Community Action Programs, neighborhood projects (e.g., Woodlawn), effective city transportation system—done with federal subsidies, black cultural programs, and subsidized public housing. *But* the breakthrough on employment, quality of education, and limited success of blacks in all bureaucracies means that most benefits are *divisible.* Substantive policies are diverted and "recognition" given instead. For a useful way of looking at the benefits class interests and ethnic groups derive from political action, see Robert A. Dahl, *Who Governs?* (New Haven: Yale University Press, 1961), p. 52. On the uses of ethnic politics, see Raymond E. Wolfinger, "Some Consequences of Ethnic Politics," p. 47.

18. This important point was suggested to me by Fred Wirt, a colleague at the University of Illinois, Urbana.

19. Cited in Hamilton, p. 643.

20. Ibid.

21. An excellent example of the use of structural barriers can be found in Lee Sloan, " 'Good Government' and the Politics of Race," *Social Problems,* 15 (1968). Cited also in Hamilton, p. 643. Also see Joyce Gelb, "Blacks, Blocs and Ballots: The Relevance of Party Politics to the Negro," in Joyce Gelb and Marion Lief Palley, eds., *The Politics of Social Change* (New York: Holt, Rinehart, and Winston, 1971), pp. 158–71.

22. Alan A. Altshuler, *Community Control: The Black Demand for Participation in Large American Cities* (New York: Pegasus, 1970).

23. David E. Apter, *The Politics of Modernization* (Chicago: The University of Chicago Press, 1965), p. 16.

24. Seymour Martin Lipset, *Political Man* (New York: Anchor Books, 1963), p. 64. Also see Hamilton, p. 644.

25. Cited in Chuck Stone, "Politics: Participate or Perish," *The Black Collegian* (March/April, 1974), p. 39.

26. Ibid., pp. 39–40.

27. These major statements are drawn from the *Champaign-Urbana News Gazette,* October 10, 1974.

28. Bryce, p. A1.

29. Alan Shank and Ralph W. Conant, *Urban Perspectives: Politics and Policies* (Boston: Holbrook Press, Inc., 1975), p. 145.

30. Jeffrey L. Pressman, "Preconditions of Mayoral Leadership," *American Political Science Review,* 66 (June, 1972), p. 512.

31. Some of the ideas developed here are drawn from James D. Barber, *The Presidential Character* (Englewood Cliffs, N.J.: Prentice-Hall, 1972), pp. 11–13.

32. Matthew Holden, Jr., "Black Politicians in the Time of 'New' Urban Politics," *Review of Black Political Economy,* 11 (Fall, 1971), p. 68.

33. The following account is drawn from the *New York Times,* February 26, 1975.

34. James Q. Wilson, "The Mayors vs. the Cities," in Alan Shank, ed., *Political Power and the Urban Crises,* 2nd ed. (Boston: Holbrook Press, Inc., 1974), p. 304.

35. Harrington J. Bryce, "Black Mayors of Medium and Large Cities: How Much Power Do They Have?" Joint Center for Political Studies, 1974, p. A1. I shall rely heavily on this article in this section of the paper.

36. Cited in Ibid., p. A4.

37. See Simeon Booker, "Washington Notebook," *Ebony,* (August, 1975), p. 21.

38. Ibid.

Part Three

# New Issues in Urban Politics

Chapter Six

# Innovations in Urban Governments: A Preliminary Model

RICHARD D. BINGHAM

Recent years have seen an ever increasing body of literature concerned with the adoption of innovations by organizations within our society. In part, many authors are concerned with innovation due to the increasing technological complexity of modern society.[1] There are predictors of doom[2] and suggestions about how to cope with the technological change.[3] Thus, today there are literally hundreds of publications dealing with the diffusion of innovations, many developing their own terminology and leaving the reader in an obvious state of confusion. Fortunately several authors have recognized the need to draw together this widely disparate body of literature and have done so with some success.[4] Unfortunately, however, most of the summaries and attempts at synthesis have very little to do with political organizations. Thus, part of the confusion lies with the fact that the literature concerned with innovation comes from a variety of disciplines, with management and business, sociology and psychology somewhat in the lead. Added confusion develops as we note the variety of types of organizations under study—business corporations, federal bureaucracies, state legislatures, local government, schools, health organizations, social clubs and dozens more. Because of problems of differing organizational goals, variations in the need for profit, varying methodologies and many other factors, it is difficult to transfer directly the findings concerning innovation in one type of organization to an organization with completely different structure and goals.

When innovative behavior in organizations is discussed, political organizations are usually the subject of serious criticism. Even introductory texts in American government often echo the complaint that the "pace of political processes is too slow to meet multiple and intense demands."[5] Criticism is even worse and more intense concerning innovation in local government. Local government is often pictured as hostile to new ideas with little capacity to design or accept new programs.[6] The Urban Institute suggests that a number of factors work against innovation in the city: institutional attitudes against change, the political risk in failure, budget constraints, distrust of industry, fear of displacement by workers and lack of evaluative capability in the city.[7] Government at all levels, but especially local government, is thus, for a variety of reasons, pictured as highly resistive to innovation.

And yet, there are significant examples of institutional success in innovation in the face of significant opposition. In the face of strong and well organized opposition, the federal government was successful in banning cigarette advertising from television and forcing manufacturers to place the following warning on cigarette packages and advertisements:

Warning: The Surgeon General Has Determined That Cigarette Smoking Is Dangerous to Your Health.[8]

In the face of some powerful recommendations to the contrary, the city of Milwaukee recently contracted for a prototype recylcing plant to dispose of solid wastes, abandoning a landfill system. This innovative behavior was accomplished in spite of Environmental Protection Agency recommendations against major commitments to large-scale facilities as long as adequate landfill capability is available until such time as recycling technology and markets are proven. Thus there are examples of innovative behavior in spite of substantial criticisms.

### Innovation

Part of the problem with innovation in local government is a definitional one. Unfortunately, the definition of innovation is critical to public policy. One student of innovation in state government defines innovation as "a program or policy which is new to the states adopting it, no matter how old the program may be or how many other states may have adopted it."[9] But is innovative behavior timeless? Probably not. There is some evidence that innovations are "fragile" issues. Two social scientists, Amos Hawley and Terry Clark, both examined the relationships between measures of the community power structure and urban renewal expenditures but with conflicting results. Hawley found a positive relationship between a high concentration of power in the community and urban renewal expenditures.[10] Clark also examined connecting links between the community power structure and renewal—but his research showed a significant relationship between a decentralized decision-making structure and urban renewal expenditures.[11] Clark reconciled these findings by suggesting that fragility may play an important part in identifying innovation. He suggests that an important component of fragility is the newness of any particular program to the community; that, in the case of a fragile issue, active opposition by even a small group of dissidents may be enough to delay or halt action on the issue. Furthermore, he suggests that fragility will decrease over time. Clark thus reconciled his differences with Hawley by suggesting that Hawley had studied urban renewal adoption when it was "innovative" (in the 1950s) while he studied renewal at a later time (in the 1960s) when the issue was "less fragile."

It appears, then, that some scholars who have equated public policy with innovation may have arrived at erroneous conclusions—not in terms of the use of federal programs but in terms of suspected determinants of innovative behavior.[12] A time constraint seems necessary in terms of defining innovation. Innovation, then, is probably best defined as "the first or early use of an idea by one of a set of organizations with similar goals."[13] Innovations are fragile, as Clark suggests. Adoption patterns change as the issue matures. It is therefore a mistake to equate all policy adoptions with innovation. Policy adoption after the maturation of an issue may or may not be "caused" by the same factors which determine innovative behavior.

### Innovation Typologies

While definitional problems have plagued innovation researchers, so has the tendency to lump together all kinds of innovation—from major policy adoptions to new fire hose nozzles. In fact, these two adoptions represent very different kinds of innovation. One way of classifying innovations, then, is by adopting unit. It is therefore helpful to think of innovation in local government in two categories—political and bureaucratic innovations. Political innovation is public policy. In local government this policy may originate from the executive section (mayor or manager), the legislative (the city council) or through a combination of both. Under our definition, then, political innovation is a first or early adoption of a new government policy by one of a set of local governments with similar goals. Bureaucratic innovation, on the other hand, is in response to political innovation or new policy, or is adopted in response to the feedback of public service. Bureaucratic innovation may encompass a change in process, a change in organizational structure and/or a new product or service. If the board of directors of a local housing authority, for example, adopts a policy of constructing or leasing housing for low income families on a scattered site basis only, and if it is one of the first authorities in the country to do so, it has accomplished a political innovation. If the authority bureaucracy then responds by reorganizing the maintenance section to provide mobile and rapid maintenance response to these scattered housing units, a bureaucratic innovation has been adopted.

Thus, the first distinction among innovations is one of political versus bureaucratic innovation. Political innovation produces new policy while bureaucratic innovation changes process, organizational structure and/or product.

A second typology of organizations is provided by the concept of operating or non-operating innovations.[14] This typology has been found to apply to bureaucratic innovations or to innovations which some policy makers believe should be adopted by units of local government. HUD, for example, was hopeful that modular or industrialized housing would be useful in alleviating the problems of housing low income families in urban areas. Local housing authorities, however, were reluctant to adopt this innovation for a variety of reasons. For housing authorities, then, the innovation was non-operating. That is, there was no particular pattern of adoption of this technology exhibited by public housing authorities.

Operating innovations fall within the incentive system of the public organization. These innovations are rational and are either adopted for reasons of need or because of their amenity value. Incentives for operating innovations include efficiency, slack, intergovernmental influence, special grants, etc.

Non-operating innovations cover a variety of new inventions or innovations which fall outside of the operating goals of the organization. Adoption of these innovations is not on a rational basis; they occur in the environment and in the organization on a random basis, strictly by chance. Non-operating innovations may be good things, but they occur outside of the incentive system of the bureaucratic decision makers. There is little direct incentive for a public housing authority decision maker specifically to want to use modular or factory built housing. The innovation is outside of his incentive system. Non-operating innovations may be interesting, but they are not essential. Bureaucratic executives have no reason to opt for something new (and sometimes risky) unless that something new will help them solve real or perceived problems.

The second typology of innovation, thus, largely applies to bureaucratic innovation. Operating and non-operating innovations are defined by the incentive presented to the organization. This incentive can be externally (e.g., by grants) or internally (e.g., by efficiency) induced, but it must be present to make innovation adoption predictable or operating.

The third typology for innovation in local government applies to both policy and process—to both political and bureaucratic innovations. The typology was first suggested by the policy oriented research of Oliver Williams and Charles Adrian in four Michigan cities.[15] Williams and Adrian suggest that certain innovations may appeal to special classes of cities. They use the term "amenities" to "distinguish between policies designed to achieve the comforts and necessities of life as opposed only to the latter." They note that city policies designed to provide amenities emphasize the home environment rather than the working environment and that certain types of cities are more prone to emphasize amenity value than are some of their counterparts.

Innovations can thus be classified according to their amenity/need base and apply equally to policy, process or product adoptions. Goals of amenity cities discovered by Williams and Adrian included safety, slowness of traffic, beauty, restfulness, where, "the rights of pedestrians and children take precedence over the claims of commerce." Need-based innovations, on the other hand, include those innovations designed to upgrade substandard performance or significantly reduce the government's operating expenses.

The need/amenity distinction is not a dichotomy, however. It is best pictured as a continuum with need on one end and amenity on the other. Innovations are seldom based entirely on one characteristic or the other but are adopted for both need and amenity reasons. A recent study of the adaptation of computer technology to public library operations, for example, found that some libraries adopted strictly on the basis of need while others appeared to adopt for status or amenity reasons.[16]

There are thus three important ways of looking at innovations in local government. Innovation may be considered political or bureaucratic, operating or non-operating, and amenity or need based. These three typologies seem to cover most innovations applicable to local government. Each innovation may be defined or discussed in terms of these three typologies. Yet while the typologies help classify or categorize innovations, they do not contribute much to an understanding of how innovations spread or are diffused from one local government to another.

### The Diffusion of Innovation

Diffusion research is fairly common in most areas of the social sciences,[17] but has been all but ignored in political science.[18] This is particularly true of innovation in urban policy where little has been accomplished beyond the few selected works mentioned earlier. Of equal importance is the complete void of comparative research in the area of bureaucratic innovation at the local level.[19] The diffusion literature in political science largely relies on the contributions of two scholars, Jack Walker and Virginia Gray, both working in the area of the diffusion of innovative policies among the states.

In his groundbreaking article, Jack Walker was interested, among other things, in developing a hypothesis concerning the geographic spread of innovations.[20] On the basis of his research, Walker suggests that there are pioneer or innovative states in different sections of the country. These pioneer states would adopt innovations or policies from other pioneers. The remaining states would then take their cues from the regional pioneers. Walker notes that the

> diffusion process forms an essentially geographic pattern, and can be visualized as a succession of spreading inkblots on a map created by the initial adoptions of new policies by states playing in a national "league" of cue-taking and information exchange, followed by other states whose standards of comparison and measures of aspiration are more parochial and who typically adopt new policies only after others within their regional "league" have done so.[21]

While taking issue with Walker concerning the aggregation of innovations into a single index, Virginia Gray's primary concern is with the rate of adoption of innovations and their cumulative distribution over time.[22] Her findings were not dissimilar to previously reported findings in other social sciences—that is, that the frequency of policy adoptions or innovations over time is normally distributed and that the adoption over time has the "S" shape of the cumulative normal curve.

In a recent essay, Walker also looks at the "S" shaped curve in terms of bureaucratic policy interest.[23] He suggests that there are communities of policy specialists in various fields made up of agency officials, journal editors and publishers, consultants, academics, administrators, etc., and that their interest in an innovation might follow the "S" curve suggested by Gray.

There are thus two ways of examining the diffusion of innovation—by geographic spread and by time-based analysis. Evidence thus far in a soon-to-be-completed study by Irwin Feller and Donald Menzel suggests that the adoption of technological innovations by local government or, more accurately, by local bureaucracy follows the expected "S" curve.[24]

Evidence also exists that substantiates, to some degree, Walker's "inkblot" pattern of diffusion. In a study of bureaucratic innovations, regional adoption patterns were noted for most of the individual innovations studied.[25] This pattern suggests a geographic spread of innovations from one city to nearby neighbors. The regional patterns, however, did not overlap with any consistency from one innovation to the next. Furthermore, correlating the scores representing levels of innovation adoption in each city for eight separate innovations produced coefficients of little significance. Thus while Walker was able to identify innovative states in terms of policy adoptions, there is no evidence that there are innovative cities—at least as far as bureaucratic innovation is concerned.

Unfortunately, there is virtually no evidence at all about the diffusion of political innovations on the local level. Beyond a few studies of the environmental base of urban government forms, this type of policy study is nonexistent.[26]

The diffusion of innovation in public organizations thus seems to be a relatively rapid process following the "S" curve common to most innovations. Findings concerning the geographic distribution of bureaucratic innovations suggest that cities tend to take cues from neighboring cities. The usual regional distributions of individual innovations suggest that emulation is a major factor in the spread of innovation. On the other hand, there is little evidence that cities tend to be particularly innovative or non-innovative. While Jack Walker was able to distinguish between innovative and non-innovative states,[27] there is no evidence that cities can be classified in this manner. Innovation adoption patterns vary with the specific policy or technology. Cities which are innovative in one area are not necessarily innovative in another. The same conclusions apply to specific types of local governments. Housing authorities, school districts, etc. also have adoption patterns which vary with the specific technology or policy. There is no evidence to suggest that a given unit of local government is innovative across all areas.

### Toward a Model of Innovation

If, then, there is no predictable pattern for the spread of innovation—if Chicago or San Francisco or Boston cannot be counted upon as innovative cities—is it possible to move toward a theory of innovation in local government? Unquestionably. There are regularities that can be observed in the adoption patterns of operating political and bureaucratic innovations. These patterns are equally observable for both amenity- and need-based adoption.

Figure 6–1 presents a model for the adoption of innovations by local government.[28] The model suggests that demands for political innovation are created by the environment and are transformed into polity by the political system. This new policy then serves as a demand for change in the bureaucracy, a change which leads to bureaucratic innovation. The output of the bureaucratic innovation is public service. A new or changed public service then acts to alter the environment and public attitudes which, in turn, lead to other innovative policies. The bureaucracy itself may also see a need for a change in the public service it provides without a change in policy. In this case bureaucratic innovation may be internally generated. Demand for bureaucratic change may also be generated without a change in policy. Availability of resources such as grants, intergovernmental cooperation, etc. also generate an opportunity for bureaucratic innovation without a change in policy.

The importance of the characteristics of the community environment as a base for innovation cannot be questioned. A multitude of urban policy studies have established the importance of the community environment in the development of public policy.[29] Socioeconomic variables appear to be good predictors of public policy regardless of whether the policy adoption is innovative or mature. In addition to the standard socioeconomic factors, the community power structure and local political culture also have a direct impact on the adoption of political innovations.

Environmental attitudes are operationalized through the attitudes and behavior of the political leaders.[30] The leaders operating through the executive, legislative and judicial branches of the political system at all levels of government produce urban policy outputs. In many cases it takes action by federal, state and local governments to produce the political innovations of local government. Recall that Amos Hawley studied the adoption of urban renewal by local government when it was a political innovation—that is, before the "fragile" issue had matured. This political innovation, like many others, required action by all three levels of government. The federal government passed the Housing Act of 1949 providing assistance to local governments for slum clearance and redevelopment. State governments then had to pass the appropriate enabling legislation and local

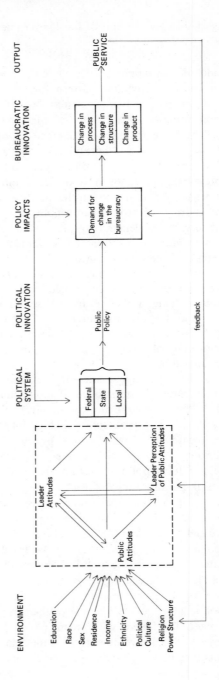

Figure 6–1.    A Model for the Adoption of Innovation by Local Government

governments had to adopt the program. Thus a local political innovation required affirmative action at all three levels of government.

Innovative public policy then demands a bureaucratic response—a response leading to bureaucratic innovation, an innovation defined as a change in process, in organizational structure or in a product used by the agency. Bureaucratic innovation then produces a change in public service, in the way a service is delivered, or in the costs involved in providing that service.

Political innovation, however, is not the only determinant of a demand for change in the bureaucracy. Two other areas also produce demand for change.[31] The political system can demand bureaucratic innovation without a change in public policy. Such system-induced change is, in fact, very common. A recent study of the adoption of computer technology by local public housing authorities, police departments and public libraries found that the adoption of these process innovations was independently influenced by intergovernmental cooperation. City governments with well-developed computer capabilities often made these capabilities available to other local government agencies. This "extra resource" provided by the city administration then allowed (and sometimes forced) other local agencies to adopt sophisticated computer-based management information systems.

The availability of financial resources from federal and state governments is also an independent contributor to bureaucratic innovation. This form of resource availability, whether provided annually or on a one-time basis, was directly related to bureaucratic innovation in public housing, police departments and public schools.

Demand for bureaucratic innovation is also stimulated by the output of the bureaucracy—through the feedback loop. Utilizing the dropout rate and the percentage of high school students going on to college as measures of the output of the public school systems in major American cities, it was found that the most successful school systems in terms of output were the most likely to adopt new and innovative programs (as measured by the adoption of individualized instruction). In this example of an amenity adoption it is apparent that feedback is thus the third independent contributor to bureaucratic innovation.

An important distinction must be made concerning the influence of the community environment on the adoption of political and bureaucratic innovations, a distinction discovered only recently. Public policy, and that class of public policy called political innovation, are directly influenced by the conditions of the community environment. Many studies of different public policies confirm this direct relationship. The community environment is directly related to policy adoptions in local government. The community environment is not directly related to bureaucratic innovation, however. The independent contributors to bureaucratic innovation beyond certain characteristics of the organization itself (e.g., size of the organization) are limited to responses to direct feedback from the public service provided, changes in public policy and excess resources made available to the bureaucratic organization by the political system. The character-istics of the local community have an impact upon bureaucratic innovation only indirectly—through the political system. The community environment, then, is directly related to political innovation, but is only indirectly related to bureau-cratic innovation.[32]

### Summary

Hopefully this article has presented an alternative way of looking at innova-tion in government. It is important, I think, to make a distinction between political innovation and public policy. Political innovation is public policy, but a policy of a very special kind—a first or early adoption of a new government policy by one of a set of local governments with similar goals. There is an inherent risk to political innovation, a risk not found in later policy adoptions built on the experience of the innovators. Much of the past research which purports to determine adoption patterns of political innovations actually con-sists of public policy studies and does not really consider true policy innova-tions. This is not to take away from such studies—most are excellent studies of public policy adoption and use. It is risky, however, to equate all public policy adoptions with political innovation.

It is necessary also to distinguish between political innovation and bureau-cratic innovation, although both types of innovation are peculiar to local govern-ments. Political innovation is a form of public policy while bureaucratic innova-tion is a change in process, organization or product leading to the actual public service output of local government. This change, of course, must also be a first or early adoption of a process, organizational form or product by one of a set of local agencies with similar goals.

Innovation adoptions are predictable phenomena—at least as long as incen-tives are presented to decision-makers. Political innovations are influenced directly by the community environment while bureaucratic innovations are not. The complex interrelationships between public policy, intergovernmental rela-tions and assistance and output feedback appear to determine bureaucratic inno-vation, with the community environment influencing adoptions only indirectly.

Obviously, the study of innovation in local government is in its infancy. Hopefully the typologies and model presented here will stimulate further think-ing about a subject that becomes more and more critical every year—the adoption of innovative policies, processes, and products by local government.

### NOTES

1. For example, Irene Taviss, *Our Tool-Making Society* (Englewood Cliffs: Prentice-Hall, 1972); Richard Kostelalnetz, *The Edge of Adaptation* (Englewood Cliffs: Prentice-Hall, 1973).

2. H. von Foerster, P.M. Mora, and L.W. Amiot, *Science,* 132 (1960), p. 1291; and later J. Serrin, "Is "Doomsday' on Target?" *Science,* 189 (1975), pp. 86, 88.

3. See part 6, "Strategies for Survival" in Alvin Toffler, *Future Shock* (New York: Bantam Books, 1970).

4. For example, Everett M. Rogers and F. Floyd Shoemaker, *Communication of Innovations: A Cross-Cultural Approach,* 2nd ed. (New York: Free Press, 1971); and Gerald Zaltman, Robert Duncan and Jonny Holbek, *Innovations and Organizations* (New York: Wiley, 1973).

5. Alan Rosenthal, "The Effectiveness of Congress," in Gerald M. Pomper, et al., eds., *The Performance of American Government* (New York: Free Press, 1972), p. 116.

6. Robert Crawford, "The Application of Science and Technology in Local Governments in the United States," *Studies in Comparative Local Government,* 7 (Winter, 1973), p. 12.

7. Urban Institute, *The Struggle to Bring Technology to Cities* (Washington: Urban Institute, 1971), summarized in Crawford, p. 13.

8. A. Lee Fritschler, *Smoking and Politics,* 2nd ed. (Englewood Cliffs, N.J.: Prentice-Hall, 1969).

9. Jack L. Walker, "The Diffusion of Innovations among the American States," *American Political Science Review,* 63 (September, 1969), p. 881.

10. Amos H. Hawley, "Community Power and Urban Renewal Successes," in Terry N. Clark, ed., *Community Structure and Decision-Making: Comparative Analyses* (San Francisco: Chandler, 1968), pp. 393–405.

11. Terry N. Clark, "Community Structure, Decision-Making, Budget Expenditures, and Urban Renewal in 51 American Communities," *American Sociological Review,* 33 (August, 1968), pp. 576–593.

12. For example, Michael Aiken and Robert R. Alford, "Community Structure and Innovation: The Case of Public Housing," *American Political Science Review,* 64 (September, 1970), pp. 843–864.

13. Selwyn W. Becker and Thomas L. Wisler, "The Innovative Organization: A Selective View of Current Theory and Research," *Journal of Business,* 40 (1969), p. 463.

14. Chapter 3 in Richard D. Bingham and Thomas P. McNaught, *The Adoption of Innovation by Local Government* (Milwaukee: Office of the Urban Research, Marquette University, 1975).

15. Oliver P. Williams and Charles R. Adrian, "Community Types and Policy Differences," in James Q. Wilson, ed., *City Politics and Public Policy* (New York: Wiley, 1968), pp. 17–36.

16. Bingham and McNaught, chapter 5.

17. For example, James S. Coleman, Elihu Katz and Herbert Menzel, *Medical Innovation: A Diffusion Study* (Indianapolis: Bobbs-Merrill, 1966); Edgar C. McVoy, "Patterns of Diffusion in the United States," *American Sociological Review,* 5 (April, 1940), pp. 219–227.

18. Jack Walker reported in 1973 that so far as he knew, only two articles with the word diffusion in their titles had ever appeared in the *American Politi-*

*cal Science Review.* Jack L. Walker, "Comment: Problems in Research on the Diffusion of Policy Innovations," *American Political Science Review,* 67 (December, 1973), pp. 1186–1191.

19. The one exception is Lawrence B. Mohr, "Determinants of Innovation in Organizations," *American Political Science Review,* 63 (March, 1969), pp. 111–126.

20. Walker, "The Diffusion of Innovations."

21. Walker, "Comment," p. 1187.

22. Virginia Gray, "Innovation in the States: A Diffusion Study," *American Political Science Review,* 67 (December, 1973), pp. 1174–1185.

23. Jack L. Walker, "The Diffusion of Knowledge and Policy Change: Toward a Theory of Agenda Setting," a paper presented at the Annual Meeting of the American Political Science Association, Chicago, 1974.

24. Irwin Feller and Donald Menzel, *Diffusion of Technology in Municipal Governments* (University Park, Penn.: Pennsylvania State University Press, forthcoming).

25. Bingham and McNaught, chapter 7.

26. See Brett W. Hawkins, *Politics and Urban Policies* (Indianapolis: Bobbs-Merrill, 1971) for a discussion of these studies.

27. Based upon his definition of innovation which concerned policy adoption without a time constraint.

28. Other policy models developed by Brett W. Hawkins and F. Ted Hebert suggested important portions of this model of innovation.

29. A good summary of this literature is found in Hawkins, *Politics and Urban Policies.*

30. This portion of the model was suggested by Warren E. Miller and Donald E. Stokes, "Constituency Influence in Congress," *American Political Science Review,* 57 (March, 1963), pp. 45–56.

31. Bingham and McNaught, *The Adoption of Innovation.*

32. Ibid.

**Chapter Seven**

# The Politics of Local Services and Service Distribution

GEORGE ANTUNES AND
KENNETH MLADENKA

## INTRODUCTION

The politics of local services is the politics of everyday life. It is the politics of the routine, the banal and, paradoxically, the frequently essential. It is the politics of school dress codes, sewer rates and the frequency of garbage collection. Topics like these at times generate rancorous community conflict and at other times are received with boredom or indifference. Yet when schools shut down, sewer plants are inoperative and garbage is uncollected these services are sorely missed.

The question Robert Dahl posed in 1961 was, "who governs?" Popular wisdom now asks whether anyone is governing. In the view of some persons local governments can no longer carry out the many tasks they are expected to perform; as a result local governments do not respond to citizen requests, to local political leaders or to major changes in the local social, economic and physical environment. In this paper we will examine the problems and politics of local services. We will examine some general aspects of determining service levels, i.e., what kinds of how much service is provided. Then we will turn to the special problem of service distribution—who gets how much of those services that are provided. Our aim in this paper is to review the various political and structural forces which affect the delivery and distribution of local services. We will explain why government behaves as it does and why, without massive structural changes in the organization, financing and politics of local services, it is unlikely that local government will ever behave any differently.

### Some Structural Conditions of Local Government.

**Fragmentation.** The most important structural condition affecting local government services is the phenomenon of fragmentation and overlap. A typical larger metropolitan area has hundreds of duly authorized and legally constituted governments.[1] There are city governments, county governments, port authorities, school districts and myriad special purpose districts providing everything from mosquito control to public hospital services. This multiplicity of governments is further confounded by overlapping jurisdictions. A citizen residing at a specific location may find himself served by, and paying taxes to, seven or eight different local governments.

Because governments are fragmented and overlapping, service provision is also fragmented and overlapping. The interested citizen contemplating the provision of local government services in a metropolitan area is confronted by a confusing jumble. Similar services are repetitiously (and often inefficiently) provided by many separate jurisdictions. It is not uncommon for each of twenty or so cities in a metropolitan area to have its own library, police department, fire department, etc. Sometimes services overlap; the same service being provided separately to the same set of citizens by more than one government. For example, persons living in Houston, Texas are served by (and pay for) both a city and a county public health department. In some areas several governments will cooperate in providing a particular service. Although this may seem a more rational and efficient approach to service provision, the political problems inherent in such arrangements tend to make them rather rare. In those instances where cooperative agreements are negotiated, they tend to be narrowly drawn and restricted to a particular type of service.[2]

Finally, there are scattered lacunae in local services. In some communities services which might be provided by government are not; they must be privately contracted (garbage collection is a frequent example).

**Inequality of Costs and Services.** Schultze notes that among the consequences of governmental fragmentation are:

1. citizen frustration and disorientation;
2. lack of coordination;
3. evasion of political responsibility;
4. inequality of costs and services and; .
5. cost shifting.[3]

Of these, the last two really represent another important structural problem of local service. Just as governments and services are fragmented, so too are local resources and need for services. Local economic conditions impose important limitations on the capacity of local government to deliver services. Jurisdictions with little economic base will be less able to provide services at the same level as more affluent jurisdictions. The fragmentation of local governments means economic resources are unevenly distributed. Since most local services are financed primarily by local taxes, some communities have great capacity to provide services while that of other communities is severely limited. Ironically, need for services is unevenly distributed in inverse relation to capacity to provide services. Those jurisdictions with the lowest economic base are generally the jurisdictions with the greatest need for local services. Level of need and capacity to provide services are important structural parameters in determining local service levels.

**Cost Shifting.** Cost shifting also affects service levels. The major cleavage in most metropolitan areas is a central city-suburban split. With only minor effort this division can be used to shift costs from the suburbs to the central cities. For example, through the use of zoning, land use regulations and tax concessions, highly desirable "clean" industries can be attracted to the suburbs, while less desirable industries and the poor can be prevented from relocating to the suburbs.[4] In this way the jurisdictional autonomy of the multiple local governments can be used further to reinforce the already uneven distribution of need for service and capacity to provide service.

**Fiscal Constraints.** Local governments are subject to a wide variety of constitutional and statutory limits which regulate their taxing and spending authority and the extent to which debts can be incurred. Frequently these limits are programmatic in nature. They set the maximum proportion of revenue or maximum tax rates that can be levied for a specific function, such as public libraries or hospitals. The result is that levels of expenditure are often determined by a combination of fiscal constraints and local tax base.

A related problem with which many local governments must contend is the requirement that tax increases or bond issues be approved by voters in a referendum. Capital expenditures as well as general revenue funds may be severely limited by a hostile electorate. As Meltsner has pointed out, the causes of tax referenda failure are complex and do not necessarily lie in the affected local governments.[5] Voters may be taking out their resentment at federal or state government in the only available forum—the local referendum. Local officials may also have to contend with taxes and revenues which are earmarked for certain expenditure categories and, by law, may not be spent for anything else. Most states have at least one such tax, the classic example being state gasoline taxes which are remitted to cities and which can be used only for local highway construction and maintenance. The Levy et al. study of Oakland found that the mix of services provided in the school system and by the street department was severely constrained and shaped by the earmarking of revenue provided by the state and federal governments.[6]

Compounding the problem of fiscal constraints is the fact that some local expenditures may be mandated by state law. Such things as minimum salary scales for public employees or mandatory contributions to employee retirement trust funds are common and further reduce the discretion of public officials in determining local expenditures. The local decision maker finds himself hemmed in by required expenditures, tax rate limits, the size of the local tax base and expectations that services and programs which have traditionally received funds will continue to be funded. Commenting on this situation Fisher and Fairbanks note that:

> decisions are incremental responses to particular pressures which are shaped by a variety of political and environmental constraints. Often, in fact, the constraints are so pervasive that few changes are made. In this case, indecision, rather than decision, characterizes the politics of finance.[7]

Even if taxes have not reached limits set by law, local officials are constrained by their reluctance to increase taxes. As Meltsner has pointed out, even though local officials generally know very little about public tolerance of increased taxes they tend to perceive the public as hostile.[8] Accordingly, they avoid tax increases whenever possible. The standard ways in which services are financed without increased taxes are the imposition of user fees (sewer charges, museum admission fees, etc.) and the creation of special districts with separate taxing authority. The latter approach adds to governmental fragmentation and, of course, amounts to the same thing as a tax increase, but it has the political advantage of isolating local officials from any adverse public response. Public outrage will be focused on the governing board of the special district, not on the government which created the district.[9]

### Some Political Conditions of Local Government

**Lack of Political Parties.** The most important political feature of local government in the United States is the almost total lack of political parties. Over sixty percent of cities with a population of 5000 or more are officially nonpartisan.[10] Most of the remaining cities, although nominally partisan, are dominated by a single party. Single party systems behave as if they were nonpartisan.[11] The major electoral contest is the primary election. Since all of the candidates are members of the dominant party, the primary election campaigns are contested by organizations established on an *ad hoc* basis by each of the candidates. The dominant local party, while it may be of great importance in state or national politics, is irrelevant to winning local elections and formulating local government policies. While it may be true that "there is no Democratic or Republican way to pave a street," political parties do aggregate and articulate interests. The lack of local political parties means the absence of a social mechanism through which citizens can contact and influence government, and government can contact and influence citizens. Without local parties citizens, in a sense, are cut off from the institutions and decisions of local government.

**At-Large Elections**. Another important feature of American local governments is the at-large election where council candidates are not elected by districts but by the entire community. In a small community this would not present much of a problem; segregation by social class or ethnicity is not as severe, and people throughout the community tend to know each other. However, in larger communities at-large council elections dilute minority representation, substantially increase the costs of campaigning for office and make government even more remote from the citizens. Over sixty percent of the cities with 50,000 or more inhabitants have at-large elections for city council seats.[12] Commenting on the impact of at-large elections Lineberry and Fowler observe that

> when nonpartisanship is combined with election at-large, the impact of residentially segregated groups or groups which obtain their strength from voting as blocks in municipal elections is further reduced. For these reasons, it is clear that political reforms may have a significant impact in minimizing the role which social conflicts play in decision-making ... [They] make public policy less responsive to the demands arising out of social conflicts in the population.[13]

**Interest Groups and Employee Unions**. If political parties do not function effectively as a part of local government, we might ask whether there are any social organizations which aggregate and articulate the interests of citizens. In this connection we will examine two kinds of organizations—local interest groups and employee unions. Interest groups are neither so well organized, extensive or effective in local political activity as they are in state or national politics. One reason for this is that the stakes in local politics are not so high as in the other arenas. While there are winners and losers in local politics, the winnings and losses are not of the magnitude associated with national or state politics. Nonetheless, there are local interest groups which sporadically endeavor to affect the course of local government policy. Local economic elites (usually represented by the Chamber of Commerce), civic and fraternal clubs, neighborhood organizations and ethnic organizations are typical of local interest groups. In addition, various service-providing bureaucracies may have an organized clientele which functions as an interest group, for example the PTA or the Friends of the Zoo. Unfortunately, not every local service has an organized clientele; as Meltsner points out, most cities do not have a Friends of the Sewer System or similar organization.[14]

Finally, there are many local organizations which may attempt to influence policy on a single issue for ideological reasons. Thus, local churches may attempt to influence local regulation of sexually explicit books and magazines, sportsmen's associations may be politicized by proposed local gun control legislation and garden clubs and horticultural societies may promote the beautification of local parks and streets. Sometimes groups are organized for the sole purpose of speaking out on a single issue, such as school busing or fluoridation of local drinking water. These *ad hoc* organizations usually disband after the issue in contention has been resolved, to be replaced by other issues and other organizations. In general, the stakes in local politics are not high enough to attract major interest groups, and local interest groups lack the resources to lobby effectively. Although there are exceptions, most local organizations lack the lobbying skill, substantive expertise and organizational capacity to mount a sustained effort which informs the government and general public, mobilizes support for a particular decision and monitors the results once a decision is made.

Employee unions are a relatively new force in local politics, but their influence has increased sharply in recent years. Although they are primarily interested in wages and working conditions, employee unions also participate in formulating the substantive policies of their particular departments. It is not unusual, for example, for a local teachers' union to speak out on questions of educational policy or for a police union to promote a particular philosophy of crime control. Beyond these obvious policy positions, the emergence of strong public employee unions constitutes yet another budgetary constraint with which elected officials must contend as they formulate local service policies.

**Low Citizen Demand**. Citizen "demand" for public services is characterized by confusion, ignorance and tolerance of the status quo. The fragmentation and overlap of local governments understandably produces a great deal of citizen confusion about what services are provided by which government, not to mention the even more obscure question of how each government finances each of its services. This confusion about the set of governments is compounded by citizen ignorance about the specifics of government operations. The average person knows little about local government policies and priorities. He does not know the proportion of funds spent in various service areas, nor how this compares with other cities. The average citizen has little direct contact with local government officials. Verba and Nie report that nationally only about 20 percent of the adult population has *ever* contacted a local government official about an issue or problem.[15] The key to the low level of citizen interest in, or contact with, local government is the fact that, in general, citizens are not unhappy with current local government services.[16] For example, an Illinois survey found that over 70 percent of that state's residents were satisfied with present garbage collection and disposal practices.[17] Fowler reported that in all but one of the ten cities he studied over 70 percent of white residents felt police protection in their neighborhood was "very good" or "good enough."[18] If residents are reasonably satisfied with local services there is little incentive to spend time and energy complaining or trying to alter existing service policies.

### The Bureaucracy
It is the public managers, the bureaucrats, who are responsible for the on-

going provision of local public services. The most important attribute of these public managers is that, within broad limits, they are not subject to direct control by the elected officials for whom they work. One of the main reasons for this situation is the civil service rules instituted by reformers bent on eliminating corruption in local government. Under civil service those holding jobs in the bureaucracy enjoy tenure; they cannot be fired except for certain narrowly specified types of malfeasance. Promotion is also regulated by civil service rules. Whenever possible, promotion is by competitive examination. When promotion by examination is not feasible (as is the case for most managerial jobs), promotion must be based on specified merit criteria. These rules mean that, once they are in, it is difficult to fire or block the careers of public managers. This in turn means that bureaucrats are subject to only limited control by elected officials.

Another factor which plays a role in the relative autonomy of local bureaucrats is the demise of the political party as a force in local politics. Even when government jobs are protected by civil service, an active local political party is an important resource to citizens seeking solutions to specific grievances. The party can bring matters to the attention of elected officials and monitor the way in which the bureaucracy acts to resolve the grievance. The party improves citizen access to government and, in effect, acts as an ombudsman on behalf of the public. The decline of local political parties has virtually eliminated this mechanism for increasing the accountability of public managers.

### The Politics of Local Services

**Budgetary Incrementalism.** We now consider the political process by which the decisions are made determining what kind of services and how much of each kind of service will be provided by a local government. Although most cities have line budgets rather than program budgets, line budgets are generally discussed and thought of in terms of the departmental activities and programs each part of the budget represents.[19] However, as Wildavsky has pointed out, the choices and decisions which the budget represents are extremely complex.[20] It is impossible to evaluate adequately the infinity of alternative budgetary configurations, priorities and outcomes. Time and resources are simply nowhere near sufficient. Accordingly, budgets are best thought of as the residue of past decisions, some of which were arbitrary, some thoughtful, some routine and some merely expedient.

In order to reduce their task to manageable proportions, officials preparing a budget proceed incrementally. They take the existing budget as an outline and make slight changes where they feel them to be necessary. As Crecine has demonstrated in his study of municipal budgeting, one of the best predictors of the allocation of funds in next year's budget is the allocation of funds in this year's budget.[21] Almost all the variance in a given budget can be accounted for by the preceding budget. The implications of this for the politics of local services are drawn out by Meltsner:

> For the most part, Oakland's resources were allocated years ago . . .
> Previous decisions determine present allocations: the decision to have a
> manager-council form of government, the decision to have a free library,
> and the decision on the fire insurance rating of the city were made by
> other participants but govern today's actions. If one allows for slight
> increases in the cost of Oakland's employees and expenses, then last
> year's budget is this year's budget.[22]

**Turning Budgets into Services.**   Once a budget has been set there remains the
task of converting the allocated funds into actual programs and services. This
task falls in part on the heads of departments. Most of the burden, however,
becomes the responsibility of the professional managers within the various
departments. These managers have great discretion in the way in which they
implement the budgetary and policy decisions of the local government. As
Crecine observes, the budget

> may have a lot to say about how many inspectors are employed in the
> Department of Building Inspection, but very little to say about how many
> buildings are inspected, the order in which they are inspected, and how
> strictly building codes are enforced. Budgeted dollar amounts provide
> many (severe) constraints on the quality of resources available to govern-
> mental units, but few constraints on how these resources are utilized.[23]

Just as incrementalism is the rule in budgeting, so too is it the rule in implementation. The best prediction about the behavior of the bureaucrats in each
department is that they will do this year about what they did last year, making
slight changes to allow for current conditions and the experiences of the past
year. There are good reasons why managers behave this way. For one thing, "in
most domestic policy areas, the production function (the relationship of inputs
to outputs) is a mystery. At best we know there is a tenuous relationship
between spending and output."[24] This means that implementation, like budgeting, is experiential and satisficing.[25] You make the best rough guess you can,
do something, and then adjust whatever you are doing in the light of subsequent
experience until it seems to be working well enough to not cause serious trouble.
Modest adjustments may be made from time to time to try to eliminate new
problems or any remaining, residual problems. The emphasis is on continuing
existing practices, with problems solved by incremental changes and fine tuning.

As might be expected, participants in such a system are resistant to radical
change and to innovations. They value highly knowledge of current procedure,
experience, rules of thumb and intuitive judgment about what is working or not
working.[26] Bureaucrats emphasize the continuing provision of routine services;
specifically, their attention is focused on doing the job (collecting the garbage,
keeping public order, cleaning the streets, etc.) as well as is possible, given the

resources available. Bureaucrats are concerned with system reliability and stability in the provision of services. As Hayes puts its, "municipal government has been typically designed as a low-change system."[27]

This emphasis on system reliability is reinforced by the structure of citizen demands and complaints. Decisions as to what services a city provides and the level at which each is funded are seldom the object of citizen scrutiny. Citizens are concerned primarily about the delivery of routine services to their own households. Burglaries must be investigated, garbage collected, streets maintained, pure water supplied and sewage processed. The typical citizen complaint to local government concerns the failure to deliver a specific service to a particular household. A person will complain about the hole in the street in front of his home, the fact that his garbage was not collected or his water supply interrupted. These are primarily problems of system reliability. They are also problems of local government service delivery and performance about which the citizen can acquire information at minimal cost. Citizens do not complain that their garbage collection is inefficient (although it may be) since they have no way to know whether or not it is inefficient. A citizen, however, does know if the city failed to pick up his garbage on collection day. Thus, citizen concern tends to focus primarily upon problems of reliability in the delivery of routine services. To a lesser extent there may be some concern with problems of equity in the distribution of services; everybody should get a fair share of what there is to get. But citizens will not normally focus on problems of inefficiency, ineffectiveness or inadequate levels of service. Problems such as these involve information about an entire service delivery system that citizens are unlikely to acquire.

**Sources of Innovation and Change.** Local services are primarily determined by the budget and the discretionary activities of the bureaucrats who convert the budgeted funds into programs and services. For the reasons we have discussed, neither budgeting nor implementation are marked by rapid change. Yet, budgets, programs and services are subject to occasional, non-incremental changes. What accounts for such changes? The sources of innovation and change in local services are varied; among the more important are crises, diffusion of professional norms within the bureaucracy, regime changes in local government and strong interest group activity. Crises are probably the major source of change and innovation in local government services. As Mayor Kevin White of Boston remarked, "I hate these constant crises, but without them would we get anything done?"[28] An important feature of a crisis is a time constraint; immediate action is required. Even though local government is a low change system, crises must be resolved by prompt action. Skillful political leaders are able to use crises as levers to obtain changes in local programs and services that could not ordinarily be obtained except by great effort exerted over a long period of time. In a sense, a crisis acts as a catalyst, making possible rapid change where only slow change or no change at all would ordinarily occur.

Another source of change is the diffusion of professional values within the local bureaucracy. Bureaucrats are professional public managers and service providers. They are plugged into a national network of similar professionals. Through each professional association's conventions, journals and other publications local professionals are exposed to a steady flow of information, norms and professional gossip, all of which can influence their skills, attitudes and behavior. Thus, a change in local refuse collection practices is more likely to occur because of the diffusion of information via the National Solid Waste Management Association than because of a decision by local elected officials. The great discretion enjoyed by local bureaucrats and their aura of professional expertise allow them to implement subtle changes and to lobby rather effectively for more serious changes. In this regard, the adoption of criteria by professional associations, such as the American Library Association, setting standards for local programs and services may be an important factor in raising service levels in communities where they are substandard.

Change may be brought about by local political leadership. The usual setting is a change in regime, the entry of a significant number of new office holders in a local government. These aspiring politicians are anxious to establish a record of achievement and often have plans for changes or innovations which they would like to promote. Unfortunately, as Lupsha has pointed out, such plans usually fall by the wayside as those in the new regime discover the many constraints which shape and limit their power to act.[29] Incumbents already know that their powers of leadership are severely limited.

Whether they are incumbents or novices, elected officials must preside over the day-to-day running of the government and at the same time establish a record of accomplishment which will facilitate their reelection. Accomplishment will almost certainly have to come in one or more of three categories: (1) expanding existing services; (2) beginning new city services; (3) providing existing services more efficiently. Expanding existing services is usually possible only if revenues can be found to finance the expanded services without increasing taxes. Thus, programs to do things like "upgrade the police" are often discussed but seldom adopted because of financial constraints.

Adding new city services also suffers from the revenue problem, but an even more serious problem is the risk of failure. As Hayes[30] and Lupsha[31] both note, innovation and change in local government are a high-risk activity, with the odds against those undertaking the change. One area of risk is the difficulty of trying to get a recalcitrant bureaucracy to implement new programs. However, an even more troublesome problem is that the organization and technology of urban services is extremely imprecise. "The plain fact is that no one really knows what to do; no one really understands many of the complex systems in which we all participate. We have learned that lesson the hard way, as we have undertaken one social program after another only to find the problems addressed were not resolved and, indeed, were frequently made worse by such interventions . . . ."[32] Thus the local official who introduces new, innovative programs in an effort to improve his standing at the polls runs a strong risk of achieving exactly the opposite result.

Trying to provide existing services more efficiently strikes a proper note of fiscal frugality but is also a high-risk venture. Bureaucratic resistance to changes in accepted procedures and "proven" ways of doing things can be a major difficulty. Middle level managers have numerous ways to obstruct, resist and sabotage changes they oppose.[33] However, as we have already mentioned, a more difficult stumbling block is our genuine ignorance about how to improve the efficiency of local services. Changes intended to improve services may wind up actually making things worse. Cities vary markedly in the apparent efficiency with which they perform routine services like police protection or garbage collection; no one knows why this is so or what to do about it.[34] This means that although local political leadership might wish to improve services, there is little they can do without a high risk of failure. Thus, such efforts will be made only rarely and then only by the most visionary or the most desperate.

Finally, interest groups, from time to time, may be a source of innovation and change in local services. Because local services are, by their very nature, personal, locality specific and highly divisible, citizen interests and demands are fragmented.[35] Most of the politics of local services occurs without the participation of interest groups; politicians, bureaucrats and isolated citizens are the only actors. Sporadically, local interest groups will become active in seeking some change in local services. A fraternal club or neighborhood organization may ask for major improvements in a park; the county medical association may seek a major reorganization of emergency ambulance services; local dentists may propose that municipal water supplies be fluoridated as a public health measure. Assuming that these proposals do not generate substantial opposition, they will be successful only if costs can be justified and if the groups concerned have the organizational resources for skillful and sustained lobbying.[36] Organizations which are not prepared to pursue their requests for months or even years will find they have little effect on government practices.

### The Distribution of Local Public Services

We now turn from our consideration of levels of service to the question of how local services are distributed. Specifically, we want to know who benefits from the policy decisions of local government.

Do the direct benefits conferred by government favor certain groups in the population? Are inequalities in municipal service delivery patterns dispersed or cumulative? Although local governments provide a variety of important services ranging from police protection to public cemeteries, researchers have only recently begun to explore the distributional dimension of the policy process. Instead of inquiring as to who benefits from the policy decisions of government (who gets the best parks, libraries, streets, schools), urban scholars have asked such questions as "who governs?" The result of this focus is that we know a great deal about how decisions are made and only a little about who benefits from these decisions. Similarly, we know a great deal about the determinants of public expenditures and only a little about the patterns of service delivery. Robert Lineberry noted that in the research on urban politics,

> ... the core question of political analysis—which I take to be Lasswell's "who gets what when how"—was overlooked. Urban political analysis became very adept at explaining the decisional process, but ignored the decisions themselves ... The tail of process came to wag the dog of policy. Less was known about the "what was gotten" than the "how it was gotten" part of Lasswell's aphorism.[37]

The policy analysis studies failed to rectify this shortcoming. Rather, this literature concentrated

> ... almost entirely on the *levels* of public policy, typically measured in dollars and cents terms. Its emphasis on "who *spent* what when how" sidestepped the distributional and allocational implications of Lasswell. If one of the objects of public policy analysis is to develop hypotheses about the benefits and burdens of policies, then it is not enough to know how big the policy pie is. It is equally important to know how it is carved up.[38]

A number of other scholars have also noted the importance of distributional analysis and have deplored the absence of extensive empirical findings.[39] In fact, Levy et al. observed that "The literature bulges with suggestions to work on the distribution of benefits ..."[40] To date, however, these exhortations have produced little empirical research.

It is misleading to maintain that we know *nothing* about municipal service delivery patterns. Instead, it is more appropriate to maintain that the available evidence is fragmentary and inconclusive. In general, three approaches have been taken to the study of the distribution of public services. The first approach emphasizes the differences in consumption levels on the basis of race and wealth. Benson and Lund reported that health and related "poverty" services were disproportionately used by low income neighborhoods while whites consumed more of such services as libraries and education.[41] Truett Chance reported a similar pattern.[42] In his study of San Antonio, Chance found that health and welfare services were used primarily by Mexican-American and other low-income neighborhoods. However, Herbert Jacob's study of Milwaukee revealed that police, health and welfare services were consumed in equal degrees by both middle and low income groups. Therefore, Jacob concludes that

Since the wealthier middle class whites 'need' public services less desparately than the other respondents, their equal use of them may be thought of as a sign of inequality.. Certainly the data do not indicate strong redistributional trends in the patterns of use of public services.[43]

A second approach to the distribution of municipal services deals with the extent of citizen satisfaction with those services. In general, these survey data strongly suggest that blacks are considerably more dissatisfied with police and recreational services than whites.[44] Although black respondents are not as negative in their evaluation of other municipal services, the differences in satisfaction levels between blacks and whites are still significant.[45] For example, Shuman and Gruenberg's study of satisfaction levels in fifteen cities found that in regard to all of the service areas studied (education, parks, police and garbage collection) blacks were less satisfied than whites.[46] Blacks were also somewhat more likely than whites to feel that other neighborhoods received better services.

The evidence available in regard to differences in levels of consumption and satisfaction raises at least two questions. First, do blacks and other low-income groups use some city services less (for example libraries) because these services and facilities are less accessible?[47] Further, how effective are local governments in responding to the variation in service preferences across neighborhoods, and what effect does an absence of effort in this direction have on user rates? Second, are blacks less satisfied with municipal services because they receive poorer services, or is dissatisfaction a function of a more general dimension of cynicism toward the political system? It may be asking too much to expect a ghetto resident to evaluate public service delivery patterns with an unjaundiced eye. Perceptions of the quality of streets and recreational services in ghetto neighborhoods are likely to be affected by those aspects of the environment for which government assumes little or no responsibility. Further, public services are probably much more salient to poor people than they are to those individuals who enjoy access to private resources. Consequently, the set of evaluative criteria blacks bring to bear in their assessment of service quality in the public sector is apt to be more rigorous than that employed by upper income individuals. In any event, the relationships between objective patterns of distribution, consumption rates and satisfaction levels have yet to be disentangled.

The location of such service facilities as libraries and parks should have a direct bearing upon utilization. In turn, one might expect citizen satisfaction to be at least partially dependent upon how equally services are distributed across neighborhoods. The Schuman and Gruenberg study suggests, however, that there is little association between the actual pattern of resource allocation and citizen satisfaction.[48] With that finding in mind we turn now to other studies of the actual distribution of local government services.

Surprisingly, there is little evidence to indicate that blacks and other low-income groups are *systematically* deprived in the allocation of resources in large metropolitan areas. A number of studies *have* demonstrated that public schools in black and low-income neighborhoods receive less money, poorer facilities and less qualified teachers.[49] However, other studies have concluded that schools in black and poor neighborhoods are advantaged in terms of resource distribution.[50] Still another group of researchers has reported a non-linear relationship between income and allocation with both upper and lower income areas receiving the highest expenditures and best services.[51] The evidence is also mixed in regard to the distribution of library services. Several studies concluded that the library services distributed to black and low income neighborhoods were inferior to those received by wealthier areas.[52] Again, however, other research has demonstrated that inequality in the distribution of new acquisitions, periodicals, total bookstock and expenditures either did not correlate with the racial or socioeconomic characteristics of the population or tended to favor poorer sections of the city.[53] In addition, two studies have found that the spatial distribution of library buildings advantaged poor neighborhoods.[54]

A similar set of findings emerges in regard to the distribution of recreational services. Two studies concluded that the allocation of resources favored wealthier neighborhoods,[55] three reported an equal distribution across neighborhoods,[56] and two others discovered a pattern that favored poor areas.[57] Finally, the evidence available in regard to the allocation of police resources and street quality suggests that black and other low income neighborhoods are advantaged in regard to the distribution of the former and deprived in regard to the latter.[58]

It is hazardous to generalize from these studies for a variety of reasons. First, too few studies of the allocation of municipal resources have been conducted. Second, only three of the above efforts investigated a range of service delivery patterns within the same city.[59] The remainder examined only one service area. Therefore, it cannot be assumed that inequalities in service delivery are cumulative. Blacks may be disadvantaged in regard to the allocation of some resources; however, they may be favored in the distribution of others. In fact, the findings from two studies suggest just such a pattern of dispersed inequality. Levy et al. discovered that black neighborhoods in Oakland tend to receive preferential treatment of in the distribution of educational resources. However, these same neighborhoods receive inferior library services.[60] Mladenka's study of several municipal services in Houston revealed a similar pattern of dispersed inequality. In addition, variations in delivery patterns were reported *within* service areas. For example, library resource distributions (expenditures, bookstock, professional staff, etc.) were found to penalize low income neighborhoods while the location of branch library buildings favored these same areas of the city.[61]

A third shortcoming in the existing body of literature on service distribution has to do with the one-point-in-time nature of most research. Few studies of resource allocation have investigated changes in delivery patterns over time. Baron did report a trend toward equality in the distribution of educational resources,[62] while Levy et al. discovered a trend toward inequality in regard to teacher-pupil ratios and a tendency toward equality in regard to teacher experience, degree attainment and salary dollars per student.[63] Also, Mladenka's longitudinal analysis of library resources and branch facilities produced strong evidence for increasing inequality, with one pattern favoring wealthy neighborhoods and the other skewed in the direction of poor areas of the city.[64] However, we do not know if service delivery patterns in large metropolitan areas have been characterized by strong redistributive trends in recent years as the result of court decisions, changes in political leadership, the heightened political awareness of blacks and other ethnic groups, the efforts of community organizations or the increased professionalization of municipal bureaucracies. Nor can it be assumed that upper-income neighborhoods have or will benefit from any redistribution of resources. The fragmentary and somewhat surprising evidence from the available body of literature should caution us against easy assumptions in regard to the distribution of benefits on the basis of race and wealth.

Few studies of the distribution of municipal services have sought to move beyond ecological explanations in an effort to account for the development and persistence of a particular distributional configuration. Those that have, however, have reported some interesting findings. For example, resource allocations appear to be controlled by the municipal bureaucracy and made on the basis of institutionalized decision-rules. Levy et al. discovered that distributional decisions in the Oakland street department were dominated by considerations of traffic volume, efficiency of traffic flow and accident rate. These engineering criteria of speed, safety and efficiency insured that those streets providing access to freeways or serving as crosstown arterials would be constructed and improved before neighborhood streets. Similarly, expenditures for the resurfacing of local streets were allocated on the basis of traffic volume, citizen complaints and an agreement with the utility company whereby improvements were deferred if the utility company anticipated work on underground lines within five years. Levy et al. and Mladenka also found that library resources in Oakland and Houston were allocated on the basis of circulation rates and were little affected by the variation in need and preference for library services across neighborhoods. As a result of these bureaucratic rules black and other low-income neighborhoods received poorer streets and libraries in Oakland and poorer libraries in Houston. In neither instance, however, was there any evidence to suggest that distributional decisions were affected by the racial and socioeconomic composition of neighborhoods. Instead, resource allocations were determined by a process of strict adherence to a set of institutionalized decision rules. It cannot be assumed, however, that those rules by which the municipal bureaucracy distributes services always result in unfavorable consequences for low-income neighborhoods. For example, Mladenka found that the Houston police allocate resources on the basis of crime rates and calls for service. Consequently, low income areas of the city are favored in the distributional process.

Another finding which emerges from these studies suggests that the distributional process is not characterized by a process of political conflict. Herbert Jacob writes about "convenient clean parks" as the "booty of the winners" while "garbage strewn alleys" are the "badge of the loser in the competition that characterizes urban politics."[65] However, the available evidence does not support this observation. Individuals and groups may complain about the quality of services in their neighborhood and resources may even occasionally be diverted as a result of these demands. In general, however, distributional decisions do not represent a balance between competing public demands. There appear to be a number of reasons why the process of resource allocation is relatively devoid of political content. First, as we mentioned earlier, many people (including blacks) appear to be fairly well satisfied with the services they receive.[66] In the absence of wide-spread dissatisfaction, the municipal bureaucracy is left to its own devices in determining service delivery patterns.

The evidence on citizen contacting indicates that relatively few citizens ever communicate a service delivery related grievance directly to municipal officials. Aberbach and Walker reported that only 35 percent of whites and 33 percent of blacks had *ever* contacted the city about poor services,[67] while Eisenger found that only 33 percent of whites and 11 percent of blacks had ever initiated a contact at *any* level of government.[68] Levy et al. discovered that the street department in Oakland received about three complaints daily while Mladenka's analysis of citizen contacting in Houston revealed that approximately 35 service related grievances were communicated to the various municipal departments on a daily basis.[69] Although blacks are less satisfied than whites with the services they receive, they are also less likely to articulate these grievances to government. Verba and Nie concluded that even when socioeconomic status was controlled, black respondents were less likely to contact government in regard to a personal matter. Although more blacks than whites perceived government as relevant to their personal problems, only 25 percent of those blacks acknowledging government's relevance had ever contacted it.[70] As a result the municipal bureaucracy apparently has little to fear from distributing resources in accordance with technical considerations or professional norms rather than in response to public demands. Also, most citizens do not perceive gross inequities in service delivery. Schuman and Gruenberg reported that only 10 percent of whites and 24 percent of blacks felt that their neighborhood received worse services than other parts of the city while Aberbach and Walker found that only 5 percent of whites and 18 percent of blacks expressed the same opinion in Detroit.[71]

The adherence of the bureaucracy to professional norms (the library system should provide "good" books rather than information on job training and health services) and decision-rules (traffic volume determining street construction and improvement, circulation rates allocating library resources, calls for service and crime rates setting neighborhood police resources) allows it to resist interference from elected officials and interest groups.

There is also some evidence to suggest that distributional decisions and patterns lack salience for elected officials. In the absence of widespread citizen dissatisfaction and public demand, officials appear content to allow the municipal bureaucracy considerable discretion in the allocation of resources. James Wilson's remarks in regard to the relationship between elected officials and the police are appropriate in describing the arrangement between political leaders and other municipal bureaucrats. Wilson observes that intervention in the affairs of the police department is limited and ". . . usually concerns the selection of a new chief or the career interests of the individual officers . . ."[72]

The more general questions—how the police allocate their resources, which laws they choose to enforce vigorously and which they choose to slight . . . are rarely raised, even in racial issues.[73]

Wilson concludes that the police largely operate in a "zone of indifference" and that control over police policies is left ". . . in many areas, to the police themselves."[74] It cannot be assumed that the elected political leadership is anxious to increase its control over the service delivery process but is incapable of doing so because of governmental fragmentation, lack of resources, budgetary and tenure constraints and the veto power of entrenched bureaucrats. It is an empirical question whether the elected political leadership is eager to embroil itself in the politically risky process of resource allocation and redistribution. Rather, elected officials may be more than willing to limit their concerns to those issues less likely to generate intense political conflict.

### Conclusion

The operation of local government in providing services is an understudied process. However, on the basis of our review of existing research we can draw some general conclusions. Levels of service are determined primarily by a complex series of constraints which include: size of the local tax base, current budget allocations, constitutional and statutory tax rate limits, earmarking of revenues and the provision of funds by the state or federal government. Political influences on the provision of local services are limited.

The level of demand for services is low. Citizens are relatively content with existing services and programs; and, although service provision is not devoid of interest-group politics, the diverse and localistic nature of local services inhibits most interest group activity. In addition, at-large elections and the absence of local parties tend to isolate the government from the citizenry, while civil service reforms isolate the bureaucracy from government control.

Elected officials can attempt to influence service levels, but they incur substantial risks if they choose to try. Bureaucrats play the primary role in the provision of services. Their professional norms about service levels are important criteria by which the service efforts of local governments can be judged. More important, however, is the discretion which bureaucrats have in turning budgets into services and in implementing programs and policies. The distribution of services appears to be primarily determined by the professional norms and decision rules of the public managers in the various departments of each local government.

## NOTES

1. Richard Leach, *American Federalism* (New York: Norton, 1970), p. 147.

2. Advisory Commission on Intergovernmental Relations, *Regional Decision Making: New Strategies for Substate Districts* (Volume 1, A43, 1974).

3. William Schultze, *Urban and Community Politics* (Belmont, Calif.: Wadsworth Publishing Co., 1974), pp. 230–232.

4. For analyses of the various ways in which costs can be shifted from suburbs to central city see Werner Hirsch "The Fiscal Exploitation by Overlapping Governments," in Hirsch et al., eds., *Fiscal Pressures on the Central City* (New York: Praeger, 1971). See also Kenneth Greene et al., *Fiscal Interactions in a Metropolitan Area* (Lexington, Mass.: D.C. Heath, 1974).

5. Arnold Melstner, *The Politics of City Revenue* (Berkeley: University of California Press, 1971), p. 259.

6. Frank Levy, Arnold Meltsner, and Aaron Wildavsky, *Urban Outcomes: Schools, Streets, and Libraries* (Berkeley: University of California Press, 1974).

7. Glenn Fisher and Robert Fairbanks, *Illinois Municipal Finance: A Political and Economic Analysis* (Urbana: University of Illinois Press, 1968), p. 2.

8. Meltsner also points out that political scientists know very little about public tolerance of increased taxes. Although vitally important to local governments, little work has been done in this area. Meltsner, p. 260.

9. A related advantage is that the special purpose district clearly connects the tax levied with the service provided and may thus increase public acceptance of new or higher taxes. The connection between tax rates and levels of service is obfuscated by the confusion and detail of most municipal budgets.

10. Eugene Lee, "City Elections: A Statistical Profile," *The Municipal Yearbook, 1963* (Washington, D.C.: International City Managers Association, 1963), p. 81.

11. Fred Greenstein, *The American Party System and the American People* (Englewood Cliffs, N.J.: Prentice Hall, 1970), pp. 63–78.

12. Robert Lineberry and Edmund Fowler, "Reformism and Public Policies in American Cities," *American Political Science Review*, 61 (September, 1967) pp. 705–706.

13. Ibid., p. 716.

14. Meltsner, p. 264.

15. Sidney Verba and Norman Nie, *Participation in America* (New York: Harper and Row, 1972), p. 31.

16. We will take up the question of satisfaction with local services in more detail later in the paper.

17. "Illinois Report Probes Citizen's Attitudes on Refuse Problems," *Solid Waste Management*, (February, 1974), p. 19.

18. Floyd Fowler, *Citizen Attitudes toward Local Government, Services, and Taxes* (Cambridge, Mass.: Ballinger, 1974), p. 163.

19. For a discussion of the merits of program budgeting see Fremont Lyden and Ernest Miller, eds., *Planning, Programming, Budgeting* (Chicago: Rand McNally, 1972). For a critical review of some of the problems in program budgeting see Leonard Merewitz and Stephen Sosnick, *The Budget's New Clothes* (Chicago: Rand McNally, 1971).

20. Aaron Wildavsky, *The Politics of the Budgetary Process* (Boston: Little, Brown and Co., 1974), pp. 8–16.

21. John Crecine, *Governmental Problem Solving* (Chicago: Rand McNally, 1969).

22. Meltsner, p. 162.

23. Crecine, p. 5.

24. Meltsner, p. 264.

25. For a discussion of these concepts in the context of budgeting see Wildavsky, pp. 11–13.

26. The public may be well served by managers who behave this way. Shoup and Mehay report an experimental investigation of traffic law enforcement production functions in Los Angeles. The object of this extensive experiment was to determine the optimal number of police assigned to traffic enforcement. The term optimal meant that the cost of enforcement was minimized relative to the injury and property damage costs of accidents. Thus optimal was the point above which the added cost of enforcement exceeded the cost of accidents. They discovered that the optimal number of police in traffic enforcement was exactly the number which had been assigned under the existing "seat of the pants" allocation. Donald Shoup and Stephen Mehay, *Program Budgeting for Urban Police Services* (New York: Praeger, 1973), chapter 3.

27. Fredrick Hayes "Change and Innovation in City Government," in W. Hawley and D. Rogers, eds., *Improving the Quality of Urban Management* (Beverly Hills, Calif.: Sage, 1974), p. 132.

28. Quoted in Peter Lupsha, "Constraints on Urban Leadership, or Why Cities Cannot Be Effectively Governed," in Hawley and Rogers, p. 610.

29. Lupsha, pp. 608–618.

30. Hayes, p. 134.

31. Lupsha, pp. 608–618.

32. Gary Brewer, "Systems Analysis in the Urban Complex: Potential and Limitations," in Hawley and Rogers, p. 152.

33. Lupsha, pp. 610–611.

34. See Louis Blair and Donald Fisk, *The Challenge of Productivity Diversity: Measuring Solid Waste Collection Productivity* (Springfield, Va.: National Technical Information Service #PB–223 116, June 1972) and Philip Schaemman et al., *The Challenge of Productivity Diversity: Measuring Police-Crime Control Productivity* (Springfield, Va.: National Technical Information Service #PB–233 117, June 1972).

35. Douglas Yates, "Service Delivery and the Urban Political Order," in Hawley and Rogers, p. 216.

36. On the necessity of prolonged lobbying see Hayes, p. 133.

37. Robert L. Lineberry, "Equality of Urban Services and the Quality of Urban Life," in William Hanna, ed., *Politics and the Quality of Urban Life* (forthcoming).

38. Ibid.

39. Robert L. Lineberry and Robert W. Welch, "Who Gets What: Measuring the Distribution of Urban Public Services," *Social Science Quarterly,* 54 (March, 1974), pp. 700–712; Werner Z. Hirsch, "The Supply of Urban Public Services," in Harvey G. Perloff and Lowd on Wingo Jr., eds., *Issues in Urban Economics* (Baltimore: Johns Hopkins Press, 1968), pp. 477–525; James T. Bonner, "The Absence of Knowledge of Distributional Impacts: An Obstacle to Effective Policy Analysis and Decisions," in Robert Haverman and Julius Margolis, eds., *Public Expenditures and Policy Analysis* (Chicago: Markham, 1970), pp. 246–270; Jesse Burkhead and Jerry Miner, *Public Expenditures* (Chicago: Aldine, 1971).

40. Levy et al., p. 9.

41. Charles S. Benson and Peter B. Lund, *Neighborhood Distribution of Local Public Services* (Berkeley: Institute of Governmental Services, University of California Press, 1969).

42. Truett L. Chance, "The Relation of Selected City Government Services to Socioeconomic Characteristics of Census Tracts in San Antonio, Texas" (unpublished Ph.D. dissertation, University of Texas, 1970).

43. Herbert Jacob, "Contact with Government Agencies: A Preliminary Analysis of the Distribution of Governmental Services," *Midwest Journal of Political Science,* 16 (February, 1972), p. 144.

44. Robert Fogelson, "From Resentment to Confrontation: The Police, the Negroes, and the Outbreak of the Nineteen-Sixties Riots," *Political Science Quarterly,* 83 (June, 1968), pp. 217–247; Joel D. Aberbach and Jack L. Walker, "The Attitudes of Blacks and Whites Toward City Services: Implications for Public Policy," in John P. Crecine, ed., *Financing the Metropolis* (Beverly Hills: Sage, 1970), pp. 519–537; Frank F. Furstenberg, Jr. and Charles F. Wellford, "Calling the Police: The Evaluation of Police Service," *Law and Society Review* 7 (Spring, 1973), pp. 393–406; Howard Schuman and Barry Gruenberg, "Dissatisfaction with City Services: Is Race an Important Factor?" in Harlan Hahn, ed., *People and Politics in Urban Society* (Beverly Hills, California: Sage, 1971), pp. 369–392; Floyd Fowler, *Citizen Attitudes Toward Local Government, Services, and Taxes* (Cambridge, Mass.: Ballinger, 1974); Roger Durand, "Race and Dissatisfaction with Urban Services," paper prepared for delivery at the 1975 Annual Meeting of the Southwestern Social Science Association.

45. Surprisingly, blacks are more dissatisfied with parks than with the police. Schuman and Gruenberg found that only 36 percent of the black respondents were satisfied with city parks while 51 percent expressed satisfaction with the police. In the Aberbach and Walker study, 40 percent of the blacks were satisfied with parks while 51 percent were satisfied with the police.

46. Shuman and Gruenberg reported that 47 percent of black respondents

were somewhat or very dissatisfied with local schools, and 64 percent expressed a similar attitude toward parks.

47. See Norbert Dee and John C. Liebman, "A Statistical Study of Attendance at Urban Playgrounds," *Journal of Leisure Research,* 2 (Summer, 1970), pp. 145–159; and Lowell A. Martin, *Library Response to Urban Change* (Chicago: American Library Association, 1969).

48. It should be emphasized that the measures of service distribution employed in this study (number of parks and garbage personnel) cast considerable doubt on the validity of the findings.

49. Patricia C. Sexton, *Education and Income* (New York: Viking Press, 1961); Kenneth A. Martyn, *Report on Education to the Governor's Commission on the Los Angeles Riots* (Report to the Governor's Commission, California, 1965); Richard A. Berk and Alice Hartman, *Race and District Differences in Per Pupil Staffing Expenditures in Chicago Elementary Schools, 1970–1971* (Chicago: Center for Urban Affairs, Northwestern University, 1971); Harold M. Baron, "Race and Status in School Spending: Chicago, 1961–1966," *Journal of Human Resources,* 6 (Winter, 1971), pp. 1–24; Jesse Burkhead, *Input and Output in Large City High Schools* (Syracuse: Syracuse University Press, 1967); Allen Mandel, "The Allocation of Resources in Urban and Suburban School Districts: Theory and Evidence" (unpublished Ph.D. dissertation, University of Michigan, 1974).

50. David W. Lyon, "Capital Spending and the Neighborhoods of Philadelphia," *Business Review,* (May, 1970), pp. 16–27; Martyn, *Report on Education to the Governor's Commission*; Mandel, "The Allocation of Resources in Urban and Suburban School Districts"; Martin T. Katzman, "Distributions and Production in a Big City Elementary School System," *Yale Economic Essays,* 8 (Spring, 1968), pp. 201–256.

51. Burkhead, *Input and Output in Large City High Schools.*

52. Levy et al., *Urban Outcomes;* Kenneth R. Mladenka, "The Distribution of Urban Public Services" (unpublished Ph.D. dissertation, Rice University, 1975); American Library Association, *Access to Public Libraries* (Chicago: American Library Association, 1963); Martin, *Library Response to Urban Change.*

53. Blanche D. Blank et al., "A Comparative Study of an Urban Bureaucracy," *Urban Affairs Quarterly,* 4 (May, 1969), pp. 343–354; Robert L. Lineberry, "Mandating Urban Equality: The Distribution of Municipal Public Services," *Texas Law Review,* 53 (December, 1974), pp. 26–59.

54. Lineberry, "Mandating Urban Equality," and Mladenka, "The Distribution of Urban Public Services."

55. Sexton, *Education and Income* (New York: Viking Press, 1961); *Comparative Recreation Needs and Services in New York Neighborhoods* (New York: Community Council of Greater New York, 1963).

56. Lyon, "Capital Spending and the Neighborhoods of Philadelphia"; Mladenka, "The Distribution of Urban Public Services"; Steven D. Gold, "The Distribution of an Urban Government Service in Theory and Practice: The Case of Recreation in Detroit," *Public Finance Quarterly,* 2 (January, 1974), pp. 107–130.

57. Lineberry, "Equality of Urban Services and the Quality of Urban Life,"

and Donald M. Fisk, *How Effective are Your Community Recreation Services?* (Washington, D.C.: U.S. Department of the Interior, Bureau of Outdoor Recreation, 1973).

58. John A. Weicher, "The Allocation of Police Protection by Income Class," *Urban Studies,* 8 (October, 1971), pp. 207–220; Mladenka, "The Distribution of Urban Public Services"; Peter B. Bloch, *Equality of Distribution of Police Services: A Case Study of Washington, D.C.* (Washington, D.C.: The Urban Institute, 1974); Levy et al., *Urban Outcomes;* Andrew J. Boots et al., *Inequality in Local Government Services: A Case Study of Neighborhood Roads* (Washington, D.C.: The Urban Institute, 1972).

59. See Lineberry, "Equality of Urban Services," and "Mandating Urban Equality"; Levy et al., *Urban Outcomes;* Mladenka, "The Distribution of Urban Public Services." Lineberry analyzed the distribution of services in San Antonio, Levy and associates studies Oakland, and Mladenka investigated service delivery patterns in Houston, Therefore, it cannot be assumed that these case studies are representative of distributional configurations in most American cities. However, the similarity of findings across cities is striking.

60. Levy et al., *Urban Outcomes.*

61. Mladenka, "The Distribution of Urban Public Services."

62. Baron, "Race and Status in School Spending: Chicago, 1961–1966."

63. The trend toward inequality in regard to teacher-pupil ratios favored black schools.

64. The distribution of expenditures, books and personnel favored upper income neighborhoods while the location of branch libraries favored poor neighborhoods.

65. Herbert Jacob, *Urban Justice: Law and Order in American Cities* (Englewood Cliffs, N.J.: Prentice-Hall, Inc., 1973), p. 1.

66. Schuman and Gruenberg found that a majority of *both* blacks and whites were satisfied with three of the four municipal services studied. A majority of black respondents expressed dissatisfaction only with parks.

67. Aberbach and Walker, "The Attitudes of Blacks and Whites Toward City Services."

68. Peter K. Eisinger, "The Pattern of Citizen Contacts with Urban Officials," in Harlan Hahn, ed., *People and Politics in Urban Society* (Beverly Hills: Sage: 1972), pp. 43–69. These figures are somewhat higher than the national rate of 20 percent reported by Verba and Nie. See note 16.

69. Levy et al., *Urban Outcomes,* and Mladenka, "The Distribution of Urban Public Services."

70. Verba and Nie, *Participation in America.*

71. Schuman and Gruenberg, "Dissatisfaction with City Services: Is Race an Important Factor?" and Aberbach and Walker, "The Attitudes of Blacks and Whites Toward City Services."

It should also be noted that the average citizen has little way of knowing whether he is receiving poorer or better services than other neighborhoods. He is, as Levy et al. maintain, in need of advice rather than a source of it. Since cities do not collect and disseminate service delivery data on a neighborhood by neighborhood basis, the average citizen is incapable of discerning and mounting an effective challenge to disparities and inequalities in patterns of resource allocation.

72. James Q. Wilson, *Varieties of Police Behavior* (Cambridge, Mass.: Harvard University Press, 1969), p. 231.

73. Ibid.

74. Ibid., p. 232.

**Chapter Eight**

# Fiscal Scarcity: A New
# Urban Perspective

DONALD H. HAIDER

Whatever lenses urbanists wore in the 1960s were likely to require substantial adjustment to analyze events and trends which had overtaken much of urban America by the mid–1970s. Where one generation of policy makers passionately debated alternative uses of the post–Vietnam fiscal dividend, the next contended with the prospects for continued high inflation, high unemployment and mounting federal deficits. The great hopes of many social engineers—to reduce poverty, to broaden educational and job opportunities and to rebuild older cities—had not been attained. Rather, exaggerated promises and exalted claims had ended with widespread disillusionment. By the mid–1970s the aggregate influences of race, poverty and economics had dealt a shattering blow to many older and larger cities from which prospects for recovery seemed bleak indeed. The National League of Cities summed up The State of the Cities—1975: "City governments, dealt double blows by inflation and recession, see no relief in the near future. Some of the nation's largest and oldest cities can see no relief at any time in the future without significant and permanent changes in America's national urban policy."[1]

With the great outpouring of resources and national attention directed at the cities in the 1960s, few foresaw that a decade later the country would be gripped by the possible default of its largest and wealthiest city—New York. President Lyndon Johnson had set the tone for urban euphoria in 1965 by proclaiming that "our nation will not be great until our cities are great." Eight years later, his successor, Richard Nixon, assured the nation that the urban crisis had peaked. "I believe we have made sufficient progress in recent years," Nixon stated in his 1973 State of the Union address; "that fears of doom are no longer justified." National leaders and the public generally had lost interest in the problems of the cities. As Anthony Downs observed, "Public perception of most 'crises' in

171

American domestic life does not reflect changes in real conditions as much as it reflects the operation of a systematic cycle of heightening public interest and then increasing boredom with major issues."[2] Thus, in a ten year period, from the rediscovery of urban America to its near abandonment, the United States had been rocked by some of the greatest changes ever to overtake a nation. Many of the assumptions motivating consumers and politicians alike in the 1960's—continued growth, abundant natural resources and energy supply, easy credit expansion, and even the desirability of urban sprawl—have been challenged by the "new realities" of the 1970s. The greatest of these changes, simply stated, is the transition from the politics of distributing more to the politics of distributing less.

Scarcity has replaced what was presumed to be abundance. High growth expectations were followed by zero growth and prospective slow growth. An era of hoped-for peace following Vietnam was accompanied by worldwide inflation, faltering economies and profound social and political dislocation. In contrast to the New Deal or Great Society periods, when federal intervention in the economy had among its principal goals promoting economic security and enhancing opportunities for the disadvantaged, the issues of government policies in the mid 1970s involved food, raw materials, energy and quality of life. The new politics of resource contraints, as Elizabeth Drew has noted, "are not subject to resolution solely by spending; they cut across the interests of a wide variety of interest groups; and they concern economic resources that are seen to be shrinking rather than expanding."[3] The solutions to these new problems involve not so much giving things to people, as did the distributive and redistributive politics of old, but asking them to give things up—something, as Drew observes, that government has usually achieved only under wartime conditions. Indeed, we have entered the post-industrial society that Daniel Bell and others have written of, where it is clear that more decisions will be made in the political arena than in the market place, resulting in greater conflict and a more fragile polity.[4]

It is my contention that the new politics of scarcity had already beset many urban centers such as New York by the late 1960s, a condition which politicians at all government levels failed to sense or respond to. Following a brief surge of employment rates in the mid–1960s, a major downturn in the economy began in the late 1960s which preceded the 1969–1970 recession in many large cities, and continued to intensify thereafter. The events of the 1970s only intensified those economic forces working against declining older cities. Specifically, we will look at a clustering of four variables operating in our political economy which are ominous indicators of further decline of, if not disinvestment from, urban America: (1) economic-demographic changes; (2) inflation, recession and government finance; (3) federal retreat from the inner city; and (4) the liquidity squeeze upon financial institutions and troubled credit markets. From this general analysis of these variables and their impact upon older American cities, we will next relate them to the New York City—New York State fiscal crisis by means of a case study. Finally, moving from the case study to broader implications, we will look at the actual or possible consequences of these trends and events upon cities nationally.

The most encompassing trend lines operating against larger and older American cities are losses of income producing residents and job producing industry. As census changes from 1960 to 1970 indicated, 38 of the 72 largest central city areas lost population. Nine of them lost more than 10 percent. Migration to suburbs continued unabated during the 1960s so that by 1970, for the first time, more Americans were found living in the suburbs of big cities than in the central cities. The 56 urban centers with populations over 250,000 contained some 20.8 percent of the United States population in 1970, while the 840 urban areas with populations of 25,000 to 250,000 contained 24 percent. By 1970 only 24 of these largest central city areas could claim over 50 percent of their metropolitan populations. Whether we look at population loss, central city–metropolitan population or per capita income, newer cities in the South and West showed vastly greater prosperity than those in the East and Midwest. These trends have only increased since 1970.

Marked disparities may clearly be seen between cities and suburbs with respect to age, income, housing, crime, government expenditures and taxes. Between 1960 and 1970, the white population declined in 40 of the 72 largest cities, while the nonwhite population increased in all but three. An increased clustering of old and poor in central cities intensified. Some 17 percent of central city households were earning under $3000 compared with 12 percent under $3000 in the suburbs, with such disparities greatly augmented if restricted to the Northeast and Midwest. For 1972, the rate for robbery was eight times as high in central cities as in suburbs; for murder, five times as high; and for rape and aggravated assault, nearly three times. In 1970, central cities spent 25 percent more per capita on government services than their suburban counterparts and had 95 percent higher per capita non-educational expenditures than suburbs.[5]

Population shifts paralleled similar changes in business and industry. Central business districts, which underpinned the city tax bases, showed a continuing decline in most older cities. As a proportion of manufacturing employment in the SMSA from 1939 to 1969, the following decline was registered: Cleveland 85 to 56 percent; Chicago 86 to 56; San Diego 94 to 78; Newark 48 to 25. These older, larger central cities have incurred a substantial economic exodus, the exceptions being those cities where annexation laws have enabled city boundaries to expand with the dispersal of population and economic activity. Industrial employees have followed their employers to the suburbs, nearly 60 percent of union membership now being made up of suburbanites.

Many urbanists in the 1960s devoted their attention to analyzing central city–suburban differences—fiscal disparities, busing, metropolitan governance and so forth. But the historic clash between central cities and suburbs tended to obscure more basic interregional shifts in growth patterns which are operating against the high density urban areas of the Northwest and North Central regions. Indeed, the problem of the declining central city in most parts of the country has been linked to the decline of the industrial belt which extends from Boston to St. Louis. This belt includes those central cities and metropolitan areas formed in the 19th Century, built on water and productive power and linked by cheap transportation. But now these same city-metro areas are becoming obsolete, their growth and prosperity lagging behind the rest of the nation.[6] Nearly all of the 12 largest SMSA's in the country, in fact, registered a net outflow of population between 1970 and 1973. Most surprising perhaps was the Chicago SMSA which, following a net population increase of 800,000 from 1960 to 1970, has registered a population loss since. This is America's heartland, the nation's leading export state internationally, and an area in which the post-industrial society has begun to arrive.

The Census Bureau's figures on the nation's population shifts from 1970 to 1975 only confirmed earlier projections. The Northeast's growth rate proved static with New York State losing population and others growing at rates well below the national average. The mountain and desert states of the West experienced heavy gains as did the South Central States—Arkansas (10%); Texas (9.3%); South Carolina (8.8%); Georgia (7.4%); and North Carolina (7.2%). The North Central States or the Midwest experienced population growth more than double that of the Northeast but significantly behind the national average. These shifts will continue to be felt in congressional reapportionment, voting power and national policies. (See Table 8–1.)

**Table 8-1. Population Shift by Region, 1970–1975**

|                     | *1975*   | *1970*      | *Percentage* |
|---------------------|----------|-------------|--------------|
|                     |          | *(millions)*| *Change*     |
| United States Total | 213,121  | 203,304     | +4.8         |
| Northeast           | 49,461   | 49,061      | +0.8         |
| North Central       | 57,669   | 56,593      | +1.9         |
| South               | 68,113   | 62,812      | +8.4         |
| West                | 37,878   | 34,838      | +8.7         |

Source: United States Bureau of Census — December, 1975

The impact of these trends upon Northeastern cities is already severe. Between 1940 and 1970, the net out-migration of whites in the Northeast totaled 900,000. Since 1970, the net out-migration of whites, some 870,000, is nearly equal to the previous 30-year period. The net in-migration of blacks to this same region was 1.6 million over the 30-year period with some indications of the emergence of an out-migration back to the South. The trend towards equalization of income between states and regions also changed dramatically. The ratio in per capita income between the wealthiest state, Connecticut, and the poorest, Mississippi, went from 2:5 in the 1950s to below 1:6 in the 1970s. The Southeast experienced the most significant per capita income increase since the 1930s while the East, although still the wealthiest region, suffered the greatest relative decline. Figure 8–1 indicates the extent to which the regional income gap closed between 1929 and 1974.[7]

These interregional trends are used by the Bureau of Economic Analysis to project to 1990 a pronounced shift in jobs and income away from the Northeast

**Figure 8-1.** The Regional Income Gap: 1929–1974 (Per Capita Personal Income as a Percentage of United States Average)

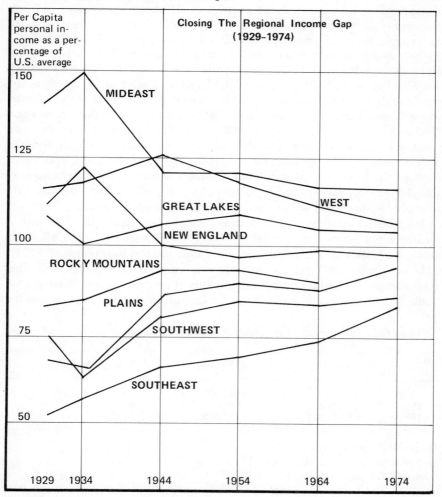

and North Central parts of the nation to the Southern and Western regions. Projected employment and population growth for the latter are far in excess of the national average, particularly in such manufacturing areas as textiles, chemicals, paper, printing and machinery. In light of the differences in labor costs, energy, and state-local tax burdens between these regions and the rest of the country, the attractiveness of these areas for industrial expansion and relocation are likely to increase.

### Inflation, Recession and City Services

Inflation has been the greatest single cause of increased city expenditures. The price paid for goods and services by state and local governments rose at an average rate of 4.2 percent annually between 1955 and 1970 compared with 3.6 percent for the federal government and 2.7 percent for the economy as a whole. As an aggregate of all general expenditures during this time, inflation accounted for well over 40 percent of the total increase in outlays. In 1965, the last year of Mayor Robert Wagner's administration, the New York City Executive Budget was $3.9 billion. In 1970–71, Mayor John Lindsay's budget was $7.7 billion, almost double the 1965-1966 figure. The most important single cause of this increase was inflation. The consumer price index in New York rose 26 percent between 1965 and 1970. A dollar earned in 1970 had the buying power of only 79 cents compared with 1965. Not only did inflation mean that the city spent $500 million more in 1970 to keep the purchasing power of the city's work force constant, with another $100 million for automatic pension costs, but also that the city had to pay another $150 million in interest costs on borrowing attributable to the impact of inflation on the municipal bond markets.

Inflation soared in the 1970s reaching double digit figures in 1974, with a consumer price index set at 100 moving up to 140 by 1975. The effect of inflation on state and local governments during the two year period of 1972–1974 was reportedly equal to the entire five year period of 1967–1972. The consequences of inflation for a local government perhaps are best illustrated by Table 8–2, the impact of inflation on the City of Chicago's expense budget for

### Table 8–2. The Impact of Inflation on Chicago's Budget

| Year | Current Dollars | 1970 Dollars[a] | Inflation Index[b] |
|------|-----------------|-----------------|--------------------|
| 1970 | $  842,974,960  | $842,947,960    | 100.0%             |
| 1973 | 993,537,251     | 888,673,748     | 111.8              |
| 1975 | 1,097,826,452   | 747,329,103     | 146.9[c]           |

[a]Formula: Current Dollars/Inflation Index
[b]Inflation Index for wholesale prices (1970 – 100.0%)
[c]Compiled for the first nine months of 1974

1970–1975. Although Chicago increased its actual budget in terms of current dollars, budget expenditures actually decreased in a relative sense, using 1970 dollars as a basis for comparing actual budgets discounted by the inflation factor. Governments, just like consumers, were spending more and getting less.

Inflation is now a worldwide phenomenon. With the exception of that of Germany, our rate of inflation, as high as it has been, was far less than that of the rest of the major industrialized nations. Also, inflation cost government more in purchasing power than it cost the private sector. The cost of goods and services rose faster at the state and local government level than at the federal level. With increased diversity in state tax sources (income, sales, excise taxes), state government has been in a far better position to capture the effects of inflation than local governments whose primary revenue source, the property tax, tends to be far less responsive to income or price-level growth. Some states, highly dependent on high yield, growth oriented income taxes, experienced serious shortfalls in revenue collections when unemployment rose and income tax yields declined. Similarly, some older cities where property tax delinquencies mounted, industry fled and new construction lagged experienced a declining tax base. The consequences of inflation-recession, translated into rising prices and high unemployment, have been to compound the squeeze upon cities. Expenditures are stimulated to a far greater extent than revenues and produced a revenue gap. Since the fiscal position of most cities was damaged far more than that of state government, city dependency on increased state assistance mounted.[8]

Many problems of the cities were approached in the 1960s from the perspective of intervention strategies to revive cities' tax bases and to blunt urban pathologies—welfare, crime, unemployment, juvenile delinquency. Ten years later the context had shifted dramatically to averting financial emergencies and developing survival strategies. Local governments no less than the federal government have uncontrollable outlays, namely fixed costs such as employee pension contributions, debt service, matched federal funds, or state-mandated expenditures. Municipal leaders in the mid-1970s confronted hard financial choices as a consequence of inflation's impact on expenditures and the recession's impact on revenues. For some, cash reserves dwindled; welfare or social service payments exceeded appropriations. Loss of jobs and population in some large cities meant a revenue base decline, but also constant, if not increased, demand for services. Limitations on most cities' ability to raise revenue made immediate tax increases difficult, if not too late to avert cash flow problems.[9] Many state governors attempted to hold the line on tax increases, while expenditure control policies in Washington held little promise of immediate relief. Indeed, the belt tightening phenomenon converged on local governments as never before, with bailout from higher government levels remote and competition over intergovernmental funds much increased.

Inflation has had an equally important impact on government debt financing. More than half of the capital outlays undertaken by state and local governments, a significant portion of their rapid growth, may be attributable to borrowing from the money markets. Total outstanding local government debt in the United States rose slowly from $1 billion in 1890 to $14 billion in 1946, and then climbed precipitously to more than $120 billion in 1973, with a projected debt of $200 billion by 1980. Aggregate state-local outstanding debt, some 50,000 government borrowers, exceeded $200 billion in 1975, with some 4 million individual debt issues outstanding.[10] Inflation plus the fallout from New York City caused interest rates on borrowing to soar. Average interest rates moved from 2.5 percent in 1955 to 4.4 percent in 1968, only to skyrocket to well above 6 percent for most governments from 1974 on. Interest rates on tax exempt securities also rose in response to the general increase borrowing costs and the moderate to tight monetary policy pursued by the Federal Reserve. Expectations concerning continued inflation and the costs of borrowing produced great concern within the public sector about the capacity of state and local governments to finance themselves. Insofar as many governments regularly engage in temporary borrowing in anticipation of revenues to meet current operating requirements, with costs of borrowing greatly increased, many local governments will move toward short-term cash flow management systems, synchronizing taxes, collections and disbursements. Long-term borrowing, particularly to acquire land or make capital improvements, will be subjected to greater public scrutiny with respect to calculable costs and benefits of such public expenditures. In short, the lost world of public finance has come alive and both elected officials and voters alike are attuned to the new fiscal realities of debt financing.

### Federal Disengagement from the Cities

Following an 18 percent annual increase in federal aid to states and localities between 1968–1973, federal grant-in-aid allocations began to return in 1974 to more moderate growth levels of roughly 8 percent annually (see Table 8–3). From state and local governments' perspective this moderate growth in federal assistance was grossly deficient both in terms of inflation (constant dollars) and

**Table 8–3. Percentage Annual Increase in Federal Grants-in-Aid (Billions), 1967–1974**

|                    | 1967–1968 | 1968–1969 | 1969–1970 | 1970–1971 | 1971–1972 | 1972–1973 | 1973–1974[a] |
|--------------------|-----------|-----------|-----------|-----------|-----------|-----------|--------------|
| Current $          | 15.7      | 10.3      | 20.7      | 18.8      | 28.5      | 8.3       | 8.1          |
| Constant $ (1958)  | 9.5       | 3.9       | 12.1      | 12.2      | 22.9      | 2.0       | −1.9         |

[a]Deflated by implicit GNP deflator for State and local Governments.
Source: Bureau of Economic Analysis, Department of Commerce.

in terms of new responsibilities and growing service demands required by the Nixon-Ford Administrations' New Federalism and the deepening recession. Federal funding thus abruptly followed the recession pattern rather than moving upwards in accordance with a countercyclical fashion as called for by state and local government leaders. Beyond an absolute decrease in federal aid to states and localities, there were ample indications that federal programs and policies had begun to reflect disengagement from the inner-city commitments of the 1960s.

The 1973 moratorium on federal housing subsidies combined with accelerated interest rates and the recession caused new housing starts to plummet nationally from a 2.3 million high in 1972 to 1.2 in 1974, the largest single year drop off in our postwar history. With a national goal of "a decent home in a suitable living environment for every American family" but a federal housing policy, as one Senator quipped in late 1975 "to build no housing," Congress responded with the Housing and Community Development Act of 1974. This act, split as it is between housing and community development sections and goals, consolidated under the latter seven separate categorical programs (urban renewal, model cities and so forth) into a single package. Beginning in 1975, more than 1300 cities and urban counties began receiving $2.5 billion of a three year, $8.4 billion community development grant program. Like revenue sharing, which from 1972–1976 dispersed some $30 billion in federal funds among 39,000 governmental units, federal CDA apportionments sprinkled too few dollars in too many places attempting to accomplish too many objectives simultaneously.[11] The planning application and certification requirements for CDA recipients (community participation, environmental statements, A #95 reviews, etc.) have resulted thus far in many local governments using their funds on short term, noncontroversial projects rather than engaging in the necessary program planning to achieve "viable urban communities" as specified in congressional intent. Indeed, some HUD spokesmen have encouraged city leaders to bypass deteriorated neighborhoods and invest their resources in those neighborhoods where disinvestment and considerable blight has not fully occurred. Caught in the transition between older urban renewal programs and the new block-grant objectives, mayors of older cities are often faced with contradictory signals from the federal government. Some cities, in fact, are using CD money simply to meet ongoing programs and to cope with inflationary and recessionary demands upon their already strapped budgets. With the very real prospect that Congress will not renew revenue sharing in 1976, CD funds may become the major outside fiscal slack cities need to meet burgeoning service demands and fiscal emergencies.

The Great Society programs of the 1960s greatly inflated state-local budget allocations as the federal government became involved as a partner in all programmatic activities of state-local governments. The New Federalism thrust of the Nixon years, while temporarily generous to subnational governments through increased funding, aimed at basic organizational and philosophical changes in intergovernmental relations. New Federalists sought to reduce the role of the federal government, to move from the service strategy of the Johnson years to an income support strategy, and to strengthen state and local governments as decision-making/resource allocation units.

Much like the Great Society programs, however, the New Federalism embraced about equal proportions of realism, romanticism and rhetoric. It may have been a realistic response to existing political and economic conditions—uncontrollable outlays, program proliferation, imbalance in federalism, and often chaotic Great Society ventures. But it smacked of a dual federalism notion without really sorting out functional responsibilities: finance, policy-making, and administration.[12] Increasingly, New Federalism became a cruel hoax to local governments, particularly to older, large cities. The initial infusion of new funds was accompanied by attendant responsibilities for programs and functions that had previously been initiated and funded at the national level. Revenue sharing allocations failed to increase at the rate of inflation, while ceilings established on social service reimbursements cost New York, Massachusetts, Illinois and California more than they received in new federal revenue-sharing money. With impoundments of some funds and cutbacks in others, cities discovered that a wide array of claimants had reassembled on their doorsteps rather than in Washington expecting local funding. This shift in programs, funding and basic philosophies left city officials in a condition of bewilderment and often demoralization.

In short, what Washington had created or stimulated in the first place had now become the burden of the cities and the states as well. Those cities that had moved far astray from traditional housekeeping roles (sanitation, police, fire, etc.) into uncharted waters of social services and human resource programs came up shorthanded.[13] New York City, the epitome of a local government that attempted to redistribute income through an extensive welfare system and a highly subsidized university and housing system, found itself teetering on the edge of default. Other large cities, caught between the legacies of the Great Society and the New Federalism, have attempted to survive in this apparent clash between stimulative national policies and new retrenchment needs. Caught between the feast and famine tradition of government spending and often contradictory government programs, local government officials have the least resources and slack with which to respond. Not surprisingly, the fallout from 1965 to 1975, euphoria to gloom, left mayors, city managers and county officials with bitter scorn toward their federal partner.[14]

The federal government's retreat from the cities may have an even more far-reaching impact in terms of its effects upon state government. Whatever else may be said of state governments, they have begun reversing a long pattern of neglect toward their largest cities. By 1974 states were spending 56 percent of their budgets—$45 billion out of a total of $81 billion—in aid to localities compared to 44 percent in 1954. During the same 20 year period, local government's dependence on state funding rapidly increased—from 42 percent of locally extracted revenues to 58 percent. Whereas in 1957 cities received no more on a per capita basis than suburbs from states and the federal government, by 1970 central cities received 31 percent more aid. Where external aid accounted for 20 percent of the nation's 20 largest cities' budgets in 1957, the figure had risen to 32 percent by 1970.[15]

Since at least the mid–1960s most older cities' survival became increasingly wedded to the "intergov fisc"; that is, the dependency of large cities on the tax revenues and funding transfers from higher governmental jurisdictions to local jurisdictions had appreciably increased. Following a record number of tax increases and a surge in revenue collections between 1972–1974, state and local governments were largely unprepared in late 1974 when the recession-inflation forces struck in full force. Aggregate municipal revenues, for example, rose to record high levels, up 17 percent during 1972–1973, only to fall to 9 percent for 1973–1974. Tax yields declined under growing unemployment, while service demands rose steadily. Simultaneously, inflation began to drive up wage demands, pension and fringe benefits, service costs, supplies and equipment. Higher interest costs meant higher borrowing costs and increased debt service. Energy prices soared as did capital construction costs. Several states reacted immediately to stem costs and cut services, while others delayed until 1975 legislative sessions. Since aid to local governments constituted the single largest expenditure for state governments, it became an immediate target for reduction. Older cities not only had to respond to declining revenues from their own tax collections, but also to a sudden drop off in fiscal assistance from higher governmental levels, both state and federal. And, once again, many of these local units were the very ones with the least slack and fewest alternative resources to cope with these new conditions.

### Financing Future Growth

While national trend lines and even government policies may not hold much hope for revitalization of older cities, some urbanists contend that a rekindled national commitment to the cities could still reverse the process of decay. Often neglected in such debates is simply the issue of resource allocation and the new position this nation finds itself in with respect to financing growth. It is notable that the public sector continues to absorb an ever increasing share of the Gross National Product (GNP), rising from 26.5 percent of GNP in 1954 to roughly 35 percent in 1975. More revealing than the dramatic increase in government spending is what expenditures are going for and how they are being financed. Where defense spending, highways, the space program and farm subsidies comprised roughly 55 percent of the federal government's unified budget in FY 1964, these expenditures amounted to less than 30 percent in FY 1974. On the other hand, federal spending for what the Social Security Administration defines as "social welfare purposes" rose from $14 billion in 1950 to $170 billion, or more than one-half of the FY 1975 budget.[16] Between FY 1974 and FY 1976 federal outlays increased by 38 percent or more than $100 billion. Due to the severe recession, unemployment compensation benefits alone climbed from $6 billion to $20 billion in this two-year period.

What has occurred in government spending is a massive shift from capital production to outright consumption, from the warfare state to the welfare state, and from relative controllable outlays to increased uncontrollability.

As Table 8–4, drawn from President Ford's 1976 budget request as submitted to Congress, indicates, nearly three-quarters of proposed federal outlays may be categorized as virtually "uncontrollable" due to existing law, prior year commitments, trust fund structures, interest on debt and mandated transfer payments. In early 1975 the President indicated great alarm at these budgetary trends, stating that "continuation of these programs at anywhere near their present rate of growth (more than twice that of the GNP) will mean that within the next two decades government expenditures at all levels could eat up more than half of our GNP."[17] The 1974 Congressional Budget and Impoundment Act provides a mechanism for Congress to establish spending goals in conjunction with revenues, and to assess various spending goals in conjunction with revenues, and to assess various spending proposals. However, whether or not Congress will moderate the rate of federal expenditures remains to be seen. But far more predictable, it would seem, is what the impact will be, both on the nation and perhaps on the cities, if it does not.

Government spending has far exceeded the rate of private sector spending or the growth rate of the economy as a whole, by roughly 50 percent since 1946. This acceleration really took hold in 1969 when government spending rose at a rate of 12 percent annually while the rate of growth in the nation's real output rarely exceeded 4 percent even in good years. The government has increasingly come to compete with the private sector for the nation's production and productive resources, reflecting the reallocation of resources between the public and private areas. To finance this surge in government spending, total taxes have risen (especially state-local tax burdens which have doubled as a percentage of total personal income since 1964) and aggregate levels of government debt have risen sharply. Not only has the federal budget been out of balance for 39 out of the past 45 years, but aggregate deficits during the past ten years, FY 1966–FY 1975, have amounted to $150 billion. Due to the enormous increase in net borrowings of "off-budget agencies" (another $150 billion) the federal government has had to borrow nearly one-third of a trillion dollars in the past decade. Adding to this figure another $175–$200 billion in new state and local government long term debt, we see that all governments have borrowed roughly $500 billion since 1966.

While government expenditures provide ample testimony to the shifting resource allocation between public and private sectors, the debt financing side further illuminates the extent to which government has become a major

**Table 8–4. Growth in Uncontrollable Federal Spending (billions), 1967–1976**

|  | 1967 | 1976 |
|---|---|---|
| Payments for individuals: |  |  |
| Social security and railroad retirement | $ 22.5 | $ 76.6 |
| Federal workers' retirement and insurance | 3.8 | 15.7 |
| Unemployment assistance | 2.8 | 18.6 |
| Veterans' benefits | 5.0 | 11.9 |
| Medicare and medicaid | 4.6 | 24.1 |
| Housing payments | 0.3 | 2.6 |
| Public assistance | 2.8 | 15.6 |
| (Subtotal, payments for individuals) | (41.8) | (165.1) |
| Spending from prior-year contracts: |  |  |
| National defense | 21.2 | 23.5 |
| Civilian programs | 15.8 | 30.5 |
| (Subtotal, spending from contracts) | (37.0) | (54.0) |
| Interest payments | 10.3 | 26.1 |
| General revenue sharing | –– | 6.3 |
| Farm price supports | 1.7 | 0.7 |
| Other programs | 3.0 | 8.6 |
| Total uncontrollable spending | 93.7 | 260.7 |
| Total spending | 158.3 | 349.4 |
| Percentage of spending that is uncontrollable | 59.2 | 74.7 |

Source: Budget of the United States, 1976

competitor to the private sector for capital funds. As government has become the dominant partner in maintaining full employment and economic growth, it has aided, as many monetarists contend, policies of excessive credit growth in the private sector—banks, corporations and individuals. Indeed, these trends of extended credit and borrowing magnify the growing liquidity problems in the economy; that is, the ability to meet cash demands when they become due without disrupting the daily operations of an organization. Firms, like individuals, may be solvent but still illiquid. Rising inflation and interest rates can (and do) compound the problem as corporations, consumers and even governments contract more credit out of fear of increased money costs.

Without explaining or fully supporting this declining liquidity argument, suffice it to say that the Federal Reserve has contributed to both inflation and expansion of credit in part out of its responsibility for maintaining orderly conditions in the government securities markets. As rising federal deficits require debt financing through sale of government securities, the Fed has had to buy many of these securities to stabilize the markets and to insure the issues are sold—a process also called monetizing the debt. This process pushes reserves into the banking system and in turn promotes credit expansion. As Murray Weidenbaum has observed, "This is inflationary because it provides a direct basis for the multiple expansion of the money supply. Issuing more Treasury debt also exerts an upward pressure on interest rates as the government is not simultaneously increasing the supply of savings available for investment."[18] Deficit financing detracts from the available supply of savings, diverting funds from investment into consumption.

With recent financial problems of major industries (Penn Central, Lockheed, W.T. Grant, REITS, banks, etc.) the economic and political pressures have mounted upon the federal government to expand the money supply, starving off economic and financial fires. One can better understand the problems of coordinating federal fiscal policy with monetary policy as the Federal Reserve gets squeezed among its not totally compatible roles—accommodating the government's borrowing needs, promoting reasonable growth rates, aiding full employment, maintaining an equilibrium in balance of payments and so forth. Not only does the official unified budget cover a shrinking part of federal spending, but fiscal policy also spills over to monetary policy to the extent that the number of "off-budget" agencies increases and the size of their outlays grows. With the growth of these new wholly federal activities (since 1972, for example, the Environment Financing Authority, the Federal Financing Bank, the United States Railway Association and others), the unified budget becomes, according to Weidenbaum, "a less complete measure of the total flow of revenues and expenditures between the federal government and the public."[19]

Table 8–5 provides an overview of growing net public and private debt from 1945 through 1973. Given the adverse financial trends previously described, the nation must soon come to grips with the growing capital needs in both the public and private sectors. To the extent that continued federal deficits and financing of debt through the sale of federal securities reduce the funds available to finance private investment, we may anticipate a shrinkage in the stock of productive capital. The United States already ranks last among major developed nations in capital investment as a portion of GNP—our 15 percent annual rate is half that of Western Europe and Japan. The Treasury estimates that the private sector will have an estimated $4 trillion in capital investment needs in the next decade alone.[20] The future pace of economic recovery will depend largely upon

**Table 8–5. Net Public and Private Debt (Billions), 1945–1973**

| Year | Federal Government | Federal Finance Agencies | State/ Local | Corporate | Individual & Noncorporate | Total |
|------|--------------------|--------------------------|--------------|-----------|---------------------------|-------|
| 1945 | 252.5 | — — | 13.4 | 85.3 | 54.7 | 405.9 |
| 1960 | 239.8 | 3.5 | 64.9 | 302.8 | 263.3 | 874.2 |
| 1970 | 301.1 | 38.8 | 145 | 797.7 | 586.3 | 1,868.9 |
| 1973 | 349.1 | 59.8 | 184.5 | 1,111.1 | 821.3 | 2,525.8 |

Source: Economic Report of the President, February 1975, p. 323.

the availability of credit across a broad spectrum of economic activity.[21] If this nation is to spur employment, increase productivity and maintain a competitive edge in world markets, it will require tremendous capitalization to do so. The prospect that heavy Treasury borrowing requirements will hit the financial markets at the same time that private sector needs are expected to increase may produce a major clash between public- and private-sector priorities. This, in turn, could lead to a credit allocation between them and enhanced national economic planning.

Hence, the political and economic aspects of scarcity may necessitate strong government intervention to promote massive capital investment, to shift much consumptive behavior into increased savings and to restrain rather than promote government expenditures, particularly in the social welfare areas.[22] As the nation enters its bicentennial year, President Ford has called for a federal spending ceiling of $395 billion with a projected $40–45 billion deficit, predicated on a 6 to 8 percent inflation range and an unemployment rate of roughly 8 percent. There is little evidence that the nation has really come to understand the implications of continued inflation or to recognize its growing capital needs. The consequences of further inflation and financial instability are already apparent in terms of interest rates, rising levels of risk and volatility in the money markets, all of which can result in lower rates of capital formation, declining rates of productivity and rising labor discontent.

The nation's high cost of energy cuts across all the problems discussed earlier: liquidity, inflation, unemployment, intergovernmental relations and the population-industrial movements in the nation. Energy prices rose less rapidly than other prices over the 20 years before 1973. Energy was a low-cost item in manufacturing, transportation and the consumer budget; so use boomed. As consumption of oil and gas rose so did our dependency on foreign suppliers— that is, until the Arab oil embargo in the fall of 1973. Considering the growing shortages of capital and materials in the United States, the OPEC nations' sharp increase of oil prices compounded our problems of economic adjustment. Higher oil prices added to inflation, reduced output and capital formation and produced profound dislocation in a number of energy-intensive industries.

The federal government's Project Independence, a goal to make the United States capable of energy self-sufficiency in the 1980s, is no closer to realization in late 1975 than it was two years ago during the oil embargo. Hopes for an atomic age of cheap and abundant power quickly faded in light of capital costs, uranium prices and safety provisions. The Ford Administration's goal of building some 600 or so atomic reactors in the next 25 years is going to require enormous government expenditures as outlined in the Administration's $100 billion Energy Independency Authority. Our capital-intensive utilities are going to require more funds in the next decade than they have previously generated in their total history. Billions of dollars are required to spur coal production and to build coal degasification plants. Still, the nation has yet to adopt a comprehensive energy program, provide incentives and funding to stimulate production and adopt sanctions to curb consumption. Unless domestic energy supplies rise considerably faster than presently expected, the nation may well suffer from unemployment higher than the projected 7 percent from 1975 to 1980, or may be forced to import vast amounts of additional energy—a further drain on capital formation and the balance of payments.[23]

The impact of the energy crisis upon older cities is unclear. Northeastern cities (where energy costs are roughly 50 percent greater than they are in the Midwest, South and Southeast) will suffer the most without a national allocation program and strong government controls. Energy producing states like West Virginia, Kentucky, Texas, Louisiana and Oklahoma have already experienced large oil and gas tax revenue increases. It will cost more to live in low density communities and to use private automobiles, which may somewhat benefit cities and inner ring suburbs. More efficient energy production and utilization may speed up plant closings and the relocation of obsolete inner city facilities. High unemployment will impact the cities the greatest. Hence, the net cost of the energy crisis will fall heavily upon older cities.

### New York City: A Political Economy
### View of Governmental Bankruptcy

New York City served briefly as the temporary capital of this country, and for many it is still the capital. Although Washington is the center of government, New York is the communications and financial center. Key national services are concentrated in the nation's most populated city which contains 35 percent of all office space, 25 percent of all apartments and nearly 25 percent of the headquarters of the nation's 500 largest corporations. The city's municipal budget of $12 billion with 350,000 municipal employees in 1974 ranks second only to the national government in size. Its range of governmental functions is unsurpassed in magnitude and kind by any state or local government. New York City is the nation's leading manufacturing center, seaport, air terminal and focus of foreign trade. Not only is the city the nation's largest and most concentrated industrial and consumer market, but it has long accounted for major proportions of the nation's manufacturing in apparel, in printing-publishing, in wholesale businesses, and in such service lines as finance, insurance, advertising and business services. With this obvious concentration of wealth, how could the nation's leading city in late 1975 be struggling to avert a headlong slide toward default?

In reconstructing the New York City fiscal crisis there are those who wish to blame the federal government. Federal housing and transportation policies aided the flight to the suburbs; urban renewal programs destroyed more housing than they helped build; the federal failure to assume the full costs of welfare placed in inordinate and fiscally inappropriate tax burden on the city's resource base; and federal redistributive programs neglected the scope and magnitude of the city's concentrated low-income population. Still others wish to blame New York State officials for failure to equalize interjurisdictional tax burdens, to accept greater load sharing for basic social services and to respond fully to the city's obvious fiscal crisis. The state is further condemned for mortgaging its own future through massive public works programs, creating a maze of independent authorities and not exercising greater oversight authority upon its corporate creature. To some, the city's political and economic leadership is to be held responsible— mayoral ineptitude, bankers' avarice, elected officials' capitulation to unions, community groups and political parties. And then there are those who lump all the city's sins into mismanagement—excessive service costs, profligate spending patterns and lack of management techniques and controls.

Explanations of what happened to New York City are likely to provide full employment to both government commissions and academics for years to come. The following case study, therefore, is merely a precursor of what will be more in-depth analytical work on perhaps the single most important event to affect urban America, and even government generally, in the postwar period—namely the default of New York City on its bonds. Four interrelated processes will be analyzed which molded the environment in which New York City—New York State elected officials operated: economic conditions, elections, budgets and municipal labor union contracts. The most important of the four is the budget, the heart of the political process through which alternatives, choices and decisions were eventually made. In New York one does not deal with the state budget or city budget as separate entities. Rather their budgets have become interdependent, budget bargaining between city and state being a unique and complex system unprecedented in scope in the American federal system. By the early 1960s budget bargaining among state and city officials had attained a certain institutionalization in terms of players, roles, expectations, strategies and even outcomes. The key principals in the game, the New York governor and New York city mayor, operated within a complex constituency system in which the governor had almost as many troubles as the mayor himself at city hall. The outcomes can be reduced to a characterization made by Aaron Wildavsky, namely "It's not what's in your estimates (revenues and needs) but how good a politician you are that matters."[24]

During the ten year period from 1966–1975, New York City's expenditures rose at a rate nearly three times that of its own revenues. Increasingly the city became dependent upon state and federal aid as a major source of its expense budget. Federal aid alone increased from 5 percent to a peak of 21 percent of the city's revenues during this time frame, while New York State's share of the city's expense budget increased from 18.6 percent to a peak of 27 percent in 1973. In both cases, federal and state aid returned thereafter to a slower growth pattern. Thus, combined federal-state aid rose from 32 percent of the city's expense budget in 1966 to a peak of 47 percent, or nearly half of total revenues, by 1973.[25]

The administration of Mayor John Lindsay (1966–1973) essentially faced three choices: (1) increase revenue from outside sources, namely federal and state aid, or conversely, transfer services (load sharing) to higher governmental levels; (2) broaden the municipal revenue base, which meant increasing taxes; or (3) reduce services and retrench. The Lindsay Administration also introduced in 1972 a much publicized productivity program designed to maintain and improve service quality. With the exception of sanitation, this approach came too late and confronted insuperable civil service and union contractual barriers to achieve any significant results.[26] Reductions of services and full scale retrenchment were never pursued with any real fervor.

The city's strategies alternated between a combination of outside aid and increased taxes on the revenue side and the neglect of the expenditure side. As the prospect of large increases in federal aid decreased (even with federal revenue sharing and hopes for federal assumption of welfare costs), the city's fiscal solvency and continued operation increasingly reflected the outcomes of budget bargaining with New York State. To understand New York City's plight, the conditions leading to its critical fiscal situation, is to analyze the process through which the city and state together dealt with these problems. It is notable that in 1973 the ACIR concluded from its lengthy study, *City Financial Emergencies,* "the survey . . . failed to locate any cities in which conditions were such that timely action by local, or in a few cases, State officials, could not avert or promptly relieve a financial emergency." The Commission further concluded that it is the state's responsibility, due to its constitutional and statutory authority, for the operation of local governments to avert financial emergencies. After all, the ACIR reasoned, "the credit and financial reputation of the State and of all the other local governments are adversely affected by a credit failure of a local government within the State."[27] The ACIR's timely but little publicized report had scant impact upon New York officials.

To comprehend further why state and local officials as well as other participants in city-state budget negotiations behaved the way they did, it is necessary to understand how political decision makers' environment is constrained or impacted by four interdependent cycles. The first, and in many respects the most crucial one, is the economic cycle. This includes not only national trends and forces but also regional and local variations. For each 10 percent increase in economic activity nationally it is estimated that New York State realizes roughly a 15 to 20 percent increase in revenue collections. Although corporate and personal income tax yields may be most responsive to economic conditions, their instability and unpredictability can often cause significant problems in revenue estimations. Corporate and personal income taxes constitute 50 percent of the state's total revenues and about 16 percent of the city's generated revenues. Revenue forecasting becomes even more difficult when a recession and inflation are working in tandem because the offsetting impact of potentially rising income and sales tax revenues are opposed to loss of revenues from unemployment, less spending and reduced corporate profits. Tax increases may follow in the wake of a recession or pessimistic economic forecasts. However, when tax shortfalls occur and budget demands for social programs rise, political decision makers may opt for avoiding tax increases and recouping lost funds in an economic upturn. Hence, the condition of the national economy, adjusted for regional economic differences, sets in motion one cycle which decision makers and other budget participants learn to live and cope with.

### Election-Tax Cycle

The election cycle tends to be the most important single variable affecting city-state budget negotiations. Most participants in the budget process since the early 1960s attest to its importance and the crucial role it plays in outcomes. When their turn to be judged by the electorate arises, legislators and executives alike are totally consumed by the election process. The New York State Constitution separates gubernatorial from presidential elections (since 1938), and also mandates local elections on odd years so as not to mix state issues with local ones (or so earlier reformers thought). During any four-year cycle, elections for the legislature occur twice—once with the governor and once coterminus with national elections. Since 1945, the New York City mayor, city council, and members of the Board of Estimate stand for reelection in odd years when no other statewide or national elections occur (1961, 1965, 1969, 1973 and 1977). Hence, there is only one year in the four year cycle when there is no federal, state or city election which means, typically, that this is the year most favorable for all elected participants to raise taxes.

Given that tax increases are perceived as being precarious to votes for elected officials, it is a reasonable guess that, whenever possible, major tax increases are sought in nonelection years. Not surprisingly, this is what has happened. In 1959, withholding of state income taxes was introduced. In 1963 no major statewide taxes were imposed, but a new means of capital financing was devised by authorizing a $500 million, nonbudgeted capital expense to be issued through the State Housing Finance Agency. This established the growing system of agency financing and of operations outside of the "voted budget." In 1965 the state finally imposed a statewide sales tax and also increased its excise levies on cigarettes. The year 1967 was an exception with no major increases, attributable in part to the yields of the recently established sales tax and in part to Vietnam War—inflated income tax receipts. But in 1969 the state sales tax was increased to three percent, and in 1971 the range of items covered by the sales tax was broadened (e.g., to meals costing less than one dollar, the "hot dog tax"), and the sales tax was increased to four percent. This was coupled with a "temporary surcharge" of 2.5 percent on the state income tax.

The pattern of nonimposition of taxes in an election year also holds true for the city. The major city increases were in 1963, with the city sales tax increased from three to four percent and gas and cigarette taxes increased as well, and in 1967, along with the city income tax, a major real estate tax increase and a large

Table 8-6. Elections and Tax Cycles, New York State and New York City, 1959–1975

| Year | New York State | | New York City | |
|------|----------|-------|----------|-------|
| | Election | Taxes | Election | Taxes |
| 1959 | No election | Income-tax withholding; gas, cigaretts, alcoholic beverages | No election | Real estate tax increase and service charges |
| 1960 | Legislature | No tax increases | No election | No tax increases |
| 1961 | No election | No tax increases | Mayor and Council | No tax increases |
| 1962 | Governor and Legislature | No tax increases | No election | No tax increases |
| 1963 | No election | $50 million non-budgeted capital authority financing | No election | Sales tax increase from 3¢ to 4¢; gas and cigarette tax increases |
| 1964 | Legislature | No tax increases | No election | Real estate tax increase |
| 1965 | No election | 2¢ sales tax; cigarette tax doubled | Mayor and Council | No tax increases |
| 1966 | Governor and Legislature | No tax increases | No election | Transit fare increase from 15¢ to 20¢ |
| 1967 | No election | No tax increases | No election | Income tax; water charges increase real estate tax increase |
| 1968 | Legislature | No tax increases | No election | Transit fare increase from 20¢ to 35¢ |
| 1969 | No election | Sales tax increase from 2¢ to 3¢; minor excise increase | Mayor and Council | No tax increases |

**Table 8–6. continued**

| Year | | | | |
|------|------|------|------|------|
| 1970 | Governor and Legislature | No tax increases | No election | Major real estate tax increase |
| 1971 | No election | Sales tax increase to 4¢; 2.5% income tax surcharge ("hot dog tax") | No election | Major real estate tax increase |
| 1972 | Legislature | No tax increases; surcharge suspended | No election | No tax increases |
| 1973 | No election | No tax increases | Mayor and Council | Major real estate tax increase |
| 1974 | Governor and Legislature | No tax increases | No election | Sales tax increase to 4¢; real estate tax increase |
| 1975 | No election | Reimposition of 2.5% surcharge; Carey proposes "temporary" tax package. Special session—$600 million tax increase. | No election | Beam proposes budget cuts; sets up major layoff program; real estate tax increase $500 million in new taxes. |

increase in water charges. Most major real estate taxes also have been increased in nonelection years, and another important political item, the transit fare, also was raised in nonelection years.

Taken together, there have been no major tax increases or impositions of new taxes by the city in a citywide election year and none by the state in a statewide election year. Conversely, the major new revenues have all been obtained in the odd-numbered fourth year of the cycle, except in 1965, when the state sales tax was imposed in a citywide election year. The participants in the process have generally accommodated their campaign styles and behavioral patterns to the "tax and election cycle." So, too, the governor and mayor responded with a pattern of expense budgeting and borrowing that adjusted election cycles to economic cycles.[28] (See Table 8–6.)

The tax-election cycle also affects legislative primaries, scheduling of special state legislative sessions (1971, 1975) and gubernatorial-mayoral relations. Insofar as the race for governor falls one year after New York City's mayoral election, incumbent chief executives developed mutual needs to satisfy in terms of tax avoidance and posturing. Even though the city's portion of the total state electorate has declined steadily (to 43 percent in 1974), the governor still requires a sizeable city vote to be (re)elected and shuns the appearance of being anti-city. Mayor John Lindsay was able to avoid a city tax increase during his 1969 reelection campaign. Even though he chose to support Democrat Arthur Goldberg against Republican Rockefeller for governor in 1970, the city gained most of its legislative package in Albany largely because of gubernatorial election-year generosity. However, in 1971, when the city's budget deficit had begun to balloon and greater state aid was desperately required, Lindsay's relations with both Rockefeller and the Republican legislature had so thoroughly disintegrated that the mayor was, in effect, closed out from negotiations over the city's tax package.

By 1974 Lindsay and Rockefeller had been replaced. Malcolm Wilson, the lieutenant governor, became governor upon Rockefeller's resignation; and Abraham Beame, the former New York City budget director and past controller, had been elected mayor. The new principals had long previous experience in the budget game. Beame decided to go soft on the new governor who was running for reelection. Accordingly, he geared his Albany strategy to request new taxes and increased state aid in 1975, the one year in the tax-election cycle when no general election would occur and tax increases would be most propitious. He limited the city's 1974 tax requests to an increase in the city's sales tax and chose not to interject the city's desperate financial condition into the 1974 gubernatorial campaign. Hence, the new mayor attempted to play both ends against the middle. If Republican Wilson were elected, Beame would have built up sufficient good will and bargaining power to support his demands for greater state aid in 1975. If fellow Brooklyn Democrat Hugh Carey were elected, the

Democrats would control the two most powerful elected positions in New York State for the first time in sixteen years.

Essentially, the city-state budget negotiations fall into four stages: budget preparation and the governor's budget message to the legislature (mid-summer—early January); regular legislative session and enactment of the state budget (early January—April 1); presentation of the city's expense budget and passage of home rule provisions by legislature (April 1–May 15); and adoption of the city's expense budget and new taxes by the Board of Estimate and the city council (May 1–June 10). These dates and sequences correspond to state law and city charter but may be altered by agreement, as has been the case in recent years. Whether major decisions governing new state aid for the city are made before April 1 or after depends largely on the governor's budget strategy as well as on prior bargaining over chips between the major and other participants in the budget game.

Nelson Rockefeller instituted a rather formalized process of budget preparation and a means of providing claimants upon the state budget with a forecast of budget conditions. Though there is no formal process for local government input into state budget making (except in education), interagency contacts provide the state with a good reading of what their city counterpart needs, expects and can live with. The city's budget bureau prepares its own budget with the uncertainties of how much state aid will be forthcoming and must devise various budget-taxing scenarios for closing what has become an expanding gap between projected revenues and expenditures.

With the governor's January budget message to the legislature and during the three-month annual session of the state legislature, the outcomes with respect to the governor's proposal, state funds for the city and the city's own legislative program are in considerable doubt. No two sessions are quite the same. Not only are relations between the governor and mayor in flux, but so are those among the chief executives, legislative leaders, party officials and interest groups. Wallace Sayre described the mayor's dilemma in that he "carries with him to Albany all the disabilities he has at city hall; he picks up no important new strength on his journey."[29] At times the mayor seeks to get as much as possible out of the legislature without requesting the governor's intervention which may have a higher trading price than dealing without the governor. Scheduling of votes affects when and how the governor and mayor interact. They may throw their mutual strengths behind measures both want. There have been times in recent years when both were fighting for their own respective survivals under a legislative revolt. Then the mayor was in a position to deliver crucial city votes. Typically the situation is reversed, however.

After the governor's message, the mayor must choose his strategy which can range from a stance of "reasoned cooperation" to a high-decibel approach. The mayor also relies on a host of "intermediaries" in dealing with Albany—elected and appointed state officials, legislative leaders, his own party's caucus and city representatives, interest group and party leaders from the city, the communications media and others who have allies at the capital. He may call on these allies, relating their strengths to his legislative goals. Such power groups have their own legislative agenda and also extract a price from the mayor in exchange for supporting him. Both sides typically wage a battle for media support in New York City as well as in Albany.

When the governor's party controls both houses and the governor has sufficient command over his party, his program may undergo only minor revision. In all but two of the past 22 years, the Republicans have controlled at least one of the two legislative bodies, and the normal pattern has been to control both. When the opposing party controls one or both houses or the governor does not have the votes, the bargaining can be fierce and divisive. From the city's perspective, the key state actors are the governor, his top aide (secretary to the governor), state budget director, minority and majority leaders in the Senate and the Assembly, the speaker of the Assembly, and the chairmen and staffs of the Senate Finance Committee and the Assembly's Ways and Means Committee. The mayor, deputy mayor and city budget director negotiate principally with these officials during legislative deliberations. The relations and interest in the city constantly changes among the four key legislative leaders—speaker, majority leader, Senate Finance Committee chairman, and Assembly Ways and Means chairman—which also affect both the governor's and mayor's strategies. The legislature is organized on a strongly partisan basis which reflects the competitive two-party system in the state. The majority party members have been able to dominate legislative proceedings beyond their actual numbers. Leadership controls the legislative budget, staffing, committee appointments and the flow of legislation. The governor still dominates the legislature through ties to legislative leaders, item veto and patronage control. In short, the New York State political process is characterized by "part-time legislators" and "permanent governors" (only five elected since 1933) and a state bureaucracy with long job tenure and high expertise.

Among chief city lobbyists in Albany are mayoral assistants and their staffs who have the responsibility for shepherding the city's legislative program through the legislature as well as reviewing the more than 10,000 bills introduced during each session. The number of bills comprising the city's program has grown tremendously: an average of 49 annually between 1940-1946; 72 per session between 1947-1956, and roughly 200 annually since then. A simple change of several words in a pension bill or a salary clause can mean virtually millions in additional costs to the city. The mayor's Albany representative thus must pore over legal technicalities of virtually hundreds of bills which affect all facets of the city's activities. The mayor's annual fiscal program has expanded as well, from three to four measures a decade or so ago (of which the mayor usually got one intact) to more than 30 separate tax measures.

The passage of the state budget sets the stage for legislative review of the city's tax package. Once again, the mayor selects from among many strategies to recoup losses, force the governor's intervention, and simultaneously calculate what new taxes may be found acceptable to the city council and the Board of Estimate. As the mayor builds a support base for his proposals, he must expend more political and financial resources to satisfy his allies, often in a classic example of diminishing returns. The mayor's efforts must be directed largely at the governor. The governor is the only participant with all the other parties to budget-making in his constituency. He is the highest elected official in the state, leader of his party and possesses an extraordinary arsenal of formal and informal powers—long a characteristic of New York State politics. The governor is the chief coordinator, the dispenser of political resources, and the final arbiter for the mayor to get his package through a legislature noted for a traditional anti-city bias. The governor-mayor relationship can be tenuous, however, even when both belong to the same party, or may deteriorate so severely, as occurred between Lindsay and Rockefeller after 1971, that the governor refuses to play the convenor role and leaves the mayor to fend for himself.

The New York City mayor is not helpless as a dispenser of resources and as a bargainer. Since at least 1970 mayors have adroitly orchestrated their budget options in terms of new taxes and municipal layoffs. In the 1971–72 city tax program Lindsay provided state legislators with four options ranging from a low budget of $7.8 billion (with 60,000 layoffs, and 30,000 others removed by attrition) to a no layoff, high budget of $9.3 billion. Some Albany legislators viewed these scenarios as scare tactics and play acting. Nonetheless, they voted for the option of attrition, no massive layoffs and no appreciable diminution of city services. They also proceeded to reject the mayor's fiscal package in which proposed taxes were predicated on elasticity, progressivity and revenue generation, substituting instead a tax package of "hidden taxes" and budget balancing gimmicks. Four years later Mayor Beame would resort to the same strategy. He threatened massive layoffs to get his tax package adopted and, over gubernatorial opposition, formed a successful alliance with upstate GOP legislators who voted for city aid and ample loans to balance his budget in exchange for more school aid for their districts.

Amidst the sound and fury over layoffs which all parties generally avoided, basic fiscal decisions are made which affect future negotiations. In 1971, for example, the state accommodated a $400 million tax shortfall partly by tax increases but mostly by freezing funds and postponing payments till the next year. The state amended the Local Finance Law to permit the city to over-estimate revenues and to borrow against prospective federal revenue sharing funds and also created a public benefit corporation—the New York City Stabilization Reserve Corporation—to allow the city to borrow funds to repay past borrowing. Thus the state agreed to permit the city to exceed its debt limitation, falsify revenue estimates and roll over its outstanding short-term debt.[30]

Once the various participants meet on behalf of the city's tax package, usually following the Easter legislative recess, the battle generally becomes lower key. The bargaining and compromises are removed from center stage. The city may already have gained more state funds than in the prior year, but less than the mayor has declared to be the absolute minimum for fiscal solvency. Now the unique politics of "gapmanship" begin—closing the gap between budget expenditures and anticipated revenues. The city charter ignores problems of unbalanced budgets and the role played by the state legislature in compensating for this deficiency. The charter calls for discrepancies between revenues and expenditures to be automatically disposed of by city council action by increasing real property taxes to arrive at a balanced budget. While no deficiency can exist in the imaginary world of the charter, the realities are such that the city's revenue gap must be closed by an assortment of new taxes and devices approved by the legislature.

The quest for a tax package, including loans, special aid, scheduling advances on state aid and types of state-approved borrowing for the city usually occurs during the time-constrained environment of April or even longer in recent years. The mayor must return from Albany with a balanced budget to submit to the council and Board of Estimate for hearings by early May. The state, in effect, has held the city captive till the end of the session. The participants recalculate revenue estimates for the city and the magnitude of the gap under various conditions and estimate the costs, risks and alternatives for each side so that the mayor, governor and legislative leaders can play the gapmanship game. Much attention is given to the range of "gimmicks" that can be employed, as opposed to new taxes, to close the budget gap. In light of the size of the city's consolidated budget, the mayor has considerable powers to shift funds and accruals and otherwise use the capital budget for emergency purposes. The city had long borrowed up to 100 percent against accrued revenues from all due real estate tax collections even though tax delinquencies had been mounting. Similarly, the city often counted as revenues in its last quarter funds to be collected after the beginning of the new fiscal year, or conversely, pushed expenditures due into the next fiscal year. Thus, gimmickery is a long-practiced art in public finance, and city and state budget officials became experts at accommodating the short-term solutions and time-compressing deadlines to political bargaining. The entire process increasingly drove out any long term perspective.

City participants generally leave to state officials the burden of proposing the various gimmicks to be employed so as not to incur state legislative wrath for fiscal irresponsibility. Such gimmicks are decried by good government groups like the New York City Citizens Budget Commission, but such opposition rarely deterred the budget makers.[31] Thus, if the state suggested that the city put off replenishing the city's "rainy day" fund, defer pension allocations or shift traditional expense items to the capital budget in place of certain taxes, city officials normally were inclined to go along. Once again, the range of gimmicks is typically discussed by respective budget heads far in advance, so that the principals have more chips with which to bargain over final settlement. But the range and application of gimmicks are not limitless. Postponements, deferrals, advances of future funds, overestimating revenues and debt financing have costs—cumulative ones that have rapidly increased fiscal burdens on the city and state, making each successive year's settlements all the more difficult to consummate.

This confrontation is not simply between the city and the state. Various taxpayer, labor, business and municipal employee groups often compete behind the scenes to alter the mayor's requests. If the mayor approves layoffs, then the focus shifts to the governor and the legislature where public employee unions seek reversal. When new taxes and increased debt threaten the city's creditors or major revenue providers, they, too, form coalitions and mobilize their Albany allies.

Thus, the mayor must deflect, channel and focus city-based interests to support his bid in Albany for greater aid. The city's home rule package has to be approved by the legislature, so tradeoffs and final settlements must be found acceptable to its leaders. In recent years, this package has included such an extensive variety of taxes, loans and gimmicks that its full consequences are not readily discernable to legislators at the time they vote on the entire package. Since most noncity legislators really are not that interested in the package, legislative leaders have enormous leverage upon rank and file. The full impact of their collective decisions awaits the next calendar year to unfold.

Even before the mayor-governor recriminations subside, the mayor must return to the city with the Albany-settled package to renew consensus building. He has a stake in keeping intact the tax package that Albany has voted. If either the Board of Estimate or the city council reject major portions of this package, the state legislators who have voted for increased taxes find themselves undercut. No legislator wishes to be on record as favoring increased taxes if they are not eventually voted. He is compromised and will be reluctant to act in a similar fashion again. However, the council and Board of Estimate must prove to their constituencies that they are not the mayor's rubber stamp—that they oppose higher taxes and find waste and inefficiency in the city's multibillion dollar budget. In recent years, there has been no real slack for budget maneuvering, even though the mayor has been forced to make some concessions to his key elected rival, the controller, and to the city council and its finance committee.

The concurrent budget setting process serves multiple political needs which, in political life, are rational and predictable. Most obvious, all participants generally avoid tax increases, which in state-local politics are an elected official's nightmare. Whatever fiscal devices can be employed to postpone or reduce the impact of taxes will be considered prior to tax leverage. A good loan is always preferable to a bad tax. However, if taxes are to be levied, the politician's cardinal rule is to enact them as far away from the next election and to hide them as effectively as possible. The other rule is that sufficient slack be left in state and city budgets to allow legislators to take some of the sting out of taxes—cut programs, force hiring freezes, reduce the rate of tax increases or their burden. In the state-city budget battle, this means that all participants must try to save face. Both the state senate and assembly must be allowed to make budget cuts, vote against some tax increases and appear as guardians of the public treasury. The city council and Board of Estimate have comparable needs to be public heroes of economy and efficiency in government. When the assembly speaker aspires to be governor or the city controller to be mayor, he must lead the charge or indulge in a special cutting exercise of his own.

Not only must the governor and mayor incorporate into their strategies the needs and expectations of other major participants, but also they must allow each other to save face as well. Each budget negotiation has an impact on the next, with participants' memories a crucial factor in outcomes. The governor accepts the early budget blandishments from the New York City media but expects his "bad guy" image to fade by the time of final April-May settlement. The mayor accepts that although he will get more state funds than last year, they will not be all that he wishes or even needs. He bears the greater burden of pressures, because for six months out of every year he must play the Albany game and as though in an annual "Perils of Pauline" can never be assured of the outcome. As the city's proportion of the state's electorate steadily falls and its proportion of the state's poor increases, the mayor's leverage in Albany declines while his need for state assistance rises. He may hope for federal windfalls and a prosperous economy. For better or worse, state government still has life and death authority over its corporate creatures—taxes, structure, functional sharing, personnel and land use. As a creature of the state, the city enjoys no powers other than those specifically granted to it, virtually all of which assume the form of state legislation.

Certain fundamentals add stability to state-city budget relations and prevent conflict from reaching even greater proportions. Economic interdependency between city and state is accepted by the major participants. The state is not out to reduce the city to a wasteland or to preside over its demise. The budget interplay between them involves a complex system where competition and conflict, negotiation and compromise, maneuver and strategy are essential ingredients. In spite of personality and partisan differences, bargaining is carried out in good faith. Nearly all parties are determined to prevent negotiations from breaking down, which has meant that fiscal consequences are subordinated to political needs.

### Labor Contract Cycle

The fourth cycle, that of New York City's municipal union contracts, is highly dependent upon the other three cycles. Labor contract settlements are increasingly important to understanding the city's financial situation. In New York State, more than 900,000 of the one million state-local employees are represented by unions—nearly one quarter of the 3.9 million employee membership nationally in 1974. Collective bargaining covers 95 percent of New York City's civil servants, more than 300,000 employees, and thus determines virtually all labor costs of city government. Roughly 60 percent of the city's expenditures represent labor costs: salaries, fringe benefits and retirement.

Mayor Robert Wagner in 1958 inaugurated the new era of municipal labor relations by granting employees the right to join unions and to bargain collectively. "Where Mayor Wagner's strategy rested on personal involvement and politicization of labor relations administration and impasse procedures," noted labor expert Ray Horton, "Mayor Lindsay sought to depoliticize the labor relations process by promoting impartial administration and impasse procedures." [32] Following the 1961 mayoral elections when Wagner ran against the old Democratic party machine with an alliance of reformers and professional organized employees and won, the six major unions in New York City became a major, if not the most significant, single actor in its politics. The unions' capacity to employ the threat or actuality of a strike, to mobilize votes and to lobby in Albany affects both the election and budgetary cycles at the city and state levels.

Exempted from the state's Taylor Law (which mandated negotiation and banned strikes except by teachers and transit workers), the city's unions have remained adamant that their demands should not be impaired by budgetary constraints and economic conditions (except for cost of living increases). During the mid-1960s the city's labor relations process became more centralized under mayoral agencies, but contract negotiations became farther removed from the mayor personally, the city's budget bureau, personnel department and legislative bodies. Collective bargaining contracts remained largely hidden from the public and from elected officials alike—no hearings, full costs of settlement rarely known, and overlaps with budget years fully accepted. Just as fiscal gimmickery overtook the state-city budgeting process in closing the city's expanding deficit, so too an identical process overcame the city's payment of labor contract settlements. New York City resorted to hiding collective bargaining money in the expense budget, making up additional costs through accruals, budget modifications, back-loading agreements (cost increases in the future), capitalizing salaries and pensions, and under retroactive settlements (where contract expiration had occurred), making up budget deficiencies through borrowing. The three uniformed service unions—Patrolmen's Benevolent Association, Uniformed Firefighters' Association, and Uniformed Sanitationmen's Association—whipsawed the city on contract settlements until the parity issue among certain ranks across services was broken in 1974. The three helped set the prevailing settlement pattern for the city's largest union, District #37 of the American Federation of

State, County and Municipal Employees. With fully one-third or more of the uniformed service workers living outside the city and many voting for suburban state legislators, the unions had both a city and a suburban power base in Albany, a base often more powerful than that of the mayor himself. Not only did New York City mayors prove to be soft bargainers with the unions, but, following the budget pattern in state-city negotiations, they deferred the full impact of labor costs through fringe and retirement benefits. (Pension benefits of nearly $1 billion in 1975 are expected to rise to an estimated $2.5 billion by 1980.)[33]

The union leaders came to understand the election and budget cycles as much as elected participants in the game. Through timing, duration and settlement of strikes, the unions could alter outcomes to their advantage. They increasingly came to gear their strategies and pressures to these cycles.

### The Outcome

For the greater part of this century it has been widely acknowledged that New York City has had a revenue problem. The city has an insufficient tax base to carry out the range of services and redistributive programs it gradually became wedded to. Hence the city has moved from one financial crisis to another for the past 20 years, with expenditures gradually but incrementally outpacing revenues. The city has no marginal revenue-raising powers of its own, subject to state approved tax-rate and tax-base limitations. From 1962–1974, the city's welfare expenditures increased sixfold from $300 million or 11 percent of the city's expense budget to $1.8 billion or 21 percent, while the state's welfare expenditure (including medicaid) rose from $200 million to more than $1.5 billion of which 70 percent went to the city. To carry out ambitious new state programs and to maintain existing services, city and state tax increases resulted in a rising tax burden. This further compounded their mutual problems by driving out job-producing industry and higher-income residents. The city and state alike operated during the 1960s on two assumptions. The one was that it was only a matter of time before the federal government assumed the costs and burdens of welfare, which would relieve them of more than $3 billion in annual social service costs. The other was the assumption that a prosperous, growth-oriented economy would enable these governments to cope with increased expenditure demands. Budgeting, borrowing and the behavior of elected officials increasingly reflected these assumptions, even when the business recession struck and their combined liquidity was impaired by declining economic activity.[34]

So long as New York City could borrow, the day of reckoning could be put off. Pinched by inflationary costs and recession-induced dropoff in revenues, the city resorted to a rash of short-term borrowings to maintain an orderly cash flow and to balance its budget. Within a single year, the city's costs of borrowing nearly doubled from a January 1974 issue of revenue anticipation notes at a net interest cost of 5.1 percent to a December rate of 9.48 percent which was nearly

250 basis points above the average for 20 year bonds. In already distressed money markets the city was paying dearly for the cost of borrowing. In a single year the amount of the city's bond anticipation notes issued rose by 37 percent and revenue anticipation notes were up 22 percent from the previous year, bringing cumulative short term debt to nearly $6 billion. This constituted some 45 percent of all the short-term tax exempt notes outstanding in the country. The city's interest on debt soared from 9 percent to 17 percent in one year. In December of 1974, Mayor Beame and City Controller Harrison Golden began a much publicized debate over the magnitude of the 1974–75 budget deficit, whether $430 million or $650 million, which extended to the amount of the bigger deficit projected for the 1975–76 budget beginning July 1.

New York has a record of never having defaulted on an obligation. Its obligations further carry the New York State constitutional requirement that debt service be provided for, that if not, moneys be set aside from first revenues, and that the fiscal officer may be required by suit of any bondholder to set such moneys aside for debt service. In spite of strong constitutional guarantees on the city's obligations, the budget deficit shook the market for the city's securities. Institutional and other holders of city bonds began liquidating their holdings. The city still had access to the money market but only at a record level of interest rates. Finally no syndicate would bid on the city's securities when buyers' interest evaporated. In February of 1975, the New York State Urban Development Corporation, formed in 1968 and supported from revenues of ongoing projects, got caught in a cash squeeze and defaulted on $100 million in notes. Considering that the city had $6 billion in outstanding moral obligation debt like that which backed the UDC, investors' concerns rose. The state legislature first blamed the new governor and his predecessor, then turned its wrath upon the banks and bond underwriters, and four weeks following default set up a new agency to redeem the notes. Consequently, not only did other state agencies backed by moral obligation bonds lose access to the credit market, but New York City's borrowing costs jumped from 7 percent interest to 8.69 percent rates within weeks.

The mayor then blamed Albany for the city's fiscal problems. He failed to take any decisive steps of the magnitude that might have restored investor confidence. The business and financial community, the media, even Washington and Albany, a base often more powerful than that of the mayor himself. Not only expenditures and systematically laying off employees. Instead Mr. Beame responded by making inconsequential housekeeping cuts and equivocating on job lay-offs.

The fiscal crisis snowballed. Cut off from the money markets and unable to borrow, the city encountered a cash flow crisis with actual default on notes being forecasted for April. The state advanced $400 million in state funds due on July 1st to get the city through the spring. Spurned by Washington in his efforts to get a $1.5 billion emergency loan, the mayor turned to Albany to avert another cash flow crisis and possible default. In June the state legislature created the Municipal Assistance Corporation (MAC), an interim borrowing agency for the city, and authorized it to sell up to $3 billion in bonds, setting aside revenues from the city sales tax and stock transfer tax to cover interest cost on the bonds. Tainted by adverse publicity about the city and rising concern about the state's finances, MAC could only sell $2 billion in new securities with interest rates above 9 percent. MAC was no more welcome in the money markets than the city, and indeed the state was being shut off from the money markets as well. Investors' reaction was not surprising. Not only had the state legislature waffled on the issue of stage legal responsibility for state agency moral obligation bonds after the UDC default, but it had also repealed the 1962 covenants governing the New York-New Jersey Port Authority; that is, when the Port Authority took over the bankrupt trans-Hudson commuter tubes, the legislatures of New York and New Jersey assured bondholders that never again would the Port Authority be required to assume any deficit mass transit operation. Faced with growing political pressures to subsidize mass transit, the legislatures and governors of both states capitulated, agreeing to repeal of the previously enacted covenant. Investor confidence crumbled in light of legislative determination to dispense with contractual obligations with bondholders.[35]

The city's financial situation continued to deteriorate. The city received no new state assistance beyond advances and obtained only $300 million in new taxing powers. MAC and Mayor Beame finally accounted for the cumulative deficit  in the city's budgets going back some ten years at $3.3 billion through 1976-1977. In late August the city's three largest banks balked at refinancing some $900 million of an intricate $2 billion plan to carry the city through December. With MAC sales stalled and the mayor still unwilling to take large scale budgets cuts, Governor Hugh Carey convened the legislature to enact a $2.3 billion package to avert default for the next three months coupled to a three year austerity plan for New York City. The New York State Financial Emergency Act for the City of New York, which the legislature passed, created the Emergency Financial Control Board which would run the city's budget and approve all spending. Control of the city's budget thus passed from the mayor and locally elected officials to a new state-dominated board which includes the governor, the mayor, the state controller and three appointees of the governor. The board takes all city revenues into its own bank accounts and disperses these revenues in accordance with a mandated financial plan which was approved by the board on October 20, 1975. This plan calls for aggregate reduction in city expenditures of nearly $700 million from 1976 to 1978, no salary increases for municipal employees, wage freezes, elimination of "discretionary" social service programs and a balanced city budget for 1977-1978.

The state then advanced $750 million to the city and MAC, the remaining $2.3 billion package financed through MAC from city-invested pension funds and further purchases by the city's banks. Besides providing legal and administrative machinery for dealing with possible city default, the state had tied its debt to that of the city. New York State, in turn, had to pay record high interest rates of 7.8 percent for notes it issued to meet the city's immediate cash needs. This was the first visible sign that the state, by pledging its backing to the city, had begun to be viewed as a growing investment risk. Once again in mid-October the city came within hours of default only to be rescued by a $150 million investment of teacher pension funds in MAC bonds.

**Table 8–7. New York's Borrowing Needs (millions of dollars)**

| Fiscal Year | Short-term debt (rollover) | Deficit | Capital Program | Total | Cumulative Total |
|---|---|---|---|---|---|
| 1976 | $2,580 | $516 | $ 992 | $4,088 | –– |
| 1977 | 250 | 470 | 1,100 | 1,820 | $5,908 |
| 1978 | 0 | –30[a] | 930 | 900 | 6,808 |
| 1979 | 0 | 0 | 1,000 | 1,000 | 7,808 |
| 1980 | 0 | 0 | 1,000 | 1,000 | 8,808 |
| TOTALS | $2,830 | $956 | $5,022 | $8,808 | |

[a]The figure represents a surplus.

The figures are based on two assumptions: (1) that the city's operating budget will be balanced by fiscal year 1978; and (2) that true capital spending will be reduced from the current level of about $1.3 billion per year to about $1 billion per year.

Source: Banking, Currency and Housing Committee, U.S. House of Representatives.

The inability of the state, the city and MAC to borrow brought the fiscal crisis to a new head in early November and forced Governor Carey to develop a three-year financial plan for the city. This complicated fiscal package included financial pledges of trust funds from the unions and the city's banks, a stretching of short term notes held by investors and new state and city taxes as well as further budget cutting measures by the city. As Table 8–7 indicates, New York City has borrowing needs of roughly $8.8 billion through 1980, some $6.8 billion of that amount being required before June 30, 1977. The Carey plan included: (1) a moratorium on the city's debt and a forced refunding of $2.6 billion in short-term notes that come due between December 1975 and June 30, 1976, which would be converted into ten-year bonds; (2) the investment of $2.5 billion of union pension funds in new ten-year city bonds; (3) advance of state funds to the city with a stretched out repayment plan; and (4) imposition of $200 million in additional city taxes and increased employee contribution to the city's pension funds.

The most controversial portion of this package and the measure strongly pressured by Washington was the one converting short-term debt into long-term debt. On November 15th the state legislature passed the New York State Moratorium Act for the City of New York, a forced refunding law based on the state's emergency powers, which asked holders of $1.6 billion in city notes (one-year obligations coming due) to exchange them for 8 percent interest-bearing MAC bonds due on July 1, 1986. Those noteholders who refused the refunding offer would receive a lower interest rate of 6 percent with a three-year moratorium on principal payments (and no guarantee that the principal would ever be paid). This forced refunding and extension of maturities, called "shotgun financing" by some, are tantamount to default. However, MAC's legal advisers and state officials, citing the precedent of a moratorium on mortgages during the 1930s, called it a moratorium. With bondholders and the banks challenging the legality of the act in the courts, a decision likely to go to the Supreme Court, a successful challenge would renew the city's crises. By November 25, the legislature had approved the Carey plan for an additional $200 million in city taxing authority; the city's banks and municipal funds agreed to the exchange offering and union leaders acquiesced to investment of pension funds in ten-year city bonds.

Thus in a six-month period the city's payroll had been reduced by 10 percent or 35,000 employees. The transit fare had been increased to 50 cents, all new construction projects halted and many under way suspended. Property taxes had been increased by 10 percent and $350 million in new business taxes had been imposed. A municipal union hiring and wage freeze had been instituted, pension fund contributions by city employees increased, and a management advisory board instituted to revamp the city's operations. Hard decisions governing the city's future now lay with the Emergency Financial Control Board, not subject to the same pressures as the mayor. New York State had exercised its full control and authority over its corporate creature falling just short of replacing Mayor Beame. At great political and economic risk it had assumed many of the city's liabilities. The state was now responsible for managing the city's fiscal affairs, acting as immediate creditor, and had begun providing for structural reorganization. In taking these actions the state had reached its limit of credit resources and, according to some, had gone too far in aiding the city.

Since May of 1974 the mayor and his allies had repeatedly directed pleas for federal assistance at the President and Congress. President Ford and his Secretary of the Treasury, William Simon, continuously refused such assistance in loans or offers of a federal guarantee for either the city or MAC securities. Chairman of the Federal Reserve, Arthur Burns, though admitting that the city's default might impair economic recovery, limited promises of aid to those banks holding the city's bonds to stemming whatever liquidity problems they may have. Simon echoed Burns' statements indicating that the economical-financial aspect of bank liquidity was both measurable and containable in the event of default. While some eight different proposals for aiding New York were being debated in Congress, President Ford campaigned nationally against aiding the city and instead advocated an immediate default. "I am prepared to veto any bill that has as its purpose a federal bail-out of New York City to prevent a default," the

President stated emphatically.[36] The President offered his own plan to amend the federal bankruptcy laws to establish procedures to avoid an avalanche of creditor litigation which otherwise would follow and to place reorganization authority under the federal courts.

But by late November the political and economic environment initially hostile toward aiding New York had completely reversed. Leading bankers stressed that the city's default could adversely affect the world's money markets and that the psychological impact of default could not be controlled.[37] Foreign leaders warned that default would adversely affect investment in this country and, as evidence, some sizeable transfers of deposits from United States to European banks transpired. Several prominent European statesmen advised the President of their anxiety lest the 1930s be repeated and a world wide depression be precipitated. Municipal bond dealers cautioned that default would collapse the municipal bond market and close out hundreds of local governments from borrowing in the near future. Once the implications of this unprecedented and unpredictable situation had begun to sink in nationally, public reaction turned in favor of some federal action. Perhaps most important of all to President Ford and his advisers, New York State had done everything in its powers to avert default and could take no further action.

Thus on November 26th, following state legislative action on Governor Carey's three year austerity plan for the city, President Ford dropped his opposition to federal aid for New York City and proposed legislation for $2.3 billion in short-term federal loans over the next two and a half years to enable the city to avert formal default. The President indicated that his position had been vindicated, that the city and state together had taken "concrete actions" to put the city's financial house in order. Rather than providing a loan guarantee, as city and state officials had requested for the past eight months, the New York City Seasonal Financing Act of 1975—the title of the President's proposal—would provide high interest loans through the state as the responsible legal entity and be implemented by the Secretary of the Treasury. "The taxpayers won't have to lose a penny and the federal government will be held harmless," the President stated, insofar as the loans would constitute a prior lien on all the city's income, including prospective federal aid. Mr. Ford further stated that, "We have always felt that they could do enough, but only because we were firm have they moved ahead to accomplish what they have done now."[38] Governor Hugh Carey also saved face, indicating that the President's action "represents a vindication of New York's case, of the merit of our position."

Once the act was signed into law by the President, federal loans began to flow into the city to the amount of $2.3 billion through June 30, 1978—a deadline for the city balancing its budget. However, these loans would cover roughly one-quarter of the estimated $10 billion the city would need to borrow over the next three years, which meant it would still have a cash flow problem unless the money markets opened up for city and state debt obligations. While short-term federal loan assistance may mark the turning point in the city's battle for financial solvency, some already questioned whether the greater damage had been done in terms of the stringent requirements to restore its economic health. Also the spillover effect upon other older cities may prove to be the catalyst, plunging them into a situation comparable to that of New York City.

No sooner had President Ford signed the bill authorizing aid to New York City than attention turned to New York State's financial crisis, which many felt was of even greater magnitude. The state had been shut out of the money markets for more than two months after trying unsuccessfuly to sell publicly notes for aid to the city. Not only had the state become entangled with the city—their debt structures now being locked together—but the state's rising debt burden raised considerable alarm from the financial community and others. The state had an estimated $900 million budget deficit for the current fiscal year ending April 1, 1976, and a projected $700 million deficit for 1976–1977. The State Housing Finance Agency required $160 million by December 16th to avert default, and the state needed an  aggregate financial package of $2.5 billion in refinancing to keep HFA and three other troubled state agencies that sold moral obligation bonds solvent over the next 30 months. This figure would be the estimated bill for allowing these four agencies to complete projects (housing, medical care, dormitory and environmental facilities) currently under construction and to generate sufficient cash flows from these projects to meet debt obligations.

On December 9th, Governor Carey sent a new package of proposals to the legislature to balance the state budget and to rescue state agencies from default. His plans included $1 billion in new state taxes, substantial cuts in social services and aid to local governments, and wage freezes for all state employees. Over protestations from Republican legislative leaders against these draconian measures, a group of city bankers publicly declared that immediate tax increases were essential to allow the state and its agencies to get back into the credit markets. The legislature responded with $600 million in new business taxes, with a 50 percent increase in bank taxes, but held over decisions on budget cuts until the legislature reconvened in January 1976.

Governor Carey also repeated his appeal to Chairman Arthur Burns for an emergency loan from the Federal Reserve Board to tide the HFA and other agencies over a time period in which more permanent financing could be put in place. Just as New York City required a work-out arrangement to possibly become solvent again, so too the state had arrived at a point where it needed both time and the infusion of capital to stem default. If any of the four state agencies defaulted on their notes, it was highly likely that the capital markets would be closed off to the state and default would be imminent. The state itself needed to borrow nearly $1 billion before April 1st, and another $4 billion in tax anticipation notes for state aid transfers to local governments shortly thereafter. It is still possible that the state could invest its own pension funds to avert default as a short-term solution. However, if the state failed to regain entry to the money markets, some $35 billion in aggregate outstanding debt of New York, its agencies, the city and all local governments in the state could well begin collapsing like dominoes. Besides New York City, the state already had to intervene in Yonkers, the state's fourth largest city, with an emergency rescue plan similar to that of New York City. New York State's collapse could well trigger a national economic panic and set back recovery from the worst postwar recession for years to come. This scenario deserves mentioning only to underscore the high-risk situation that had gradually emerged over the years from the city-state budget game. Given that nearly 1,000 banks in 33 states hold more than $6 billion in New York City and New York State obligations and the possible bank chaos that would result from city-state default, it is likely that the Treasury and the Federal Reserve will be compelled to intervene to defuse the problem. After all, 1976 is a presidential election and the Ford administration can not afford a serious setback to economic recovery which the New York State situation represents.

To illustrate just how precarious the condition of New York State had become, one only has to examine the state's rising debt load. Total New York State debt grew from $3.1 billion in 1961 to $13.4 billion in 1975. This 318 percent increase in state debt would not itself be so alarming if it were not accompanied by equally troublesome economic indicators. New York already has the highest per capita state-local taxes. On taxes as a percent of personal income, New York's combined state-local taxes also rank the highest. More important, New York ranked last in population growth, personal income and industrial employment growth among states from 1969 to 1973. Where creditworthiness analysts once stressed risk of default as a criterion, they use a more meaningful benchmark termed "relative ability to pay"—a debt to personal income measure. Table 8-8 indicates the rates of total state debt to state personal income for New York and four other major industrial states with similar credit ratings for the period from 1961 to 1974. The rates of total New York State debt to personal income nearly doubled over the 14 years from 6.81 percent to 12.84 percent while three other states either reduced their burden or increased it only slightly.[39]

**Table 8-8. Ratio of Total State Debt to State Personal Income (Percentage)**

| State | Moody's Rating | 1961 | 1971 | 1974 |
|-------|----------------|------|------|------|
| Florida | Aa | 3.06 | 4.09 | 3.93 |
| Michigan | Aa | 4.63 | 3.25 | 2.85 |
| New York | Aa | 6.81 | 9.91 | 12.84 |
| Massachusetts | A-1 | 9.74 | 7.97 | 10.39 |
| Pennsylvania | A-1 | 5.80 | 8.26 | 8.57 |

Governor Nelson Rockefeller embarked on an ambitious course in the 1960s to make state government a powerful force in New York's economic and social life. The Governor began a new system of capital financing by creating public authorities and corporations authorized to issue revenue bonds and to enter into lease-purchase bonds. Many of these agencies are financed through "moral obligation bonds," non-full faith and credit backing which circumvented the state constitutional requirement that full-credit borrowing be secured by voter referendum. The state entered into lease-purchase and lease-rental agreements with local governments whereby the debt to finance state agency facilities is issued by a local government for a rent or amortization equal to the debt service of the project. Moral obligation debt and lease-purchase agreements rose from $300 million or 18 percent of long-term state debt in 1963 to 64 percent or $7.2 billion (moral obligation plus lease-purchase) which is non-guaranteed. Much of the state's construction program in housing, education, hospitals and medical facilities was financed in this manner, largely hidden from legislative oversight and budgetary review. Governor Nelson Rockefeller, with strong legislative backing, established government-financed construction as the state's biggest growth industry. Just as the growth of the New York City government helped offset some of the loss of city jobs, so too, the state-financed construction programs provided jobs and employment throughout the state. Between 1960 and 1970, the city's fastest-growing industry was government, which provided 75 percent of the new jobs. In the state the construction industry rapidly became two tiered: government contracts and private. The Rockefeller Republican constituency came increasingly to reflect support from the building trade unions, while the New York mayor came to rely on the bureaucracy and organized municipal unions. Support for both involved the intricacies of budgeting and capital financing. While most state legislators, the press and others may not have fully understood the extent to which the state had mortgaged its future, the support for these bold ventures in state financing was nonetheless substantial.

"And thus it is," noted one observer of the city's fiscal crisis, "that the city's fiscal deliverance, however historic and ingenious it might be considered, must now be viewed as only the prologue to the 1976 legislative session's need to find the mechanisms for this fiscal rescue of the state and its construction agencies."[40] In short, the city's brief respite from default has placed increased pressure upon the state. With rising interest on debt and a glut of debt instruments already on the tax-exempt market, the state's finances are in serious trouble. A further diminution of its credit rating would further raise the cost of borrowing, assuming reentry into the fiscal markets, and reduce even further the liquidity of outstanding bonds in the secondary market. This country has not experienced in modern times the problems of a state being shut out of the credit markets or even possible widespread state default. Indeed, the New York State and New York City fiscal crises should be viewed as the most serious strains to the federal system since the Civil War whose effects and implications may well prove to be as pervasive.

## Conclusions

The late Wallace Sayre and Herbert Kaufman wrote their definitive treatise on New York City in 1960. *Governing New York City* became a seminal work in urban politics, noted for its comprehensiveness and the pluralist interpretation later applied by urbanists to their own research. "What other large American city is as democratically and as well governed as the City of New York?" Sayre and Kaufman concluded.[41] In a sequel to his earlier masterpiece, Sayre summarized the major actors in the city's political life in aggregate form: (1) the political parties, elected officials and city electorate; (2) the bureaucracies, career and appointed agency heads and municipal unions; (3) the interest groups; (4) the electronic and print media; (5) state government at Albany; and (6) the federal government in Washington. Sayre asserted that each of these aggregated actors tended to be splintered internally with no durable tendency toward cohesiveness and alignment. According to Sayre, it is the mayor's principle job to understand and to mobilize these constituencies rather than to allow them to lead him.[42] But beginning in at least 1965 a gradual transformation of the city's political process occurred with the result that the formal structure of the city's government had been revolutionized by 1975.

Fifteen years following the Sayre and Kaufman book, and after the city fiscal disaster, the nation's largest city was being governed by a new ruling class, including the banking and business community, the state of New York through the Emergency Financial Control Board and the Municipal Assistance Corporation, and the United States Department of the Treasury. The emerging power groups of the 1960s, notable municipal unions and civil rights, welfare and community groups, have in varying degrees been displaced. Until financial order is restored, the issue of restoring popular control to the nation's premier city can not be raised. And when popular control is restored, the one thing that may be said with reasonable assuredness is that it will be a far different city than it has ever been before. Query, if the Sayre and Kaufman pluralist interpretation of the city's politics failed both as theory and ideology, how and why did this happen? No other recent studies of New York City politics or of big city mayors adequately explain the last decade of New York City politics.*

This article provides only the roughest beginnings of an explanation set within the context of four cycles—economic, budget, election, and municipal union contracts. Each of these successive and overlapping cycles had time dimensions which helped shape elected leaders' options and strategies and led to certain outcomes. It should be noted that New York City and to an extent New York State as well never recovered from the recession which struck in 1969.

*My gratitude to Dr. Raymond Horton of the Columbia University School of Business for first raising these essential questions.

Similarly, the state failed to adopt a retrenchment program when the storm warnings of fiscal trouble began to mount in the late 1960s. Beginning in 1967, Governor Nelson Rockefeller issued shrill warnings concerning the coming fiscal crisis in American federalism and began his national campaign for revenue sharing. New York State had reached its practicable taxing limit, and the governor asserted that the state could accomplish little more without massive federal assistance. In his final budget message as governor Rockefeller reflected on the 1971–1972 fiscal crisis the state had just weathered with cautious optimism about the future. Indeed, as the city and state were to learn so painfully, the full impact of that crisis had not yet fully unfolded.

There were ample signs to political leaders that New York City was undergoing the same processes of transformation that other, older industrial cities had been experiencing—industry and jobs moving out, a gradual erosion of the tax base and a sizable increase in the poor and citizens demanding high service. Beyond their sheer size and scope, New York's economic and social conditions were not that different from what dozens of other major cities had to cope with and respond to. Since 1969 the city has lost more than 500,000 jobs, mostly from what were once New York's key industries—apparel manufacturing and retailing; securities and insurance; wholesale trade; water transport; and the restaurant trade. But state and city leaders chose to respond to these conditions and storm warnings, implicitly or explicitly, in three ways.

The first was to substitute public sector generated capital for disinvestment by the private sector with the purpose of stemming job loss through public employment. The 100,000 new jobs created in the city—in schools, hospitals and state and city agencies—as well as the growth in construction were largely a function of increased state-local government expenditures, aided by federal stimulation. Another alternative was to alleviate the impact of job loss through social welfare expenditures for the poor, policies which overlapped with public job creation. A policy of generosity and compassion for the poor, laudable as it may seem, was totally inappropriate for a city with its tax base and taxing powers to carry on.[43] Once committed to such policies New York State only compounded the problem by becoming more and more deeply involved in the tradeoffs required between city and state priorities to allow the city to continue on its course. But once city and state officials were convinced that social welfare was the national government's responsibility, the third strategy emerged—that of relying on Washington for fiscal salvation.

One can readily condemn the bankrupt operating ideology of New York leaders.[44] Rising social expenditures and taxes tended to be largely counterproductive in a rapidly spiraling fashion. More corporations and industries fled the city, and many high income tax payers moved to the non–income states of Connecticut and New Jersey to avoid the city and state combined tax burdens. Once caught up in these policies of job creation, rising municipal wages and social welfare expenditures, political leaders could only retreat from these incremental policies at higher and higher risks—public union strikes, demonstrations and confrontations, and possible reelection defeat. Also, with the state and city tax structures tied to a growth-oriented economy, many leaders came to believe that renewed growth would provide sufficient revenues to compensate for tax shortfalls and increased borrowing. However, the four operating cycles provided little relief to elected officials in rethinking strategies and extricating themselves from the road to default. Budget deadlines, labor settlements and electoral demands came totally to consume the state's and city's highest elected officials.

The governor and mayor alike frequently held wildly optimistic hopes for direct federal aid to their treasuries. Washington held the keys to their survival quests, as the least risk-laden and highest payoff strategy. Federal grant programs had cumulative costs both to city and state. Short-term federal commitments often were met by long-term city commitments only adding to the city's burdens. Following revenue sharing's enactment in 1972, federal aid to the city and state returned to more modest growth levels and the viability of a federal aid strategy declined precipitously. Also, the prospects for new multibillion federal programs declined as well with mounting federal deficits and a White House committed to slowing the pace of expenditures for social welfare programs. With half of the AFDC recipients residing in four states (New York, California, Illinois and Massachusetts), Congress was not about to pass a massive new income security program largely for the benefit of four states. Although the OPEC-generated energy crisis and deepening recession in late 1974 drove home the new politics of scarcity nationally, the scarcity phenomenon had already begun in New York—in New York City as early as 1969.

To many the image of the city's economic strength and the constitutional backing of the city's obligations cloaked the reality of its ebbing tax base and mounting deficits. As one major credit rating service stated of the city on the eve of its being shut out of the money markets, "the strong legal backing of the city's obligations and the city's unique position in the American economy provide a considerable amount of assurance to the creditor. These assets, managed by political leaders of even average competence would represent adequate backing for any city's securities."[45] Few appreciated how little maneuverability and slack existed in the state's financial structure, particularly following the UDC default, repeal of the Port Authority covenant and state moratorium law. Once again, the reality of the liquidity problem faced by financial institutions was far greater than the politicians sensed. Their attempt to continue the budgeting-financing game as usual subsequently forced the intervention of the banks and business interests into the political process. The days of reckoning had come to New York City and New York State alike. It now seem likely that the state will have to regain entry into the money markets sometime in 1976 to prevent further default. If if does not, then the state may well become some kind of semi-federal dependent.

New York City's "postponed payment" on its notes had a fallout on municipal borrowing nationally which has undergone and will continue to undergo fundamental changes. As long as defaults remained rare and the economy was reasonably prosperous, municipal bond investors had considerable freedom from worry and assuredness of payment. After all, individual investors, who hold some 30 percent of all outstanding state-local debt either directly or through bond funds, had found these securities increasingly attractive due to safety and rising yields. Inflation and increased income drove individuals into higher tax brackets which made purchases of municipal bonds profitable. So, too, commercial banks, which hold another 40 percent of these bonds, had increased their purchases over time. Following New York City, the weakening of state and local governments' promises to repay borrowed money, and easing of default laws, the element of risk had entered the municipal markets, driving up interest rates. Not only did a two-tier market spread emerge between high grade, high quality bonds and the rest, but also between borrowing rates for the Northeast and the rest of the country.

One estimate of the spillover costs of New York City on state-local borrowing in 1975 was roughly $3 billion in added interest over the life of the debt. Many older cities like Chicago, Detroit, Philadelphia and Boston had to pay record high interest rates in borrowing which added to inflation and the interest on debt these governments would have to finance. Some governments outside of New York have been unable to market their new issues of long term debt altogether. Those governments employing debt financing other than full faith and credit backing discovered a more probing and even hostile investment community. Particularly hard hit have been state housing finance agencies and various city redevelopment agencies which now seek co-insurance of their bonds from the Department of Housing and Urban Development to avoid the demise of much of the nation's housing construction. Consequently hundreds of local governments have postponed debt offerings, curtailed capital expenditures and begun retiring overall debt. Some institutional investors have reacted to this new world of public finance by "red-lining" much of the Northeast and older cities as being actual or potential credit risks. Large and small municipalities alike, highly dependent upon easy access to money markets to balance budgets, maintain cash flows and support capital construction, ponder their survival lest their access to credit lines be impaired.

The federal government reacted to the New York City situation by making municipal bonds subject to rules of the Securities and Exchange Commission and holding underwriters responsible for full and accurate information on public offerings. These rules will not just change financial and accounting practices of local governments, but also will force underwriters, banks and bond-rating houses to exert much greater pressure upon the operations of local governments. Marketing securities will take greater time, be more costly, and likely limit underwriters' bids where creditworthiness of a local government is in question. Witnessing the entanglement of New York State in New York City's finances and the statewide impact it had upon borrowing, a number of states have taken steps to exercise greater control over their local governments' finances. Some have strengthened borrowing and auditing requirements, mandated fuller funding of employee pension funds and drawn in home rule powers. In short, public sector debt financing specifically and local government finance generally will never be the same again following the New York City debacle.

Between 1966–1974 state and local governments increased spending from their own sources by 140 percent, about one-third greater rate of increase for domestic expenditures than the national government. Since 1955 employment in state and local government has surged, increasing over 125 percent or at three times the rate of private sector employment. But by the mid–1970s indications are that these subnational governments are going to be considerably less expansionary than in the past two decades. Their expenditures have slowed to adjust for reduced growth of receipts and less federal aid, with many local governments finding their revenues to be falling behind the rate of inflation. Caught between rising service demands and revenue shortfalls, some state and local governments have adjusted their total operating budgets by as much as 10 percent. These cutbacks may be translated into layoffs, hiring and wage freezes, shorter working hours and other measures to reduce personnel costs. Indeed many local governments have already dropped revenue-sharing funds from their projected budgets in the expectation that Congress will fail to renew the program in 1976. In short, the rate of expenditure increase for state-local governments, roughly 12 percent annually since 1969, is likely to run at a much slower pace for years to come. The economic dilemma of state and local governments is that their retrenchment could well slow down economic recovery, increasing the very fiscal problems that they are struggling to overcome.

For many older cities the politics of distributing more had already shifted to a far different politics of distributing less. In this respect New York State-New York City's response to the new realities of scarcity and economic change can only be considered atypical. Some states, like New Jersey in its relation to financially strapped local governments like those of Newark, Jersey City and Hoboken, have maintained strong fiscal control over their local governments in revenue estimating, budgeting against uncollected taxes, emergency appropriations and accounting systems. An Ohio law governing cash basis of accounting for local governments forced Cleveland into massive municipal layoffs in the light of its cash deficit. One may fault state governments for not coming to the rescue of their largest cities, but the fact remains that they have the primary responsibility under our federal system for the fiscal management of local governments. Still, in the midst of the projected further decline of our older and heavily populated urban centers the new post-industrial cities are flourishing— Houston, San Antonio, Dallas, San Diego, Phoenix and others. Economic trends and cycles have proven thus far to be more durable than the constituency-oriented politics of mayors, congressmen and their allies who have fought, largely unsuccessfully, the movement of jobs, population and industry. The new politics of scarcity, it can be argued, has only intensified these national forces of economic and social change long recognized throughout the country. To adjust to and cope with the anguishing human problems resulting from these trends is likely to challenge our political system for years to come.

Finally, for years federal brick-and-mortar programs directed at the cities forced hard decisions on mayors, or as James Q. Wilson put it, "A mayor soon discovers that he has to hurt the poorest and weakest citizens to provide for the general welfare."[46] So, too, federal policy makers who have operated within an incrementalist value perspective of the past are now being confronted by scarcity issues as never before. The shift from growth to stability or even decline necessitates adaptation and change to which our political institutions are not equipped to respond, nor our political leaders yet fully prepared to face. Our national leaders must now deal with many of the same choices under which mayors have long labored. Their decisions will affect not just whither goes urban America, but where goes America.

## NOTES

1. *Nation's Cities,* 13 (December, 1975), p. 4.

2. Anthony Downs, "Up and Down with Ecology," *The Public Interest,* 28 (Summer, 1972), p. 39.

3. Elizabeth B. Drew, "The Energy Issue," *The New Yorker,* (July 21, 1975), p. 35.

4. See Daniel Bell, "The Year 2000—The Trajectory of an Idea," in Daniel Bell, ed., *Toward The 2000* (Boston: Houghton, Mifflin, 1968), p. 7.

5. Advisory Commission on Intergovernmental Relations, *American Federalism into the Third Century* (Washington, D.C., 1974), pp. 6–7.

6. George Sternlieb and James W. Hughes, "The Decline of Post-Industrial America," *Nation's Cities,* 73 (September, 1975), pp. 14–20.

7. ACIR, *Intergovernmental Perspective,* 1 (Fall, 1975), p. 18.

8. See Roy W. Bahl, "Recession, Inflation, and the State/Local Fisc," *Public Management,* 57 (March, 1975), pp. 2–4.

9. See Anne R. Markusen, "Inflation, Recession, and Metropolitan Public Sector Structure," *Governmental Finance,* 4 (August, 1975), pp. 8–13.

10. See Moody's Investors Service, *Pitfalls in Issuing Municipal Bonds* (New York: Moody's 1974).

11. See *National Journal,* 7 (November 29, 1975), pp. 1634–1640.

12. See Donald Haider, *When Governments Come to Washington* (New York: Free Press, 1974), chapter 7; and Jesse Burkhead, "Revenue Sharing: New Federalism or New Conservatism," paper presented at the Metropolitan Studies Conference, Syracuse, New York, March 8, 1974.

13. Patrick Healy, *The Nation's Cities: Change and Challenge* (New York: Harper & Row, 1974), chapter 1.

14. See National League of Cities, *State of the Cities–1974* (Washington, D.C.: NLC, 1975).

15. ACIR, *American Federalism: Into the Third Century*, p. 7.

16. See David Stockman, "The Social Pork Barrel," *The Public Interest*, 39 (Spring, 1975), and *Uncontrollable Federal Outlays* (Tax Foundation, 1975).

17. Reported in *The National Journal*, 7 (February 8, 1975), pp. 199–200.

18. Murray L. Weidenbaum, "Federal Finances and Inflation," in C. Lowell Harris, ed., *Inflation* (New York: Academy of Political Science, 1975), p. 82.

19. Ibid.

20. Remarks by Sidney L. Jones, Assistant Secretary of the Treasury for Economic Policy, Northwestern University, November 5, 1975.

21. "U.S. Debt Financing Is Being Felt in Money Markets," *Treasury Papers* (Washington, D.C.: October, 1975), p. 7.

22. See Alexander P. Paris, *The Coming Credit Collapse* (New Rochelle, New York: Arlington House, 1974).

23. *Business Bulletin–Cleveland Trust*, 56 (July/August, 1975), p. 1.

24. Aaron Wildavsky, *The Politics of the Budgetary Process* (Boston: Little, Brown, 1964), p. 64.

25. See Donald Haider, "The New York City Congressional Delegation," *City Almanac*, 7 (April, 1973).

26. See David A. Grossman, "The Lindsay Legacy: A Partisan Appraisal," *City Almanac*, 8 (October, 1973); and Edward K. Hamilton, "Productivity: The New York City Approach," *Public Administration Review*, 32 (December, 1972), pp. 784–794.

27. ACIR, *City Financial Emergencies* (Washington, D.C., 1973), pp. 3, 49.

28. See Donald Haider and Thomas Elmore, "New York At the Crossroads," *City Almanac*, 5 (February, 1975).

29. Wallace S. Sayre, "The Mayor," in Lyle Fitch and A.H. Walsh, eds., *Agenda For a City* (Beverly Hills, Cal.: Sage Publications, 1970), p. 587.

30. See Allen Schick, *Central Budget Issues under the New York City Charter* (State Charter Revision Commission for New York City, 1974).

31. See the *New York Times*, April 7, 1975, p. 54; May 29, 1975, p. 26; July 7, 1975, p. 33.

32. Raymond D. Horton, *Reforming the Municipal Labor Relations Process in New York City* (State Charter Revision Commission for New York City, 1975), p. 7.

33. Bernard Jump, *New York City Pensions* (State Study Commission for New York City, 1973).

34. See Donald Haider, "The State and the Federal Government," in R.H. Connery and G. Benjamin, eds., *Governing New York State: The Rockefeller Years* (New York City: Academy of Political Science, 1974), pp. 85–94.

35. See Ken Auletta, "Who's to Blame for the Fix We're in?" *New York Magazine*, 8 (October 27, 1975), pp. 29–41.

36. *New York Times*, November 27, 1975, p. 43.

37. Ibid., October 19, 1975, p. 1.

38. Ibid., November 27, 1975, p. 1.

39. *Daily Bond Buyer,* September 11, 1975, pp. 2, 18.

40. *New York Times,* December 22, 1975, p. 28.

41. Wallace S. Sayre and Herbert Kaufman, *Governing New York City* (New York: W. W. Norton, 1965), p. 738.

42. See Sayre, pp. 564–566.

43. See *New York City: Economic Base and Fiscal Capacity* (Maxwell School Research Project on the Public Finances of New York City, 1973).

44. See Irving Kristol, "New York Is a State of Mind," *Wall Street Journal,* December 10, 1975, p. 20.

45. Moody's Investors Services, Inc., "Municipal Credit Report—City of New York," April 8, 1975, p. 1.

46. James Q. Wilson, "The War on Cities," *The Public Interest,* 3 (Spring, 1966), p. 30.

Part Four

# New Dimensions of Urban Decision Making: Internal and External Influences

Chapter Nine

# New Federalism: Centralization and Local Control in Perspective

PETER A. LUPSHA

Harry N. Scheiber, in a brilliant essay written in 1966, laid to rest the accepted model of the evolution of American federalism.[1] Rather than the "cooperative federalism" or "marble cake" of intergovernmental sharing presented by Professors Grodzins and Daniel Elazar with its supposed continuity over time, Professor Scheiber correctly noted that a more accurate view is one of a period of "Rivalistic State Mercantilism," 1790–1860, followed by "Centralizing Federalism," 1860–1960, and blooming of centralization of power in the federal government with the "New Deal," 1933–1941.[2] While there have been fluctuations in the pattern—the Eisenhower years, the JFK-OEO period, Lyndon Johnson's "Great Society" and Richard Nixon's revenue sharing—it is the contention of this paper that political centralization, like economic centralization, has been as Scheiber describes it. It is the basic and the continuing theme of American federalism despite occasional rhetoric and gestures to the contrary.

The importance of the Grodzins-Elazar model which is today the accepted textbook and "informed citizen" view of federalism must not be underestimated. For, as Scheiber notes:

> ... it lends the weight of historical authority and precedent to the *status quo,* or indeed to any centralization of power that is accompanied by arrangements for the sharing of administrative functions. It has the further

I would like to thank the following for giving of their time and thought to advise, criticize and comment on this paper in its various forms and to provide it with their insights, although they may not fully agree with its views: Dorothy Cline, Art Blumenfeld, Jim Jaramillo, Frank Coppler, Lee Zink, Herb Smith, Robert U. Anderson, Joe Trujillo, Roy Cornelius, Dan Weaks, Richard Weissman, Paul Hain, Robert Locander, Ursula Hill and Sylvia Banes.

advantage of discrediting those who fear centralization because they attribute the historic strength of representative government in America to a tradition of dual federalism. "One cannot hark back to the good old days of State and local independence," Grodzins declared, "because those days never existed. This refrain was echoed, with good political effect, by Lyndon Johnson . . ."[3]

Lyndon Johnson is not the only liberal to echo this refrain with political effect. It has become a part of the litany of American liberal thought. The centralization of power in the federal government over the states, cities and citizens has been part of the liberal credo since the New Deal with its NRA, TVA, WPA, welfare and social security programs and its stress on the Keynesian economic theory. In the Kennedy years it returned to Washington with the academic cadre, OEO, Peace Corps, and the belief that brains, rationality, good will and a little money could solve basic social problems. And, in the back of the minds of most of us policy oriented political scientists, the elitist perspective of this centralist position remains today. The following are some of the basic premises of this centralist perspective.

**Premise One**: *That the United States is a national community with a relatively homogeneous culture.*
If one travels by plane, lives within the Bos-Wash, Chi-Pitts, San-San, Sea-Tac urban strips, watches only network news, and buys mainly the products of the petrochemical majors and agribusiness giants—that is, the "name brands"—we Americans appear to be wrapped in very similar plastic. But these are superficial indicators and represent neither the needs or reality of the American people.
Rather than a national community, the United States is still a very hetero-geneous community containing highly urbanized and cosmopolitan bands along its coasts and inland seas, but also containing vast rural and underdeveloped areas. Cultural and political pluralism is still the norm in America even if corporate centralization has provided a veneer of homogeneity. Unfortunately for rooted people, the less mobile masses who travel by bus instead of plane, power in America rests with airborne cosmopolitan elite. The social scientist or social engineer who makes policy, the corporate or union head who promotes it, the congressman and administrator who implement it, are a rather homogeneous national community, but they do not necessarily represent either the culture and needs of the people in the 50 states or the people's values.
Robert Merriam, Advisory Commission on Intergovernmental Relations Chairman, puts it this way:

> . . . The answers of people in the Ozark Mountains will not be those of the people of the areas of Puget Sound, . . . in each area the definitions and priorities may change more rapidly than any Washington-level administra-tor could envisage. People in Maine's Washington County may be willing to

cope with what the rest of us would call poverty if they can be left alone
to take their living from the sea and the land . . . a set of problems . . . far
better bargained out in (the locality) than on the Potomac.[4]

I find it somewhat amusing that the heterogeneity of the American people
has once again been discovered by political science. Ira Sharkansky in his most
recent work, *The United States: A Study of a Developing Country,* illustrates his
firm grasp on the obvious by finding that the American system suffers from
economic and racial dualism.[5] In fairness to Sharkansky, it is nice to find an
intelligent establishment scholar writing about the social and economic disparities to be found in the United States. Being a liberal, however, Sharkansky's
solution is another centralist premise, the setting of national goals and priorities.

**Premise Two**: *That there exists a set of national priorities.*
It would be nice if this were true. One centralist, Michael Reagan, in his book,
*The New Federalism,* states that anything that can get through the maze of
Congress is a national priority.[6] This view of our priorities seems as short-sighted
as the Congress often is. If we define priority in this manner, actions and
inactions of merit and expedience all become part of our collective goals as does
the Vietnamese War, tax breaks for Lockheed and TWA, as well as tariffs for the
chocolate covered cherry lobby and subsidies for New England ski operators
who lost money because of poor weather and insufficient snow.

If only there were a federal public agency doing long-range national planning,
assembling and offering for debate a set of national priorities, one could be
much more sympathetic with the centralist perspective. But, unfortunately, such
an agency does not exist. There is no long range domestic policy planning, or
setting of national priorities at the federal level at the present time, and to look
to Congress as the agency to set policy is a poor solution.

The problem with priorities is that we are not a homogeneous nation that is
in agreement on its values. Even within a given community or classroom, one is
not likely to find a complete value consensus. Thus the priorities question
becomes one of "It depends." That is, if the decision reflects my values it is fine;
if not, it is a mistake. Certainly there are certain sets of values that most of us
can agree upon: fairness, safety, opportunity, the first amendment freedoms; but
as Stouffer long ago found, we Americans often agree on them more as abstractions than as concrete realities.[7] Thus it is difficult simply to give over to that
small national community of policy makers, often with elitist biases and little
contact with the hinterland, the full freedom of priority setting.

**Premise Three**: *That the federal government is more sensitive to the majority
of American citizens and better able to withstand the assaults of vested interests
than are the states and local jurisdiction.*
This argument rests on the historical inefficiency and corruption found in

state and city government, the mistaken view that the "best" men are in Washington, and the out-of-date belief that Washington is less likely to be subject to the pressures of special interests than are state and local governments which are often dependent on a single or very narrow economic base. Given recent history, one would have to say, "It depends." For the key issue is visibility, and until recently a citizen had an extremely hard time finding out what went on in Washington; now he only has a difficult time. At the state and city level, pressure and corruption were easily observed and leaked to a muckraking press—a kind of press which was not considered good form in Washington until Watergate.

As Katznelson and Kesselman put it in their new text on American government:

> . . . local governments are responsive to a different set of interests than the national government. The latter is closely allied with corporate capital and to a lesser extent, consumer and organized-labor interests. Local governments are more responsive to small scale capital.[8]

Certainly these differences will lead to differences in responsiveness. But while the federal government may be more responsive at one time, there are real questions about whether it is responsive or responsible at all times and in all jurisdictions. The Federal Emergency Highway Act forced states to establish 55 mile per hour speed limits or lose federal highway funds. This may be a responsible act in the crowded urban coastal areas, but it may not be a responsible or economic policy for the wide open spaces of Texas, Wyoming or New Mexico. Federal gun control may make sense in a crowded city, but not where the sheriff is 100 miles from your door. Similarly, the HUD regulations that no subsidized low-income housing can be built in neighborhoods (census tracts) where 15 percent or more of the housing is already subsidized, may be fine for promoting the dispersion of poverty populations in overcrowded Eastern cities, but it does not help the mountain villages or barrios of New Mexico. For where people have lived in a community for hundreds of years, they simply need new housing and not the dispersal and death of their neighborhood.

Indeed, it took five years and seven site visits to get HUD to recognize adobe, the most popular building material in New Mexico, as adequate for HUD construction because, being a homemade product, it was not part of the standard engineering list of accepted (corporate made and tested) building materials. Given that adobe homes have been constructed, are standing and have been lived in for over three hundred years, HUD's attitude does not suggest that the federal government, in this case, was either sensitive or responsive to the poor of New Mexico. And, unfortunately, this is not an isolated example of bureaucratic insensitivity.

**Premise Four**: *That innovation and experimentation tend to come from federal proposals and initiatives, not from state or local governments.*

This premise may not be accepted by all centralists; but one, Michael Reagan, presents it as an important part of his thesis for centralization. Regan points to the National Defense Education Act (NDEA), the Economic Opportunity programs, Head Start and Community Mental Health Programs as examples of Washington centered innovations.[9]

But this, like the earlier premises, can only be answered, "It depends." For every federal innovation cited by centralists such as NDEA, Community Mental Health Clinics, NSF programs, one can cite examples of state and local innovations. Contrary to Reagan's view that O.E.O. was a top-down Washington innovation, much of the O.E.O. idea came from below, from city innovations, community ideas stimulated by private foundations and then assisted as pilot projects by federal funds until they received national funding.[10]

One can also cite other examples of local governments undertaking innovations, such as Pittsburgh taking the initiative to clean up soft coal pollution decades before there was an EPA. Or one can site Seattle, Washington; Jacksonville, Florida; and states like Illinois which had model emergency medical systems years before they were seen as a national priority and incorporated into federal legislation. To this list one can add other state innovations such as tax circuit breakers for the poor and aged, passage of equal rights provisions for women, progressive educational equalization funding formulas and child labor laws, many of which were traditionally part of the textbook litany on the experimental value of the states in the federal model.

**Premise Five**: *That given the imbalances in the fiscal relations and activities of the various levels of government, only the federal government has the wherewithal to meet state and city needs.*

This premise is based on Walter Heller's now famous dictum: "Prosperity gives the national government the affluence and the local governments the effluents."[11] This view has been reinforced of late by New York City's fiscal plight. Heller's view was the basis for much of the so-called redistribution strategy contained in the "New Federalism." Fiscal disparities, local structural taxing constraints and governmental fragmentation all pointed to the need for a redistribution of money in some sweeping manner that would go beyond the limitations and difficulties of the categorical and bloc grant programs.

Because one of the key premises of the centralist view is that the national government should use its affluence to equalize local resources at the same time it establishes national standards and priorities, revenue sharing and grant consolidation seemed to offer an answer. For the liberal economists like Heller this had an added advantage. It would tax surpluses and spend them in the public sector rather than returning them to the people in the form of tax cuts.[12] At the same time the entitlements of special revenue sharing would make sure that national priorities are addressed in the six functional areas (law enforcement, manpower training, transportation, rural development and education). Administrative oversight would remain in these areas, continuing to upgrade and improve the quality of local administration. The now common federal "boiler plate" of non-discrimination and affirmative action would help ensure that these national social objectives were achieved. Thus to many, while revenue sharing might need improvement and incremental alteration, it was a "good" thing.

Michael Reagan is of special interest as a centralist, for he takes an extreme position. To him the new federalism revenue sharing is a mistake that will permit the inadequate, inefficient, oft times racist, weak local and state governments to undermine the national community. But once again Reagan speaks more eloquently than I:

> . . . The essence of the so-called New Federalism is in fact reactionary (in the literal sense) notion of moving back toward a day when there were no national priorities, when there was no particular content to the concept of national citizenship, when to speak of one's "community" usually meant one's home town, and perhaps sometimes one's state, but never the United States as an integrated national entity. The New Federalism is, in short, simply romantic rhetoric, a facade behind which the national government is to abrogate its domestic role to that of an onlooker.[13]

Was Reagan correct? Enough research has been done to illustrate the general trends and directions of this shift in intergovernmental relations under new federalism and what these might imply for the future.

Reagan, one finds, is rather prescient on this, and so before proceeding, it is well to sum up his view of the future of intergovernmental relations. First, he feels the predominant mode of federal assistance will still be categorical grants with some attempts to consolidate block grants. Revenue sharing "in the true sense of funds supplied without programmatic strings of any kind is not likely to amount to much."[14] Second,

> . . . the fundamental trend in the development of our intergovernmental system will be the continued further development of the notion of a national community and a further ideological acceptance of the corollary proposition that it is proper for the goals and standards of public service to be set by the national government as a basis for uniform rights for citizens no matter where they live.[15]

Third, Reagan's ideal is "Permissive Federalism," in which "the state's share rests upon the permission and permissiveness of the national government."[16] Fourth, federal aid is used for purposes selected by the national legislature and that this in turn "has created a nationally dominated system of shared powers and shared functions."[17]

If one accepts this view, and it is increasingly the dominant view of the upper middle-class, academic liberal, socially concerned and policy creating opinion leaders of this country, then the future of intergovernmental relations for our cities is simply more of what we have seen under the era of grants-in-aid.

There may be some slight adjustment of the intergovernmental pendulum in the direction of loose money general revenue sharing and special purpose "entitlements," but the pressures from the "concerned community" as well as Washington will probably mean that in the long run Reagan is correct and revenue sharing will become "simply romantic rhetoric."

Indeed, a recent HEW memo dated July 18, 1975 and sent to the cities reinforces Reagan's position. Entitled "Strengthening Public Management in the Intergovernmental System," this memo summarizes a three-volume study recently completed for the agency under the same title.[18] It finds basically that the new federalism has failed because the states and cities lack the management capability to interface with the federal agencies and regional councils. While citing the rhetoric of decentralization, its message is clear. Here are some conclusions:

1. The Executive Branch and Congress have taken significant steps to devolve decisions on allocation of Federal resources and to decentralize and simplify the administration of federal programs.
2. These measures have been insufficient to meet even the most minimal criteria for establishing a genuine partnership with State and local governments for the design, execution and coordination of federal programs by place or jurisdiction.
3. The responsibility for improved Federal-State-Local partnerships in the achievement of national domestic program objectives does not rest with federal government alone. But Federal government leadership is required.[19]

One need not read further to see between the lines that it is Michael Reagan's permissive kind of partnership. Or as Governor Lamm of Colorado put it at a recent energy conference:

The federal government said this was to be a partnership. Now I know what kind—not an equal partnership, but one where they are the senior partner.[20]

This is the decentralization of the new federalism. An administrative decentralization where the state and local governments dance to music written and choreographed in Washington and checked by a regional office to make sure no essential steps are missed.

What about revenue sharing? Isn't that free money which the cities can play with to write their own tune? In some sense it is, but as I will argue, it has often created expectations and demands which, while satisfying short-run problems, often lead to long-run, even permanently crippling, problems for our cities. But first, let's see what the experts have found in their studies of the "new federalism" of revenue sharing.

Most cities have played (politically) the revenue sharing game rather poorly. From the beginning most cities panicked, taking the view that revenue sharing was likely to be a one-shot phenomenon, and placed their initial entitlements into bricks, mortar, equipment and other one-shot projects. Richard Nathan's study for the Brookings Institution, for example, found that close to half of all local revenue-sharing money (46%) went to new capital improvements.[21] Given the inconsistent and vacillating behavior of the federal government toward cities in the recent past, this behavior can be seen as rational, although short sighted. A far more politically astute and social-change oriented strategy would have been to put the bulk of the funds into the social (youth, poverty and aging) programs that were cut as revenue sharing was created and mobilize a long-term national constituency to maintain and enlarge the redistribution of the federal tax wealth.

But it is perhaps foolish to chide the cities on this, for the demands were many and the resources slim. The most hard-pressed cities used revenue sharing, as Nathan found, for "substitutions" to provide tax breaks and lessen the threat of taxpayer revolts.[22] While this lowering of pressure may have been good news to harassed local officials, city employees and taxpayers, substitution also meant that the uses reported of revenue sharing may hide the real use, i.e., of "freeing up" funds from the regular budget for use elsewhere.[23]

In terms of the theme of this paper, however, we can say that one effect of general revenue sharing has been an increase in the short-run freedom of cities, particularly the hard pressed ones, by "freeing up" local revenues to meet demands (especially demands for larger, better equipped police departments, salary increases to increasingly stronger and more militant municipal employee unions), perhaps at the long-run expense of the broader public interest and national priorities. The Clearing House study for example found that "revenue sharing has not been a significant resource for social services; less than 2 percent in 1973 and 1974. In contrast . . . 75 percent of the GRS dollars went for public safety, chiefly police departments."[24] This is a finding worthy of further exploration.

A brief case study. Albuquerque, New Mexico, in 1972, was said to have a crime problem. It ranked number one on the FBI's list of high property crime cities. One rarely felt unsafe walking the streets at night, however; more than 80 percent of the people surveyed during the period said they did not feel afraid. Indeed, there was a crime problem, but part of it was because the then chief of police wanted to build a "L.A. type" professional department. All "crimes" were religiously reported to the FBI, and the value of stolen goods was often inflated to meet insurance requirements as well as to make the FBI crime charts. The Safe Streets Act, LEAA, and revenue sharing all combined to make the chief's dream a reality. On the first year of the new federalism, 100 new officers were hired; through LEAA, new computer technology and hardware were bought; the crime problem declined. The force went from 381 officers to 505 in less than three years. Their salaries make up more than 10 percent of the city's total budget. In the summer of 1975 they struck for higher pay; 324 policemen resigned, and for two weeks the city was patrolled by 181 administrative and desk officers working twelve-hour shifts. What happened? The crime rate continued to fall.

The point of this example is to highlight what New York and every other major American city is experiencing: an overcommitment to provide services and the overemployment of personnel to provide them. In New York, there is one city employee for every 24 citizens; Los Angeles has one for 55; Chicago one for 73.[25] This may mean good service, but is it really necessary? And more important, would this overservice have occurred without the inducement and lure of federal funding and programs? Certainly Albuquerque would have had fewer policemen but equally adequate service if the extra resources of revenue sharing had not been available; perhaps for other cities—cities like New York or Newark—the picture is more clouded.

Another early finding is that revenue sharing funds have apparently breathed new life into many archaic, overlapping and dysfunctional political and jurisdictional units. Many counties, special districts and townships that were about to die a natural death were given new power and influence through the funds provided by revenue sharing.

Whether this is a "good" or "bad" happening depends on the values one brings to the issue. From the standpoint of this paper, one can note simply that general revenue sharing has again increased the short-run freedom of these units, if not their effectiveness.[26] One study states the issue this way:

> In some cases distributing revenue-sharing funds to essentially all general purpose governments regardless of size or fiscal condition tends to perpetuate inefficiency by reducing fiscal pressure which might otherwise cause units to consolidate with other units to form more economically viable governments.[27]

While it is easy to think of this as a short-range freedom, it is likely to be a long-run fetter. To foster the continuance of non-viable units only frustrates the citizens and the system's ability—whether local or nations—to meet their needs. An additional problem for rural small towns and an interesting twist on the dilemma of intergovernmental relations is that not only were the allotments insufficient to be of real value, but that federal demands and requirements in other program areas often resulted in the revenue sharing funds simply being transferred from one federal project to another. Many small cities in New Mexico, for example, spent their entire revenue-sharing allotment on backhoes and bulldozers to meet federal EPA sanitary land-fill requirements.[28]

For such cities, revenue sharing is a freedom only in the sense that it allows the community to continue accepting the demands of other federal programs without having to use local money and alert the local citizenry to the reality of the federal demands.

From the value perspective of the centralists, perhaps the most critical finding of the revenue sharing studies is that the early results seem to indicate that (a) increased citizen participation is not encouraged and (b) that spending reinforces local patterns of sex and racial job discrimination.[29] Naturally there are wide variations from area to area. In one study 44 percent of public officials polled in Michigan said their communities had taken poor measures to encourage citizen participation,[30] while in another study Phoenix, Arizona and Los Angeles, California and several other cities were given "high marks" for encouraging citizen participation.[31]

The finding concerning job discrimination and both a lack of compliance and a lack of enforcement by federal officials is quite serious. According to data from ten cities, there are disproportionately fewer minorities and women in public employment, particularly in areas where the bulk of revenue sharing money has been expended—police and fire department hiring.[32] If this pattern is nationwide and these preliminary findings hold, it will have important consequences for revenue sharing and future intergovernmental relations.

In addition, the finding that the cities have not in general picked up the social service programs for the poor and aged which were cut by the federal government could also have important ramifications. To my knowledge, the city of Salem and Lane County, Oregon are the only political subdivisions in the country to make an active and coordinated attempt to use revenue sharing money to this end.

But it is perhaps unreasonable for the centralists to expect that cities, with their vast problems, limited resources and unmet traditional demands, should use their general revenue funds for social programs, particularly federally initiated programs that cities had not expected to be saddled with. The need, the demand, and most important the organization, however, are there; and thus if the Clearinghouse study is correct, one can expect that community organizations in 1975 will increase their demands for entitlements and what they feel is their proper share of federal revenue funds.[33]

From these revenue-sharing studies one can conclude that the new federalism is not working as planned. One might also conclude that the emphasis on money and fiscal federalism is misplaced. For it now appears that money creates problems as well as solving them.

While it is true that the federal government has too big a share of the nation's tax revenue, simple redistribution may not be the whole answer. In the long run, it might have been better simply to give the money to the people and let them solve their own problems.

**Premise Six**: *That the states and localities lack the talent and resources of Washington and are thus less effective and efficient than the national government.*

As liberal academician Christopher Jencks commented, the best men

> are the most mobile, and in any community the "natural elite" is likely to be composed largely of the recent arrivals. Such men usually think in national terms taking little interest in state [and local] politics.[34]

Jencks, however, most clearly captures the elitism of the centralist perspective when he goes on to say:

> Similarly, the trouble with Massachusetts politics is not that Boston and Newton have too few votes; it is that people like the Saltonstalls, Lodges, and Kennedys do not spend their time trying to clean up the State House; they want to use their home state as a springboard to Washington.[35]

**Premise Seven**: *That state (and local) governments tend to be "structurally inadequate and politically weak, even when not actually corrupt."*[36]

They simply are not up to the job (with a few notable exceptions: New York, California, Wisconsin) of delivering to the needs of their people as well as is the central government in Washington.

These premises are as debatable as those that preceded them, but taken as a total *Weltanschauung,* they make up the core of the centralist philosophy. They also make up the political reality, if not the verbalization, of new federalism. Under this system, state and local governments may appear to have new freedom and discretion, more money and more control, but in the long run, this is more appearance than reality. For this new freedom is offset by new administrative demands, new judicial and planning controls, and continued categorical grants. For, along with the new federalism and its rhetoric of decentralization has come the development of "supersessive" legislation—legislation which deprives the state and local governments of jurisdiction and gives it to federal agencies, federal guidelines and federal control.

James Croy, as far as I know the first to examine this new aspect of intergovernmental relations, notes five classes or types of federal supersession.[37] They are:

1. *Overt supersession.* Here the federal intent is clear and the wording

blunt ". . . this Act shall supersede any and all laws of the States and political subdivisions thereof. . . ."

Examples are: the Civil Rights Act of 1964; the Fair Packaging and Labeling Act; and the Noise Control Act of 1972.

2. *The Unless-Surprise type:* Here the intent is not to supersede state law "unless" state law disagrees with the federal legislation and then ("surprise") the federal act supersedes the state law or that of its political subdivisions.

Examples are: Gun Control Act of 1968; the Drug Abuse Control Amendments of 1965; the Federal Metal and Non-Metallic Mine Safety Act.

3. *The "if-then; if-then" type:* If a state does not issue regulations acceptable to the federal government, then a federal agency or department will; and if the state does not adopt and enforce these laws, then the federal government will assume jurisdiction over that area.

Examples are: the Water Quality Control Act of 1965, the Occupational Safety and Health Act of 1970, the Clean Air Act Amendments of 1970.

4. *The "fiat" type:* Here the federal legislation, by stating that only the provisions of this particular act shall apply in a given situation, blocks the ability of states or local governments to act in that area.

Examples are: Federal Cigarette Labeling and Advertising Act, and the Marine Mammal Protection Act of 1972.

5. *The "administrative directive" type:* Here federal regulations give authority to federal agents to act or make decisions in states or their political subdivisions. For example: the Secretary of Agriculture is given authority to determine what the *county* wheat acreage allotments will be. HUD officials determine how much new publicly subsidized housing will go into a neighborhood, etc.

There is also the modified impoundment process used in the Emergency Highway Conservation Act, which could be called the "do this, or lose your federal money form." In addition to this legislative and administrative supersession, categorical grants with all their administrative rules and guidelines continue to grow and to hamper initiative.

Overall, the real problem with the new federalism, as with any Washington created format, is *administrative federalism.* It is the problem of the translation of congressional intention "to end poverty," "to insure an adequate and full life for all our senior citizens," and other such abstractions, into federal guidelines, accounting forms and administrative rules and procedures.

Daniel Elazar has noted one aspect of this problem:

The federal government does exert a potentially negative influence on municipal governmental organization through the impact of its own administrative structure . . . at the local level the federal government is represented by the outermost projections of its bureaucratic pyramid—a profusion of specialized agencies and bureaus, each with its own programmatic concerns and professional biases. Quite frequently—one is tempted to say invariably—the federal bureaucratic fragmentation, which is a legitimate organizational concomitant of the administration of several different programs, becomes a source of extreme fragmentation and disharmony at the community level as different federal line agencies make differing demands upon local governments.[38]

I quote this at some length, for Elazar illuminates a critical problem of intergovernmental relations for the cities, particularly under the grants-in-aid programs, a continuing problem for cities now under general revenue sharing and particularly special revenue sharing entitlements.

An example of this problem: In Albuquerque, New Mexico, the Department of Transportation (DOT) funded a computer routine for the local Council of Governments (COG) to do transportation surveys. Part of this system contained a license check through which all past and current motor vehicle violations on a given car were recorded. The purpose of this was supposedly to pinpoint areas of the city where speeding most commonly occurred and the type of vehicle involved. At the same time LEAA granted funds to the municipal court system to improve calendar organization by developing a computerized system of warrants outstanding on moving traffic violations. A short time later, LEAA also funded a computerized system for the Correction and Detention department to find out at what point in the judicial process each outstanding police warrant was. In this way, the federal government not only funded a threefold duplication of effort, but none of the systems can interface. Different machine languages and formats were used and different consultants hired to design the systems.

As a result, COG can tell you a traffic violator's past record, while the municipal court has to find out by a hand search; and only Corrections and Detentions have the process data needed by the judicial system. This happened because of federal and local administrative fragmentation and because even with the OMB A–95 review, no one, state, local or federal, is responsible for making sure duplication is avoided. Combine this with each agency's desire to spend its allotment, to look good, be modern and be professional, and it all adds up to waste.

The problem of bureaucratic organization and administration is the most important problem of intergovernmental relations today. For despite all the changes and attempts at administrative streamlining that have occurred in recent years, the lack of a clean, simple, standardized mesh between local governments and federal agencies and administrators complicates and increases the problems of intergovernmental relations, trust and of fast, efficient management of program adoption, adaptation and delivery.

Thus the problem of the new federalism is basically the problem of all interrelations—communication, regulation, agency myopia and self protection, and a lack of willingness by all parties to serve the people instead of their agency or personal interest.

In sum, the new federalism, when placed in perspective, is nothing more than another rhetorical rock thrown into the stream of the continuing centralization of power in America. It may divert the course momentarily, but the historical current of Washington-based authority is too strong to change the reality of a continuing loss of state and local autonomy and control.

**NOTES**

1. Harry N. Scheiber, "The Condition of American Federalism: An Historian's View," Subcommittee on Intergovernmental Relations (Washington: Government Printing Office, October 15, 1966).

2. Ibid., pp. 4–14.

3. Ibid., p. 2.

4. Robert E. Merriam, "American Federalism—A Paradox of Promise and Performance," address given at Advisory Commission on Intergovernmental Relations National Conference on American Federalism in Action, Washington, D. C., February 20, 1975, p. 24.

5. Ira Sharkansky, *The United States: A Study of a Developing Nation* (New York: David McKay, 1975).

6. Michael Reagan, *The New Federalism* (New York: Oxford University Press, 1972), p. 11.

7. Samuel Stouffer, *Communism, Conformity and Civil Liberties* (New York: Doubleday, 1955).

8. Ira Katznelson and Mark Kesselman, *The Politics of Power* (New York: Harcourt, Brace, Jovanovich, 1975), p. 130.

9. Reagan, pp. 65–68.

10. See Russell Murphy, *Political Entrepreneurs and Urban Poverty* (Lexington, Mass.: D. C. Heath and Company, 1971, and Fred Powledge, *Model City* (New York: Simon and Schuster, Inc., 1970).

11. Walter W. Heller, *New Dimensions of Political Economy* (Cambridge, Mass.: Harvard University Press, 1967), p. 129.

12. Cited by Reagan, p. 82.

13. Ibid., p. 163.

14. Ibid., p. 154.

15. Ibid., p. 155.

16. Ibid., p. 163.

17. Ibid., p. 145.

18. Memorandum to City of Albuquerque from Department of Health, Education and Welfare, Dallas Regional Office, July 18, 1975.

19. Ibid., p. 6.

20. Videotape interview, 6 O'Clock Reports, Channel 13 News, July 28, 1975. Western Governor's Energy Conference, Santa Fe, New Mexico.

21. Richard P. Nathan et al., *Monitoring Revenue Sharing* (Washington, D.C.: Brookings Institution, 1975). Cited, *The Brookings Bulletin,* 12(Winter, 1975), p. 4.

22. Ibid.

23. National Clearing House Study, cited "Revenue Sharing Progress Report," *Nation's Cities* (February 1975), p. 21.

24. Ibid., p. 22.

25. *Newsweek,* (August 4, 1975), p. 20.

26. Tom Littlewood, "Washington," *Illinois Issues,* (January 1975), p. 31.

27. Tax Foundation, *Tax Review,* 35 (November 1974).

28. Roy Cornelius, "The Impact of Revenue Sharing in New Mexico," paper presented at the Western Political Science Association Meeting, Denver, 1974.

29. National Clearing House on Revenue Sharing, *Revenue Sharing Clearing House,* (Nov./Dec. 1974), p. 4. Also see Joint Center for Political Studies, *Focus,* 3 (March 1975), pp. 4, 5.

30. Ibid., p. 1.

31. *Nation's Cities,* p. 24.

32. *Clearing House,* p. 5.

33. Ibid., p. 6.

34. Christopher Jencks, "Why Bail Out the States?" *The New Republic* (December 12, 1964), pp. 8–10. Cited by Reagan, p. 113.

35. Ibid., p. 10.

36. Reagan, p. 111.

37. James B. Croy, "Federal Supersession: The Road to Domination," *State Government* (Winter 1975), pp. 32–36.

38. Daniel Elazar, "Fragmentation and Local Organizational Response to Federal-City Programs," *Urban Affairs Quarterly,* 24 (December 1969), p. 24.

**Chapter Ten**

# Urban Government as a
# Policy-Making System

**DOUGLAS YATES**

## Introduction

Whether or not there is a "new" urban politics, there is unquestionably a new tradition of urban political analysis. It has been almost twenty years now since Lawrence Herson wrote bleakly of the "lost world of municipal government."[1] Since then, there has been a significant resurgence of interest in the urban political system. That interest was kindled at first by the community power debate and was given urgency by the discovery of an "urban crisis" and the concomitant outbreak of urban rioting in the 1960s. And although the community power debate has proven notably persistent—generating a small library of research and analysis—various other approaches have sprung up to extend and enrich urban political analysis.

Thus, we now have a variety of comparative approaches[2] which seek to identify significant differences between urban systems, as well as studies of taxing and spending,[3] poor non-white communities,[4] citizen participation and protest,[5] and urban bureaucracies.[6] What has been lacking in urban research to date, however, is an exploration of the urban policy-making process—viewed from the perspective of mayors and high-level administrators who deal with urban problems and policies on a day-to-day basis. Aside from the various frameworks provided by the pluralists and anti-pluralists (e.g., executive centered coalitions, non-decisions, etc.), we lack concepts and categories for understanding and evaluating the character of urban policy making. Further, as will be seen below, the main theories of political decision making in national government (rational analysis and incrementalism) are inadequate for urban analysis because they miss the intricacy, uncertainty and instability of decision "games" in the city.

The aim of this paper is to develop an analytic model of urban policy making

235

which reflects the distinctive characteristic of urban government and politics. The point of this paper is to explain why urban policy makers seem to be constantly crisis hopping: bouncing from one problem to another and from one hopeful solution to another. The implication of this paper is that given the level and range of demands that are placed on urban policy makers and the instability of the resultant policy-making process, the prospects for "orderly" agenda setting, planning and implementation are very slim. Rather seen as a policy-making system, urban government looks to be fundamentally "ungovernable." That is, city government seems to be out of control, lacking a rudder or perhaps steered by 100 rudders working in opposite directions. More concretely, I will argue that urban policy is fragmented, erratic, reactive and unstable because the urban policy-making process is fragmented, erratic, reactive and unstable.

### Three Caveats

I should make it clear at the outset that I am not seeking here to add to or revise the corpus of community power analysis. The structure of community power obviously shapes policy making but it is not my concern to examine that linkage. Rather I am concerned to illuminate how city government, understood as a system as compared to state or national governments, reacts to its characteristic problems: service complaints, conflicts between neighborhoods, busing controversies, demands for participation and the like. This focus calls attention to the nature and impact of different urban problems, issue contexts, configurations of participants and bureaucratic settings. And it places emphasis on the decision routes and networks along which demands travel and through which decisions are worked out (or not) between different urban policy makers. The presumption of this policy-making approach is that the outcome of any given policy-making "game" is powerfully shaped by the problem, issue context, bureaucratic setting and configuration of policy makers involved. Put in its strongest and most debatable form, my argument is that the structure of the urban policy-making process will largely determine the content of public policy—whatever the nature of the "power structure" in a particular city.

This approach has its roots in the decision-making approaches of Lindblom and Allison[8] and in the organization theory of March and Simon.[9] Further, it draws on Norton Long's provocative notion of local government as an "ecology of games"[10] and Theodore Lowi's argument that to a large extent policies determine politics in American government.[11] In general, the approach takes a close-up "interior" problem-solving view of urban policy making. It attempts to "model" the way the urban world looks to central policy makers seeking to sort through a bewildering array of problems, deal with constantly changing sets of policy contestants and find appropriate policy responses in an uncertain, unstable, decision-making context.

A second caveat is that I am making no attempt here to present a comparative analysis of urban policy making. Clearly, I have in mind big city politics; that is, politics in Detroit, Boston, Chicago, Cleveland, Baltimore, New York or Philadelphia. But beyond this distinction, I will avoid comparisons between cities for the simple reason that I am concerned to illuminate what is common and shared in urban policy making. Rather than asking how Chicago differs from New York or Baltimore, I want to ask how the urban policy-making system differs from state or national policy making. My premise is that a main reason we have not made more rapid progress in understanding urban policy making is that analysts have not paid sufficient attention to what is distinctive, i.e., "special" about the urban political and governmental system. And lacking a persuasive characterization of what makes the city different, we equally lack a strong justification for doing "urban" political analysis rather than simply public policy analysis or the analysis of American government in general.

A final caveat is that in constructing an analytical model of what urban problems and policy-making processes look like to a central urban policy maker, I am not speaking about the mayor or the police chief *per se*. For mayors or police chiefs, in fact, do not encounter all of the problems and demands that bubble up from the street level—although they certainly see many of them. Thus the central policy maker, whose perspective we take in this paper, is an analytic construct designed to provide an overview of the full range of urban problems, demands, decision "games" and policy responses.

### Power Analysis Versus Policy-Making Analysis

I have said that this paper does not follow the contours of the community power debate. Rather we ask: how do different demands and problems arise and how does government respond to them? What are the main decision networks in urban policy making and how do different problems and issues travel along them? The difference between a community power analysis and a policy-making analysis can be clearly seen if we examine the case studies of decision making found in Dahl's *Who Governs?*[12] and Banfield's *Political Influence*[13] from the two different perspectives.

Dahl looks at the structure of power and decision making in the areas of urban renewal, education and party nominations. What interests him, given his concern to evaluate the power elite thesis, is that different actors (and configurations of actors) exercised power in the three cases. This suggests to Dahl that power and decision making are not monolithic in New Haven but rather pluralistic—characterized by an executive-centered coalition, revolving around Mayor Richard C. Lee.

From a policy-making approach, what catches our attention about the three cases is that they involved such different problems and issues that they represented very different policy-making processes. Two of the cases, urban renewal and education, involved the delivery of public services—services which have a tangible impact on urban residents. But there are significant differences between the goods and services involved. Renewal involved large-scale capital construction that, as Dahl notes, initially seemed to offer something to everybody. In this sense, renewal at first appeared to be a classic public good—a benefit to all members of the community because it promised to revitalize the city as a whole. For this reason, citizen demands and interests were not at first sharply articulated or sharply conflicting. The mayor found that he had considerable room for maneuver in designing his renewal strategy. What is more, renewal was in an important sense a "free good"—paid for largely by the federal government and thus not requiring a reallocation of funds away from competing bureaucracies (such as schools and police). Had it required such a transfer of funds, renewal would almost certainly have plunged the mayor into a difficult bargaining process with his own government agencies rather than allowing him, as it turned out, to present renewal as a wondrous gift to the city. Further, the logic of urban renewal pointed toward central planning and administration. The federal government wanted to see a "workable plan" for the city's future development, and the very task of redesigning the central city called for a broad overview for a coordinated, central perspective. Also, few if any cities had the administrative equipment in the 1950s to plan for and carry out renewal programs. Thus, in New Haven and elsewhere, mayors built redevelopment agencies as extensions of the mayor's office, and this only reinforced the centralizing pressures created by renewal. In short, renewal required expertise, long-range planning, and intricate (sometimes secret) negotiations with the federal government, and this was a kind of policy making that an energetic mayor and his professional planners would naturally and easily dominate. Dahl, indeed, found that the executive-centered coalition was an overwhelming political success in renewal but, in my view, this does not reveal nearly so much about the power structure *per se* as it does about the nature of the policy problem and decision process created by urban renewal.

By contrast to renewal, public education is an urban service that many citizens and administrators are continually involved in and care about deeply. Residents have long been involved in educational policy making through the central Board of Education and local PTAs, and various community groups as well as the teachers' unions regularly press their demands and interests on city government. In addition, there is a long-standing, well-entrenched system of fragmented decision making in public education. The members of the Board of Education, the superintendent, the assistant superintendents, principals, supervisors and the teachers themselves all figure into the policy-making process. For a mayor to imagine that he could centralize planning and administration in education, as he might well do in his own newly-created redevelopment agency, would be foolish. (Aside from all the competing forces he would have to contend with, he would lack legal authority to give direct orders; the Board of Education has legal authority over the schools and, even in cities where the mayor appoints Board members, there are many slips between political appointment and mayoral control of decision making.) Finally, Mayor Lee and other mayors quickly discovered that the issues and problems facing the school system were very different and far more politically difficult than policy problems in urban renewal—at least in its early days. Instead of dealing with the free public goods of renewal, mayors faced in education the divisive, sometimes explosive issues of integration and busing, of unequal school facilities and expenditures. These were zero-sum issues or so they seemed. There was no way to satisfy pro-busing forces without alienating anti-busing forces. Given these issues and the decision-making processes that existed in the schools, it is no surprise that, according to Dahl, no single power elite ran the New Haven schools or, for that matter, that Mayor Lee's executive-centered coalition did not operate in the sphere of educational policy making. And again, this analysis does not appear to reveal as much about the general power structure as it does about the character of urban policy making in a particular policy area.

In general, community power analysis tends to disguise the specific policy-making contexts and processes that, when viewed carefully, reveal and explain the shape of urban decision making. Consider another example. In his *Political Influence,* Edward Banfield presents a "new theory of urban politics" in which policy making is characterized by a "mixed decision choice process." Put simply, this process is pluralistic in that it involves bargaining and compromise between several political institutions or actors. But the process also has elements of what Banfield calls "central decision." This centralized policy making lies in the active and powerful role that the governor, the mayor and the county board play in Banfield's case studies of urban decision making. As Banfield puts it, "there is, nevertheless, an important element of central decision in the Chicago system. The governor, the mayor and the president of the county board are all in positions to assert the supremacy of 'public values' and, in general, to regulate the workings of the social-choice process."

What is crucial here for our purposes is that Banfield's conclusions about power relations are in large measure a reflection of the decisions he is examining. And to that extent his "new theory of urban politics" is an artifact of certain distinctive policy contexts and processes—which happen to generate a particular policy-making pattern (one which Banfield takes to be general). What is so distinctive about Banfield's cases? The answer is that most of the cases are either about major city-planning decisions in which both high-level city hall officials and major private sector (especially business) leaders were intimately involved or they were about organizational conflicts between different levels of government. Note: the cases do not concern at all the daily conflicts in urban government about police, education and other types of urban service delivery—conflicts that routinely involve myriad citizens' groups and lower-level urban officials. In short, these are not cases where the mayor has to deal primarily with conflicts between citizens and city government or internal conflicts between different institutions in his own government. Rather the cases capture city hall in what might be called *foreign relations* with private enterprise and with county and state governments. The cases are not insignificant for this reason, but they are quite distinctive. On the one hand, in these cases, the mayor lacks the power to try to control policy making directly. He cannot order the state or the business community around. On the other hand, he does not have to deal with the fragmentation of interests and demands that he finds within his own government. Instead, in Banfield's cases, the mayor is dealing with other princes, the central decision makers in the state or the business community. And since the other players are independent and powerful, he deals through bargaining and compromise. The result is a "mixed decision-choice process"—in part centralized because it involves a small number of high-level leaders—in part pluralistic because competing independent institutions are involved and also because other interests have been expressed along the way. The point is that, given the context, issues and actors involved, we would naturally expect the result that Banfield discovers. It is built into the policy-making process that operates in his cases.

In sum, both Dahl and Banfield have tried to find the essence of urban power relations by looking at a series of case studies of decision making. But what they have really turned up is certain distinctive policy issues and contexts in which the policy-making process strongly determines power relations, not the reverse. Thus, if Banfield had looked at school policies in Chicago, we would expect him to talk more about fragmented decision making. And if Dahl had looked at the conflicts between New Haven and the State of Connecticut, we would expect him to find Banfield's pattern of "mixed decision-choice." What is most important, this analysis of Dahl and Banfield suggests that the most profitable way to gain an understanding of policy making and the exercise of power in the city is to examine particular policy contexts and issues with a view to illuminating significant similarities and differences in the policy-making process.

This leads one to believe that any persuasive analysis of urban policy making must carefully specify and distinguish between different structural and policy variables in decision making. The implication, which will be spelled out in detail below, is that we cannot talk about urban policy making in simple, general terms. Rather, to talk meaningfully about urban policy, we must break the concept of "policy making" down into particular decision "games": particular combinations and permutations of urban decision-making variables.

### What Makes City Government Different?

Still, even a carefully specified and differentiated model of urban "policy making" will appear to come out of thin air if it is not clearly anchored in, and does not grow out of, the substance and structure of urban government and politics. The questions are: what is that "substance"? What are the defining characteristics of the urban political structure?

It would take another paper if not a full length book to do even rough justice to those questions. So I offer the following "distinctive" characteristics of the urban system briefly and schematically as assumptions on which my model of urban policy making is built. By "distinctive" characteristics, I mean that the urban system either possesses the relevant characteristic and other levels of government lack it completely; or in a somewhat weaker sense, the characteristic is far more strongly manifest in the urban system than elsewhere. The argument is that the differences between the city system and other systems on the following twelve characteristics constitute in aggregate a fundamental "difference" that justifies calling the urban system distinctive.

The city's distinctive characteristics are as follows:

(1) The basic function of urban government is service delivery. In particular, urban services are daily, direct and locality-specific. That is, fire and police protection, garbage collection and public education are delivered to particular people, in particular neighborhoods, every day. With many of these ordinary urban functions, citizens can immediately tell whether or not a service has been "delivered"; they can see whether the trash has been picked up or whether the pothole, broken traffic light or ruptured water main has been fixed. In these cases, urban services are distinctly *tangible* and *visible*.

(2) In addition, urban service delivery often involves a street-level relationship between citizens and public employees that is not only direct but *personal*. Consider, for example, the relationship between citizens and city government in police, education, welfare and health services. In these policy arenas, the character of "service delivery" is heavily dependent on the attitudes, values and behavior of the particular citizen and public employee involved. And to this extent, urban service delivery tends to be distinctively individualistic, even atomistic.

(3) Unlike pure public goods like national defense or national parks, urban services tended to be highly "divisible"—they can easily be divided (in quantity and quality) between different individuals, blocks or neighborhoods. Indeed, one of the most familiar citizen complaints in city government is that a particular block or neighborhood is receiving inadequate services—not receiving its fair share. Conversely, urban administrators can make countless small adjustments and reallocations both in their deployment of street-level bureaucrats and in their definition of what service policies and procedures should be followed in a particular neighborhood. For example, police administrators may decide to crack down on prostitution or teenage gangs in one area of the city but not in other areas. And school administrators may develop bilingual programs or "enrichment" programs or strict disciplinary procedures in certain classrooms and schools but not others.

(4) What is more important, there is enormous variation in individual needs and demands for city services. More precisely, service demands may vary from individual to individual on a block, from block to block and from neighborhood to neighborhood. They also vary according to the race, economic position, age, sex and family composition of urban residents. To take one extreme case, elderly women on a block may demand police action to quiet "rowdy" juveniles,

while the demand of the juveniles is that police not harass them when they are "hanging out." Given the number and diversity of cleavages in citizen service demands and given the fact that citizens tend to have a well-crystallized sense of their own service interests (because the services are tangible and visible), the structure of citizen demands for service is deeply fragmented. This demand structure reflects what Robert Dahl calls "conflictive pluralism"[14] where, in the extreme case, every individual is his own interest group.

The distinctiveness of ordinary urban services, viewed in terms of divisibility of supply and variation in citizen demand, can be presented as shown in Figure 10-1.[15]

**Figure 10-1.** A Logic of Public Goods and Services: Service Divisibility and and Variation in Need

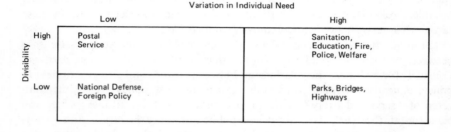

| | Variation in Individual Need | |
|---|---|---|
| | Low | High |
| **High** Divisibility | Postal Service | Sanitation, Education, Fire, Police, Welfare |
| **Low** | National Defense, Foreign Policy | Parks, Bridges, Highways |

(5) Another distinctive feature of urban services is that evaluations of service delivery by both citizens and public employees tend to be highly subjective (in part because the service relationship is often personal and individual). What constitutes a clean block? Is an older area of the city a deteriorating slum or a valued old neighborhood? Is a policeman guilty of harassment or "brutality" in dealing with a suspect or is he merely doing his job vigorously? Is a principal sensitive to students' needs, responsive or unresponsive to community concerns? The reason service appraisals are so subjective is that they rest on the most fundamental personal values of citizens and street-level bureaucrats alike. These are the values that shape judgments about what a good community ought to be like. What constitutes prejudiced or threatening behavior, and what is immoral, antisocial or destructive of civility or tranquility in public places?

(6) These diverse, fragmented citizen interests have produced a bewildering array of street-level community organizations that seek to give voice to one neighborhood demand or another. Typically, they represent highly segmented and crystallized political interests: any given neighborhood is likely to have scores of these small, competing community organizations. Some of these organizations are long standing and familiar: churches, neighborhood associations, PTAs and ethnic social clubs. A great many more arose in the 1960s as a result of what Bell and Held called the "community revolution."[16] These were

the organizations stimulated by the civil rights movement and the War on Poverty: tenants' councils, neighborhood corporations, block associations and Model Cities' planning committees.

(7) The formal system of political representation in the city is notably weak. City councils are typically ineffectual—both in representing local interests and in making policy. City councilmen are often part-time, unpaid officials with little or no staff assistance. In addition, urban representation is confused and weakened by overlapping political constituencies. Who does the urban resident turn to for "representation?" His or her city councilman, state representative, state senator, congressman or senator? Or to the competing and equally fragmented system of "informal" community organizations?

(8) Because service delivery lies at the heart of city government and because service delivery involves at root an ongoing "service relationship" between citizens and street-level bureaucrats, city politics has a distinctively bureaucratic and administrative character. That is, the demands of citizens and community organizations are focused on urban administrators—beginning with the mayor.

(9) Mayors are distinctive as American political executives because of their proximity to their constituents (which paradoxically makes it easier to "fight city hall" than the state house or the White House); their daily involvement in the administrative details of service delivery; and because of the public presumption that the mayor is directly responsible, accountable for street-level service problems. Presidents take credit for their foreign policy accomplishments, and governors may focus on and take credit for their new highways and community colleges. But the men in city hall are the custodians of the sidewalks. They are the "dirty workers" of American government who must deal every day with the most ordinary and personal needs of their constituents.

(10) But if mayors are the primary target of citizens' service demands, they are not in a structural position to control service delivery within their "own" administrations. For mayors operate in a political system of deeply fragmented authority and fragmented administration. The institutional fragmentation of urban government has, of course, been widely noted and discussed. But the fact that this structural fragmentation is so well known does not make it any less important. Simply put, the city's governmental fragmentation is manifest in the division of public authority between city hall and independent boards and commissions and among scores of city departments and agencies with overlapping and conflicting street-level jurisdictions.

(11) What is less frequently noted but equally important is the vertical fragmentation of public control within city bureaucracies. That is, given the discretion that urban bureaucrats possess in the street-level service relationship, it is difficult for administrators "downtown" to exercise strong control over urban services. This lack of bureaucratic control over the service relationship is evident in recurrent outbreaks of police corruption as well as repeated allegations of police brutality and abuses (of power) by teachers or social workers. What is

most important about the decentralization of discretion and administrative judgment in urban bureaucracy is that it grows out of the distinctively individualistic character of street-level service delivery.

(12) Finally, urban policy making is deeply fragmented by the conflicting authority and policy jurisdictions of national, state and city governments. For many of the programs and policies of all governments in the American system come to rest—have their direct impact—at the street level. Put simply, every level has its claim and source of control in setting urban policy. The result is that urban policy is often pulled apart from several directions; and, in this context, policy coordination is made difficult and direct conflict and competition between one or more levels of government over the determination of street-level policy are frequent.

### Summary: Urban Fragmentation and Street-Fighting Pluralism

The twelve "distinctive" characteristics presented above add up to a striking picture of fragmentation in the urban political system. This fragmentation grows out of the very nature of urban services, and it is reinforced by the structure of community organization and service bureaucracies, the structure of city government and the competing policy initiatives and jurisdictions of national, state and city governments.

Now this pattern of systematic fragmentation might appear to be a curiosity of urban governmental political architecture. That is, fragmentation might arguably be theoretically uninteresting or unproblematic. Indeed, some political analysts would argue that political and governmental fragmentation merely creates the conditions for a political marketplace that allows for "public choice" or mutual adjustment—analogues for efficient allocation in economic markets.

My argument is that urban fragmentation profoundly affects policy making in the city but not in the way suggested by the optimistic political analysts. Rather, the systematic fragmentation leads to a political and governmental free-for-all that makes urban policy making chaotic and unstable. More precisely, the fragmentation of urban government at every level produces an almost anarchic structure of demands and policy conflicts. It produces scores of different individual and institutional interests which "fight" over urban programs and policies in a policy-making context (of procedures and decision networks) that may vary with every different "fight." I call this unstable political free-for-all "street-fighting pluralism" and use the concept to describe a pattern of unstructured, multilateral conflict in which the many different combatants fight with one another in an almost infinite number of permutations and combinations. Street-fighting pluralism exists when five different groups in the neighborhood struggle over programs and expenditures in a local school and when they enlist different city administrators, representatives or agencies as allies in the fight. It exists too when organizations in five different neighborhoods, along with opposed factions in the police department, fight to keep a local police station from being closed down. Or when the mayor, a neighborhood group and one or more bureaucracies are arguing about an urban renewal project. Or when five agencies within a department or eight city departments are fighting over a policy that concerns them all. Or when national, state and city government fight over the environmental consequences of a proposed sewage treatment plant.

More precisely, I define street-fighting pluralism by the following characteristics:

1. *diversity* of interest: from individual to individual, block to block, neighborhood to neighborhood, policemen to teacher, department to department, city hall to state bureaucracies to federal bureaucracies;
2. *crystallization* of interest: because service problems tend to be concrete and particular, so that interests that arise from them tend to be sharply defined and locality specific;
3. *variability* of conflict: with a few exceptions, it is easy to imagine a conflict breaking out between any pair or set of urban combatants;
4. *complexity* of conflict: an urban decision "game" is likely to be multifaceted, to involve 3, 4 or 5 or 10 different individuals, groups or institutions;
5. *instability* of conflict: the players, demands, problems and conflicts constantly change—and change rapidly—in a free-for-all street fight;
6. *entanglement* of urban contestants: the main institutional actors in urban policy making constantly get in each others' ways. In large measure, this is because the different pieces of service delivery—health, housing, education, welfare, police—are so highly interdependent;
7. *directness* of conflict: urban conflicts tend to be direct, personal, face-to-face. This reflects the direct, personal qualities of urban service delivery described above.

What are the implications of street-fighting pluralism for urban policy making? We can start to answer this question by viewing the street fight from the perspective of our hypothetical central policy maker. In the first place, the central policy maker confronts a continuous stream of demands and problems, arising from the street level, coming from all directions. These demands and problems reflect all aspects of urban service delivery, and they pop up from the neighborhoods spasmodically and unpredictably, for the possibility always exists in urban service delivery that something will go "wrong" somewhere or somehow and that community groups and/or street-level bureaucrats will seize on the problem and make it an "issue" for city government. So the central policy makers must deal with a constant barrage of street-level problems, and in the face of this barrage, it is difficult—to say the least—for city government to structure a stable agenda for decision making, and hopefully, problem solving.

More precisely, because street-level demands are not filtered, channeled, assigned priority and otherwise mediated by formal political representatives, they provide a constant supply of new and unfamiliar issues for urban policy makers.

What should city hall do (if anything) about the recent rash of murders in one neighborhood, the tenant strike in another, or the unpopular principal, the harassment of firemen, the newly-created and newly-menacing youth gang, the protest against plans for a secondary sewerage treatment facility, the new X-rated movie or the massage parlor, the recently broken street light, water main, or catch basin, the garbage that hasn't been picked up for a week on a particular block, the outbreak of fighting between white and black students in a recently redistricted high school, the discovery of corruption in the police department or in a municipal loan program, the vandalism of benches in a popular neighborhood park (or in school buildings), the outbreak of fires in an abandoned building, the suspicion that drug pushers have been hanging around a local school, or that a large number of children in a neighborhood are suffering from lead poisoning, the discovery in a community that a hospital plans to expand down the block or that private developers intend to tear down a block of three family homes in an old, "stable" neighborhood, or that a public union is close to calling a strike, and finally the allegation that police are beating up teenagers in a "racially tense" neighborhood?

Which problem should our urban policy maker deal with first? Some of them are serious, some are routine. Some call for an emergency response, some do not. Some of the "problems" can be immediately verified, others are hard to pin down and get an accurate reading on. (In fact, in a large proportion of cases, it may be very difficult to find out exactly what is going on out at the street level.) Nevertheless, in every case, some group of citizens will feel that "their" problem is enormously important—an emergency that must be dealt with immediately.

Obviously, the first point to notice about this spontaneous "agenda" is the length of the list. And before the list of problems can be sorted out, assessed, "dealt with" (or ignored), a new list of problems will have sprung up, demanding attention from our already overloaded central policy maker. The main implication of this "demand" structure is that central policy makers are forced to be reactive. They cannot easily plan for tomorrow's problems when they are fully occupied responding to today's, yesterday's and last month's accumulated inventory. More important, given the constantly changing barrage of demands and problems, our central policy makers are likely to get caught in a frantic movement from one problem or issue to another. And if our policy makers set their agenda by responding to the most dramatic problems and the loudest complaints, they will be seen to be crisis-hopping—caught in the process of rushing to the next fire. So the first point about street-fighting pluralism is that it puts urban policy makers in a highly reactive posture.

The second main point about the urban policy agenda is that the items on it present so many different kinds of problems, call for so many different kinds of policy responses and create so many different decision games. That is, as we will see below in some detail, different demands carry with them very different policy making characteristics. More concretely, different demands involve, among other things, different types of policy problems, issue contexts, configurations of participants and institutional settings. This means that the character of decision "games" is constantly changing from demand to demand, and this makes urban policy making highly unstable. (Of course, urban policy making is made unstable in the first place by the simple fact that a constant stream of new and diverse demands is flowing into the urban policy making system.) What is most important, an effective response to or process of deciding on one demand may be totally inappropriate to another.

In sum, street-fighting pluralism gives urban policy making two central characteristics: reactivism and instability.

### A Penny Arcade Model of Urban Policy Making

So far, I have offered a verbal description—a sketch really—of urban government as a policy-making system. To gain a clearer picture of the uncertainty, instability, and reactive character of urban policy making, it is useful, I think, to present a metaphor of the city's decision processes based on three familiar "games" of chance found in most penny arcades. First, we can think of the process of urban problem-generation and agenda-setting in terms of a "shooting gallery"—not the addict hang-out (which is also an urban phenomenon) but the game in which a player (urban policy maker) is faced with a large number of moving targets—rows of ducks, pinwheels, etc. The point of the metaphor is that, as in urban policy making, the "shooting gallery" player has far more targets than he can possibly hit and they keep popping up in different places or revolve around and around in front of him. So the player is constantly reacting to a new target (problem) and, at the same time, is faced with the choice of which target (problem) to fire at (with the knowledge that firing at one target means letting the vast majority of targets go past until the next go round). The implication is that faced with this need to react quickly and to deal with such a bewildering array of targets (which, incidentally, have different pay offs), the player will frantically move from target to target—relying on reflexes rather than on any considered plan of action. Now there may be some extremely rational souls (or expert marksmen) who can manage to impose an orderly agenda of action on the shooting gallery game—i.e., shoot the ducks in the top row first or use all their shots on the pinwheels. But anyone who has played the game or observed it being played will probably agree that it is intrinsic to the structure of the game that the player is forced to be reactive and is likely to become frantic. And so it is with urban agenda setting given the structure of demands that arise from the city's street-fighting pluralism.

Second, we may think of the urban policy maker's ability to predict and control the decision "games" he must deal with in terms of the workings of a slot machine. We have said above that urban policy making variables include the nature of the problem, the issue context, the configuration of participants and the institutional setting involved. The point of the metaphor is that the policy making characteristics of a given urban demand or problem will vary just as independently (randomly) as the apples, oranges and cherries in a slot machine. For example, the first combination to turn up may be a resource problem in the context of health delivery in which a neighborhood group is pitted against a group of hospital administrators. This problem combination may call for the policy maker to hold a bargaining session and free up some extra budget lines from his budget director. Having followed this policy making procedure, the central policy maker may then encounter a second problem combination:—a conflict over busing involving several neighborhoods and the board of education as well as agencies of state and national government. Clearly, the first policy response is not appropriate to this case; the latter problem may require instead legal action, appeals to higher-level governments and an immediate police response at the neighborhood level to prevent actual street fighting between black and white residents. Having adopted this policy response, the central policy maker may then face a third problem combination: a charge by several community groups that several principals in a school district are "unresponsive" or "insulting" and should be removed. In such a case, the board of education may have its own independent or quasi-independent authority and the teachers' union may threaten a strike if the city accedes to community demands. This kind of problem combination may plausibly call for "crisis management"—round-the-clock negotiating sessions—or perhaps the decision to implement a new plan for citizen participation and decentralization. Having responded in this way, the central policy maker may face a fourth problem combination: a complaint by the administrators in the welfare department that the city and state housing bureaucracies are refusing to help them arrange temporary shelter for welfare families who have been evicted from their apartments. Such a problem may call for the creation of a new interdepartmental task force or the development of a new state-local policy agreement (to be negotiated directly with the governor). But the appropriate policy response bears little resemblance to the responses called for by earlier problems. Finally, consider a fifth problem combination: two policemen, along with several journalists, tell the policy maker that there is widespread corruption in the police force and that the internal police watchdogs are either ignoring the problems or covering it up. What should our policy maker do, and how much would the problem and plausible policy responses differ if the allegation concerned police brutality in a low-income, non-white area? (For one thing, it is obvious in the latter case that community groups would raise the issue into a dramatic controversy and, as a result, the policy maker's range of options would look very different.)

The point of the slot machine metaphor is that our central policy maker never knows what kind of problem he will be dealing with from moment to moment and also does not know which of his available policy responses or procedures will be relevant or useful. This underscores the point that urban policy making is highly unstable. For a policy maker who wishes to rely on one or two standard responses—or to develop a "standing plan" for decision making—will find that he has guessed wrong much of the time—or most of the time. That is, imagine a central policy maker who relies on any one of the following policy making strategies: (1) systematically analyze the benefits and costs of different policy alternatives; (2) bargain and compromise with the principal combatants; (3) appeal to state or national governments for more money; (4) create new mechanisms for citizen participation; (5) create new coordinating committees or planning task forces within city government; (6) stall or put off decision (in the hopes that many problems will go away); (7) adopt a moralistic, crusading posture including symbolic expressions of commitment or opposition to a particular policy; (8) assign blame for problems to rigid bureaucracies, stingy higher-level governments, the economy, suburbs, white "racists," militant blacks, etc.

Of course, few actual policy makers would adopt any one of these strategies rigidly—to the exclusion of all other strategies. But the point is that given the "slot machine" character of urban decision games, a "rational" policy maker who wished to tailor his policy response to each different problem would constantly be forced to change policy making procedures and strategies and would never know what strategy or procedure would be called for tomorrow. And this is what I mean by the fundamental instability of urban policy making.

Third, we can think of the process of implementation in urban policy making in terms of the operation of another familiar penny arcade game: the pinball machine. Given our central policy maker's weak control over his own administration, his street-level bureaucrats, and higher-level governments, decisions, once taken, are likely to bounce around from "decision point" to "decision point," to use Pressman and Wildavsky's term.[17] The implication is that even when a decision or policy is arrived at in city hall, it will be knocked off course by both known and unforeseen obstacles by the time it reaches the street level. If this is true, the implemented policy is likely to raise a new set of problems and demands that will enter into the "shooting gallery" of agenda-setting all over again. And to that extent, urban policy making will become a continuous process in which a particular problem receives brief, often frantic attention; some kind of decision is made which bounces around in the implementation process, and then the problem pops up again in a new or slightly altered form. This means that problems are not dealt with in a steady and sustained fashion, but rather they are fired at erratically. This means too that policy making on any given problem or set of problems is unlikely to develop in a linear fashion or in small closely-related incremental steps. Rather the development of a given urban policy is likely to trace an unstable, uneven course: either zig-zags, circles or possibly unrelated targets. To this extent, urban policy making will have a distinctly evolutionary character: the shape and substance of urban problems and policies will continually change—in a protean fashion.

Consider the following examples:

1. A strict code-enforcement program leads to housing abandonment which requires a new set of policy responses.
2. Urban bureaucracies are centralized and professionalized to overcome the perceived defects or decentralization, but it is not long before demands for decentralization arise in response to the perceived defects of centralization.
3. Policies toward drug addicts, criminals and juvenile delinquents veer back and forth between community treatment and institutionalization. Each strategy is offered hopefully as a solution to the problems caused by the other.
4. Public concern over prostitution, massage parlors and other issues of "public morality" erupts sporadically in one neighborhood or another and then quickly dies down.
5. Youth gangs come and go. Sometimes they are viewed as a menace; at other times they are perceived as a possible instrument of community development. At times, the gangs provide protection against outsiders; at other times they run protection rackets.
6. An old neighborhood evolves from a working-class neighborhood to a black slum to a high-rent area population by "brownstoners" with a decade.
7. The "drug" problem rapidly shifts from heroin to cocaine to pills to alcohol and back to heroin.
8. The police department moves to car patrol to increase coverage and visbility and begins to receive community demands that patrolmen be put back "on the beat" in the interests of responsiveness and visibility.

In the face of these protean problems, the question is validly asked: What is a mayor (or other policy maker) to do?

### Rational Decision, Incrementalism and Reactive Policy Making

In sum, the penny arcade model presents a stark metaphor of the uncertainty, instability and reactiveness of urban policy making. In fact, it somewhat exaggerates the randomness of urban policy-making games. For there are certain emerging patterns in the structure of urban problems and demands that, as we will see below, reveal a great deal about the character of the "new urban politics."

Nevertheless, the penny arcade model serves to sharply distinguish the city's policy-making system from the national system as it is depicted in the two most influential models of policy making: rational decision and incrementalism. The model of rational decision presumes that a problem can be defined clearly, that it can be isolated for analysis—frozen like a laboratory specimen—and that through the application of knowledge and reasoning, some better, more efficient solution can be found for the problem. The rational decision model also presumes a very simple policy-making process. To slightly exaggerate its simplicity, it implies a world in which the policy analyst has direct access to a central policy maker who has previously set a clear set of goals for the analyst. The policy analyst then reports policy recommendations to the central policy maker who uses his authority to bring the desired program and policy into being. This model is clearly at variance with the characteristics we have posited in the urban policy-making model: the number of contestants (street-fighting pluralism), the difficulty of focusing steadily on a particular problem (as in the "shooting gallery" metaphor), and the complexity of implementation (as in the pinball machine metaphor).

The model of incremental decision does not presume the same conditions for systematic, scientific analysis, but it does presume a relatively stable set of decision games and a steady process of agenda setting and policy development. For, in essence, incrementalism depicts a political system in which established policies are changed marginally and through a consistent process of bargaining and mutual adjustment. The latter point is important because it means that whatever the particular features of a given decision game, it displays the fundamental characteristic of bargaining and accommodation between familiar contestants over familiar policies. Again this model is clearly at variance with the instability and variability of urban decision games. Most important, even though both the incremental model and the penny arcade model allow for a large number of players, the players in the former case play the same game (i.e., are willing to play the bargaining game), whereas the players in urban government find themselves in highly dissimilar games (depending on the problem combination) and are by no means always willing to trade and negotiate in the interests of mutual partisan adjustment. Rather urban players often find themselves in stalemates, confrontations and "non-decision" games in which opposed players do not bargain or adjust at all because each has a separate piece of authority or policy jurisdiction and can therefore operate in feudal isolation from competing players and baronies. In short, the many players in the incremental model find established, predictable channels and mechanisms for working out their bargains, whereas in our model of urban policy making the players enter into an unstructured, unpredictable policy process: the free-for-all of street-fighting pluralism. As a last point of contrast, there are simply not as many players per decision-game in incrementalism as in the urban system of street-fighting pluralism. In Lindblom's and Wildavsky's accocounts,[18] the main players are the familiar ones in the national system: presidents, bureaucratic agencies, congressional committees and interest groups; whereas in the urban system, the players run the gamut from individual residents to community organizations, to policemen, to city departments, to mayors, to higher-level governments. We can summarize the central difference between the models of national decision, incrementalism, and reactive policy making as shown in Figure 10–2.

**Figure 10–2.** Instability, Uncertainty and Number of Participants as Properties of Policy-Making Models

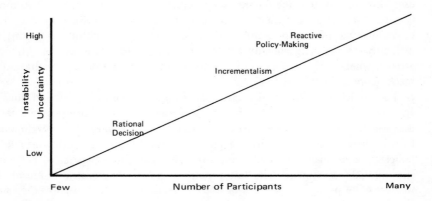

Finally, as may be clear by now, the three models differ dramatically in the kinds of search processes they produce in decision making. In the rational decision model, the dominant search process is a search for knowledge and efficient policy in bargains. But in the reactive policy-making model of city government, the search process is harder to specify. It is clearly not a consistent, controlled search. Rather it would seem to involve an *erratic* search process when policy makers veer back and forth between available (and often opposed) strategies. And, it is a *blind* search process when, in the extreme cases of uncertainty and instability, urban policy makers are looking for something—anything "that will work."

### The Elements of Urban Decision Making

To this point, we have stressed the uncertainty and instability of urban policy making. In particular, the slot machine metaphor suggests that the basic elements of urban decision games may vary almost randomly—creating constantly changing problem combinations that call for very different policy responses. The next step of this analysis is to flesh out this rather abstract analytical model by examining each of the elements of decision making in some detail. We noted above that the basic elements of urban decision include (1) the nature of the problem; (2) the issue context; (3) the stage of decision; (4) the configuration of participants; (5) the institutional setting; and (6) problem definition.

In examining these basic elements, we will be able to see more clearly what is the actual stuffing of urban decision games and also be able to detect emerging patterns in decision making. More precisely, my argument is that although decision games will always vary in a bewildering way, there are significant trends and consistencies in the character of the different elements of decision that are likely to shape the future of urban policy making.

**I. The Nature of the Problem.** What are the defining characteristics of urban policy problems? In the 1960s, the dominant answer to this question was that the city's problems were essentially money problems that could only be "treated" through commitment of new financial resources. In the 1960s, city hall and higher-level governments followed the resource strategy in the urban renewal program, and in various education, health, manpower and welfare programs. Now it should be clear analytically that a resource strategy is necessary to deal with certain kinds of urban problems. You cannot build new public housing, schools, parks or mass transit systems without substantial financial resources. In general, public works and capital construction projects are going to be resource problems for the city unless urban administrators find a way to make bricks and mortar out of garbage or good intentions.

On the other hand, the experience of new urban "spending" programs in the 1960s suggests that the most persistent service problems—in education, police, health and welfare—are not merely resource problems. For the billions of dollars spent on these service problems simply did not have the impact that the architects of urban programs had hoped for. The reason for this is that there were other equally fundamental problems involved—problems that reflect both the distinctive features of the street-level service relationship and the intergovernmental character of urban service delivery.

In addition to the resource problem, then, our central policy makers face four other fundamental problems which we will call the problems of: (1) responsiveness, (2) trust, (3) regulation, and (4) restructuring government itself. That is, if we ask what urban problems are "about," we will often hear the following replies (in addition to the standard reply that the city lacks financial resources):

1. City government is out of touch with citizen needs—is not close enough to the neighborhoods—and, therefore, does not respond quickly or flexibly to particular neighborhood service demands (the responsiveness problem).
2. Citizens feel that street-level bureaucrats do not understand their problems and are hostile, insensitive, or possibly prejudiced against them. At the same time, street-level bureaucrats feel that residents do not respect them, are hostile and uncooperative, and do not understand the difficulties of their work (the trust problem).
3. City government is unable to control the performance of policemen or teachers or, for that matter, the behavior of community-based service organizations. The result is corruption, sloppy administration and a lack of accountability in government (the regulation problem).

4. City government will be unable to improve its service delivery unless it dramatically restructures its own organization and its relationship with other governments (the restructuring problem).

Quite different claims and complaints come together in the last articulation of the "urban problem." Some point downward to a need for greater decentralization and the creation of mechanisms for citizen participation and community control. Others point upward and outward to a need to plan and finance urban services on a metropolitan or state-wide basis or a need to create new revenue sharing and policy-making arrangements between city governments and the national government.

What is most important for our purposes here is that the character of urban policy making will vary according to which problem (resource, responsiveness, etc.) is emphasized in a given decision game. To be more concrete, the politics of resource problems involve a politics of allocation—either distributive or redistributive. By contrast, responsiveness problems lead to a quite different kind of politics: an administrative politics concerned with the architecture of service bureaucracies. For example, recent government strategies for dealing with responsiveness problems have led to the creation of little city halls, neighborhood service centers, the appointment of ombudsmen and the delegation of increased decision-making power to neighborhood-level service administrators. Equally, trust problems also lead directly into the tangle of administrative politics—with the emphasis placed again on street-level strategies. These have included community relations programs, minority recruitment efforts, and civilian review boards. To reiterate, the central political task arising from trust problems is how to alter the administration of service delivery in order to bridge the social, psychological and often racial gaps between the servers and the served.

Regulation problems also lead to an administrative politics in which central policy makers argue with one another about the best way to "tighten up," monitor or evaluate the work of urban bureaucracies. The main difference between the politics of regulation problems and the politics of responsiveness and trust problems is that the former imply a centralization of power and control. For example, in trying to deal with regulation problems, city governments have created departments of investigation, special prosecutors, central policy planning offices, project management programs, productivity programs and various other devices for improved management and evaluation.

Finally, restructuring problems leads to a very different kind of politics, involving city governments in both (1) "foreign relations"—bargaining games with outside players (suburbs, higher-level governments)—and (2) renegotiations of local authority relationships as in the case of plans for community control.

There are several emerging trends in the incidence and salience of the different problem types. First, resource problems will always be central, but, for two separate reasons, decisions about new expenditures and resource strategies are likely to engage the energy and imagination of urban policy makers far less than they did in the 1960s. For one thing, in the wake of its frustrating experience with the War on Poverty, the federal government has moved away from innovative public spending programs that tend to focus urban policy making on new resource strategies. Further, given the austerity budgets of city government, the resource problem is taking on a different character. Instead of leading to decision about how to allocate new expenditures, the resource problem now leads to decision games in which all players must lose something or in which the city government is asked to redistribute existing resources from one bureaucracy or neighborhood to another. In this context, resource problems impose strong constraints and political costs on urban policy makers rather than providing opportunities and political benefits.

The second trend is that problems of trust-responsiveness and restructuring are emerging as arguably the most critical urban problems. Regulation problems are always present and tend to erupt from time to time when charges of corruption or racism or brutality are made against one urban bureaucracy or another.

On the one hand, trust and responsiveness problems, which are the fundamental problems of street-level service delivery, have become dominant in recent years (a) because of the perception that urban spending programs were simply not getting implemented at the street level and (b) because racial tension and polarization have greatly increased the mistrust between street-level bureaucrats and- an increasing percentage of urban residents. Notice too that these are the kinds of problems that push urban policy making in the direction of decentralization strategies and citizen participation. Restructuring problems also have a decentralizing thrust to the extent that they involve demands for neighborhood government. And to this extent, responsiveness, trust and restructuring problems all come together in their focus on the need to reform the street-level service relationship. However, restructuring problems are increasingly pulling in a different direction: to an emphasis in policy making on the city's relationship with other governments. The problem here is how to reform neighborhood-city-metropolitan-county-state-national relationships so as to provide planning and equitable financing in the future in policy areas such as education, health, welfare, environmental protection and urban growth. Thus, urban policy making is simultaneously being pulled in opposite directions: to a concern with the street-level service arrangements, on the one hand, and to a concern with the structure of intergovernmental planning and policy making, on the other. (We will examine the sources and implications of this urban schizophrenia in more detail below.)

**II. Issue Contexts.** A major source of the instability of urban decision games is that the demands arising from the city's street-fighting pluralism present so many different issue contexts. Below we will identify the main variables that distinguish different issue contexts and will attempt to indicate the significance of these variables for urban policy making. These variables are as follows:

*1. Private Versus Collective Goods.* The most familiar urban services take the form of private goods—that is, highly divisible goods that can be delivered differentially to different individuals, goods for which individuals typically have different private needs. Indeed, as was argued above, street-fighting pluralism grows out of the fragmentation of a citizen demand structure oriented to these private goods. However, there are other kinds of public goods being provided by city government that have different implications for urban policy making. For example, in the great era of city building in the 19th century, urban governments supplied public goods that benefited the entire population of a city collectively. Among these city-wide public goods were the development of city water supply systems, the draining of mosquito swamps to prevent disease, the construction of bridges, and to a lesser extent, the development of "central parks." More recently, other kinds of collective goods have appeared on the urban agenda and have produced new and difficult issue contexts. One kind of "new" collective good might be called a neighborhood good and involves the claim that a particular zoning, busing, or highway-routing decision vitally affects the interests of an entire neighborhood. A second kind of new collective good is one that involves the interests of residents in a metropolitan area, in a state, or a multi-state region. For example, decisions concerning environmental protection, energy allocation, economic development and educational financing typically impinge on the collective interests of these larger "communities." Thus, the distinction between private and collective goods is not a dichotomous one, rather it involves a continuum which can be expressed as follows:

| Private Goods | Individual→Neighborhood→City-Wide→Metropolitan→State-Wide→Regional | Collective Goods |
|---|---|---|

The point of this analysis is straight forward. It is that it is hard enough for urban policy makers to deal with the myriad demands for private goods that give rise to street-fighting pluralism. But it is that much harder for urban policy makers to deal with demands based on the supposed interests of neighborhoods and larger-scale communities. In the first place, conflicts between neighborhood interests pose controversial issues of redistribution and preferential treatment. That is, does the urban policy maker favor poor neighborhoods, "solid, working-class neighborhoods." or affluent neighborhoods? The very language involved in describing these issue contexts suggests the political difficulties involved. Further, issues involving the interests of even larger communities impose a different kind of burden on urban policy making: they lead to "foreign relations" with other governments and thus to a policy-making process in which city government has even less control over policy outcomes than it does on issues that arise entirely within city limits. Our empirical proposition is that urban issues increasingly involve neighborhood and larger-scale issues; and that, to this extent, urban policy making has become all the more complicated.

*2. Benefits and Costs.* Issue contexts also differ according to the benefits and costs involved for different participants. In general, we would logically expect that the easiest issues to deal with are those that distribute many benefits to urban residents and impose little or no costs. These issues are also hard to come by. Next best for urban policy makers are issue contexts in which particularistic benefits are given to certain individuals without cost to others. Historically, many service delivery issues have been of this character as city government has acted to take care of a pothole here, a broken water main there. However, given the increased awareness of citizens about their private and neighborhood service needs (an awareness that is a hallmark of the "new urban politics"), it is now much harder for urban policy makers to take care of service demands on a piecemeal basis. Urban government is perceived as making deliberate choices about which pothole to fill, and residents with unfilled potholes are likely to conclude that their demands have been slighted or ignored.

Consider, too, the cost side of urban issue contexts. It is logical to believe that decisions that impose concentrated costs on particular neighborhoods will be difficult ones and strongly resisted—to say the least. And this will be true even if the decisions involved produce dispersed benefits. The difficulty of dealing with issues involving concentrated costs and dispersed benefits is evident in many recent urban controversies: neighborhood renewal projects, scattered-site housing, busing programs, the siting of methadone clinics, sewerage treatment plants and prison halfway houses. Our empirical proposition, related to the last section, is that the rise of self-conscious neighborhood interests greatly increases the likelihood that any given issue will be seen to impose concentrated costs and therefore will be highly problematic for urban policy makers.

*3. Symbolic Versus Material Issues.* The classic problems of urban service delivery have always been tangible, specific, *material*—things that needed to be fixed, requests for an additional school or number of policemen. And the demands that arise from these problems could therefore be clearly met. Both the servers and the served could easily tell when the service problem had been taken care of. Recently, however, as a result of the greater political self-consciousness characteristic of citizens in the new urban politics, material issues have frequently been defined in highly symbolic terms. That is, problems are often described, not in terms of the specific service complaint, but rather in terms of "inequality" or a lack of sensitivity or institutional racism. In addition, issues are now being defined symbolically that were never defined at all when urban policy making was focused on material service problems. Thus, recent controversial urban issues have involved references to "quality education," neighborhood "development" or "decay," and "alienation" from government. Because these concepts are symbolic and hard to pin down, it becomes that much harder for urban policy makers to define the problem and figure out a way of responding to it (assuming that they want to in the first place).

*4. Independent Versus Intertwined Issues.* Historically, the most familiar service issues also had the characteristic of being relatively independent of one another. That is, the task of building a school in one neighborhood was clearly independent from the task of policing the street or fixing the now proverbial pothole. Separable issues of this sort present clear advantages to urban policy makers, for they can be rather easily sorted out, assigned, and monitored. By contrast to these "simple" urban issues, the issues that confront policy makers in the new urban politics are increasingly intertwined. That is, with these intertwined issues, it is hard for even the careful policy analyst to figure out where one dimension of the issue begins and another dimension ends. Such issues involve not only multiple problems but also impinge on the work of several different urban bureaucracies. A good example of this kind of intertwined issue is lead poisoning, which is at once a health problem, a housing problem and possibly too a problem of public education. Or consider street crime (as related to drug addiction), or educational problems (as plausibly related to health, housing and nutrition problems), or problems of discipline and crime in schools (which are at once problems for teachers, policemen and, often, social workers). Our empirical proposition is that urban issues are increasingly intertwined, and again this makes it harder for urban policy makers to cut into a problem and develop a policy response. Here policy makers are faced with the difficulty of choosing which facet of the issues to attack and of trying to figure out whether they can treat one facet of the problem without treating all facets of the problem at once.

*5. Means-Ends Relationships.* The classical problems of urban service delivery had the final characteristic of being patently solvable. That is, city governments knew how to build schools, hire policemen and pave streets. Having, in fact, solved many of the most easily solvable (and often technical) urban problems, city governments find themselves left with an increasing proportion of issues where they literally do not know how to solve the problem (again even if they wanted to). Such problems include the prevention of street crime, the treatment of drug addiction and the education of children in low-income neighborhoods. This leaves urban policy makers in the new urban politics in the awkward position of focusing on precisely those problems that they have been least able to deal with in the past.

*6. Problem Definition.* Related to the last point, the most familiar and traditional urban service problems—problems of cleaning the streets, filling potholes, putting out fires and building new schools or hospitals—had the further characteristic of being easily and unambiguously *defined*. In short, the business of delivering old-fashioned urban services to individuals could be managed effectively because the problems involved could be clearly defined and workable solutions could be applied.

By contrast, consider the world of the "new urban politics"—the world of street-fighting pluralism in which myriad groups and interests fight over issues that are increasingly intertwined and symbolic; that involve concentrated costs and demands for neighborhood goods; and that have no easy (or known) solution. For these reasons, in the new urban politics it is often very difficult to define the nature and boundaries of policy problems. The consequences of weak and ambiguous problem definition are straightforward. In the first place, it is hard to see how a problem can be solved (or how any plausible solution can be mounted) if the problem at issue has not been clearly defined. Second, and perhaps more important, to the extent that the process of problem definition itself becomes the subject of many-sided arguments and conflicts, to that extent the policy-making process will become even more *unstable* (since problem definitions may change rapidly) and also *fragmented* (since different urban policy-makers may act on the basis of different and conflicting definitions of the problem).

**III.  The Stage of Decision.**  A third element that adds to the variability and instability of urban policy making is what we will call the "stage of decision." In the simplest terms, the problem that pops up on the city's slot machine of pressing issues may be a brand new one (that no one has ever encountered before) or an old familiar one that the city now deals with routinely and effectively. Or it may be an entirely different kind of old problem—one on which numerous constraining decisions have been made in the past, and, as a result, decision making is now deeply embedded in existing policies, programs and expenditures. In this latter stage of decision, the city is locked into its treatment of the "old" problem, and any new approach would require a basic restructuring (or rewiring) both of policy and of existing administrative organization. Now, of course, urban policy makers will often deal with problems that are at still other stages of decision. For example, some problems (such as the problem of drug addiction or prostitution) may regularly pop up and force some policy response only to reappear shortly in a slightly different form. Or consider problems like a serious water shortage or a public union strike or a fiscal "crisis" or a rash of murders or rapes in a neighborhood. These are recurrent problems that are treated each time they appear as brand new crisis issues.

Finally, in terms of crisis issues and crisis-hopping, we can distinguish several very different stages of crisis decisions. In the first stage of crisis decision, the mayor may make some quick statement or literally rush to a fire (or disaster) and then move on rapidly to the next crisis. Here the mayor's reaction is similar to what Mayhew calls "position taking":[19] getting on the public record but not taking any particular action on a problem.

What if the "crisis" does not go away after the mayor has paid momentary attention to it? In the second, slightly more protracted state of crisis decision, the mayor will move rapidly to provide some new program or policy (or reverse an existing one). For example, he might move to prevent demolition of an old building that a neighborhood has been fighting to preserve or he might order police into the schools to deal with a sudden increase in vandalism, theft or fighting. In this stage of crisis decision the mayor feels compelled to do something about the problem. But because of pressures to "do something" quickly about *other* crises and non-crises, the mayor typically reacts by reaching for an "instant solution" in the hope that the crisis will be reduced by his brief spasm of action and attention.

In the third and most protracted stage of crisis decision, the mayor faces a "crisis" that simply will not go away and that drives all other problems and decisions off the city's agenda. In this stage of crisis decision, the mayor cannot continue to rely on his standard crisis reactions: making a public pronouncement or appearance (position-taking) or quickly developing a new program or policy (the "instant solution"). Rather, the problem at hand requires more sustained attention, for the problems involved are those of a city-wide strike that cuts off a vital service, a riot (or series of riots) that turn racial conflict into actual streetfighting, or a fiscal crisis that requires the firing of city employees and cutbacks in city services.

Curiously, this is the only kind of urban crisis decision that resembles "crisis decision making" in foreign policy, where policymakers work around the clock to come up with a response to a clear emergency. The emergency decision places heavy burdens on urban policy makers because it physically exhausts them and places heavy psychological stress on them to act decisively in the face of unusually great risk and uncertainty. And there is no doubt that a mayor who had to deal with one emergency decision after another would find the city increasingly ungovernable. This is an obvious point, I think, but it is not the point we are concerned with mainly in urban policy making. Rather our proposition is that it is the succession of small, variable "crises" coming from so many directions and involving so many different participants that makes the city so difficult to govern. It is the constant, small-scale crisis-hopping that fragments city hall's attention and makes its policy making reactive and erratic.

In more general terms, let us consider what difference the different stages of decision make for a central policy maker. A central policy maker who wished to control (manage) his city as easily as possible would clearly prefer to deal with problems that he is familiar with and has learned how to treat routinely—as against problems that are either brand new or that cannot be routinized. Our central policy maker would prefer to deal with relatively small issues as opposed to relatively large ones. At least, as we have seen above, the historical urban administrator demonstrated his competence by producing many tangible, divisible services to urban residents.

Our proposition is that in new urban politics city hall policy makers are forced to deal not only with a more difficult range of issues, but they also encounter these issues at stages of decision which themselves are more difficult to manage and control. The basic distinctions developed above may be presented graphically as shown in Figure 10–3.

**Figure 10–3.** Stages of Decision

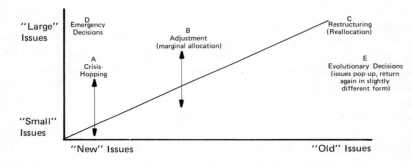

What this analysis suggests is that the "best" (most manageable) decisions are found at and around point B. This equilibrium point represents decisions that the policy maker is familiar with and knows how to respond to. In this context, policy making involves either relatively small adjustments in policy and program or incremental allocations of existing services. As noted above this is the kind of policy making that traditionally occurs when city hall responds to tangible service requests such as a demand to fix a pothole or repair a traffic light or collect the garbage.

Thus, our proposition is that in the new urban politics, city hall policy makers must increasingly deal with issues at points A, C, D, E, all of which exists at a distance from the equilibrium point B where decisions involve only small adjustments and allocations. In particular, our proposition is that urban issues cluster at point A, the point of constant crisis-hopping, where the attention and energy of urban policy makers are severely fragmented and dissipated. To a large extent city hall administrators also face issues at the emergency, evolutionary and restructuring stages of decision; and, these "stages" also carry high costs for decision making.

**IV. Configuration of Participants.** In the interests of space, I will present the last two major elements of urban decision rather briefly. The first point is straight forward. It is that if our central policy maker could control his political environment, he would doubtless choose to deal with street-level demands one at a time, and he would avoid complicated multilateral decision games with various city bureaucracies and higher-level governments. As against this desired issue context, when the central policy maker has to trade-off the claims of different urban groups, he inevitably winds up in the position of disappointing as many interests as he pleases. In addition, to the extent that the central policy maker has to operate through multilateral decision games with other agencies and governments in order to work out a policy response, the less likely he is to be able to respond quickly and flexibly to the given demand. The simple point is that urban issue contexts increasingly involve a multiplicity of participants. This is in part because of the proliferation of neighborhood-based interests, in part because of the intertwined character of urban issues (drawing in different bureaucracies), and in part because of the increased involvement of other levels of government in urban issues. Thus, our empirical proposition is that in the new urban politics, the policy maker is likely to be increasingly involved in multilateral decision games involving community groups, city bureaucracies, and higher-level governments. And this multiplicity of participants imposes high transaction costs and makes it all the more difficult for city government to make coherent decisions—or, for that matter, any decision at all.

**V. Institutional Setting.** Different urban issues wind up on the doorstep of particular urban institutions. Some are directed at the police department, some at the school system, some at independent boards and commissions, some at city hall itself. Seen in this light, the character of urban issue contexts depends crucially on the character of the principal urban institution involved. Of course, the structure of urban institutions differs in various ways. Some are relatively closed to citizen involvement, such as police departments or redevelopment agencies. Others have a tradition of providing far greater access to citizens, such as the school system. In addition, some urban institutions, such as the fire department, exercise relatively strong control over their internal administrative processes, while others are perpetually searching for effective mechanisms of internal control as are the police department and the school system. A careful examination of the variations in the structure of urban institutions requires a lengthy treatment, but it is possible to note two general trends that have critical implications for urban policy making. In theory, our central policy maker would doubtless wish to preside over a bureaucratic structure that was both open to citizen involvement and was in control of its internal operations.

For such a combination would presumably provide greater responsiveness to street-level demands and greater confidence that central decisions were actually being carried out at the street level. However, the dominant pattern in urban bureaucracies is just the opposite. It is typically one of weak citizen involvement in policy making and at the same time weak control of internal operations. And it should be obvious that these institutional patterns further complicate and frustrate the process of urban decision making.

### The Politics of Urban Decision Making

We have not as yet considered the central policy maker as a political actor. Let us imagine that he wishes to be liked by his constituents and, as a result, to stay in office by retaining broad electoral support. If we imagine further that our central policy maker can best gain support by taking credit for "solving" citizen problems, we find that the new urban politics, as depicted above, makes life very difficult for him. Our central policy maker does not even have to be a perfect rational economic man to realize that he is best off dealing with private goods that confer particularistic benefits (and avoid concentrated costs) and that are not symbolic in character, intricately intertwined, and unsolvable (given his present knowledge and resources). Further, our politically-motivated policy maker would like to avoid multilateral decision games so that he can respond as he sees fit, and he would like finally to have bureaucracies working for him that are accessible to citizen concerns but also are capable of controlling the implementation of their services.

However, the simple point of this analysis is that on every count our central policy maker is likely to be disappointed, and is apt to become involved in decision games that disadvantage him systematically both as a "problem-solver" and as a politician.

### The Future of Urban Policy Making

To put this analysis into a broader structural context, our central policy maker is required by the new urban politics to deal with two quite dissimilar problems. He is asked at once to work out a more effective street-level service relationship that meets the twin problems of trust and responsiveness, and at the same time to bargain effectively with other governments on the growing number of issues that extend beyond city limits. On both counts, the urban policy maker is in severe trouble and therein lies the troubling suspicion that urban government has become increasingly ungovernable.

### NOTES

1. Lawrence J. R. Herson, "The Lost World of Municipal Government," *American Political Science Review,* 51 (1957), pp. 330–45.

2. See for example, Terry N. Clark, *Community Structure and Decision-Making* (San Francisco: Chandler, 1968).

3. In particular, Arnold J. Meltsner, *The Politics of City Revenue* (Berkeley: University of California Press, 1971); and John P. Crecine, *Governmental Problem-Solving: A Computer Simulation of Municipal Budgeting* (Chicago: Rand McNally, 1969).

4. See for example, Stanley Greenberg, *Politics and Poverty* (New York: Wiley, 1974).

5. Michael Lipsky, *Protest in City Politics* (Chicago: Rand McNally, 1970), and Douglas Yates, *Neighborhood Democracy* (Lexington, Mass.: D.C. Heath, 1974).

6. See for example, James Q. Wilson, *Varieties of Police Behavior* (Cambridge: Harvard University Press, 1968); and David Rogers, *110 Livingston Street* (New York: Vintage, 1968).

7. C. E. Lindblom, *The Intelligence of Democracy* (New York: The Free Press, 1965).

8. Graham Allison, *Essence of Decision* (Boston: Little, Brown, 1971).

9. James March and Herbert Simon, *Organizations* (New York: Wiley, 1958).

10. Norton Long, "The Local Community as an Ecology of Games" in *The Polity* (Dubuque, IA: William C. Brown, 1972).

11. Theodore Lowi, "Four Systems of Policy, Politics, and Choice," *Public Administration Review,* (July/August, 1972), pp. 298–310.

12. Robert Dahl, *Who Governs?* (New Haven: Yale University Press, 1961).

13. Edward Banfield, *Political Influence* (New York: Free Press, 1969).

14. The concept is developed in Robert Dahl, *Autonomy and Control* (draft manuscript, August, 1974).

15. This analysis and the figure that follows appear in a slightly different form in Yates, p. 6.

16. Daniel Bell and Virginia Held, "The Community Revolution," *The Public Interest,* 16 (Summer, 1969), p. 142.

17. Jeffrey Pressman and Aaron Wildavsky, *Implementation* (Berkeley: University of California Press, 1973).

18. See Lindblom, *The Intelligence of Democracy;* and Aaron Wildavsky, *The Politics of the Budgetary Process* (Boston: Little, Brown, 1964).

19. See David Mayhew, *Congress: The Electoral Connection* (New Haven: Yale University Press, 1974), pp. 61ff.

# ✳ About the Editors

**LOUIS H. MASOTTI** is Director of the Center for Urban Affairs and Professor of Political Science and Urban Affairs at Northwestern University. He has
coedited numerous books, most recently *The Urbanization of the Suburbs,
Suburbia in Transition* (both with Jeffrey K. Hadden) and *Urban Problems and
Public Policy* (with Robert L. Lineberry), and has written articles on suburbs,
metropolitan development, and civil disorders. He is the editor of *Urban Affairs
Quarterly*.

**ROBERT L. LINEBERRY** is Associate Professor of Political Science and
Urban Affairs at Northwestern University. He is the coauthor (with Ira Sharkansky) of *Urban Politics and Public Policy* and coeditor (with Louis H. Masotti)
of *Urban Problems and Public Policy* and has written on the subjects of metropolitan politics, urban policy and urban service distributions.

**GEORGE C. ANTUNES** is Associate Professor of Political Science at the
University of Houston. He is currently doing research in criminal justice and is
coauthoring (with Kenneth Mladenka) a book on urban service distribution. He
has contributed articles to *International Studies Quarterly, Criminology, Journal
of Urban Law, Journal of Criminal Law and Criminology, Sociology and Social
Research, American Journal of Sociology* and *Administration and Society*.

**RICHARD D. BINGHAM** is Assistant Professor of Political Science at the
University of Wisconsin-Milwaukee and is on a one year leave of absence completing a similar appointment at Marquette University. His teaching and research
interests are in urban politics and public policy analysis. He recently completed a
National Science Foundation project on the adoption of innovations by local
government. Recent publications include *Public Housing and Urban Renewal:
An Analysis of Federal-Local Relations* (Praeger, 1975).

**DONALD HAIDER** is Associate Professor of Public Management and Urban
Affairs at the Northwestern University Graduate School of Management. He is
author of *When Governments Come To Washington* (Free Press, 1974) and has
served as a financial consultant to New York State, New York City and Chicago.

**E. TERRENCE JONES** is Associate Professor of Political Science at the University of Missouri-St. Louis. He is the author of *Conducting Political Research*
(1971), and his articles on urban politics, policy analysis, research methods and
voting behavior have appeared in more than ten professional journals. He is also

an editorial board member of and contributor to *The St. Louis Journalism Review.*

**IRA KATZNELSON** is Associate Professor of Political Science at the University of Chicago. From 1970 to 1975 he was the editor of *Politics and Society.* His published works includes *Black Men, White Cities: Race, Politics, and Migration in the United States, 1900–30 and Britain, 1948–68* (Oxford University Press, 1973) and *The Politics of Power: A Critical Introduction to American Government* (Harcourt Brace Jovanovich, 1975), written in collaboration with Mark Kesselman.

**PETER A. LUPSHA** is Associate Professor of Political Science at the University of New Mexico. He is interested in the linkage between the theory and practice of urban decision making. He has written on political violence, housing and water policies as well as on intergovernmental relations.

**KENNETH R. MLADENKA** is Assistant Professor of Government at the University of Virginia and Research Associate, Institute of Government. He has published articles in *Criminology* and the *International Journal of Group Tensions.* He has also taught at Rice University.

**KENNETH NEWTON** is a Research Fellow at Nuffield College, Oxford University. An interest in comparative urban politics led him to the United States, where he was Visiting Professor at the Department of Political Science, University of Pittsburgh in 1972 and an American Council of Learned Societies Research Fellow at the Department of Sociology of the University of Wisconsin, Madison in 1973–74. He is the author of *The Sociology of British Communism* and *Second City Politics* and a number of articles on local politics in Britain and the United States.

**MICHAEL B. PRESTON** is Assistant Professor of Political Science at the University of Illinois at Urbana. He is the author of *The Politics of Reorganization* (University of California Press, forthcoming) and has written book review essays for *Political Science Quarterly* and *Urban Affairs Quarterly.*

**FREDERICK M. WIRT** is Professor of Political Science at the University of Illinois at Urbana. He has also taught at the University of California, Berkeley and the University of Maryland. He has written widely in the fields of urban government, suburbs and educational politics, including *Power in the City: Decision Making in San Francisco* (University of California Press, 1974) and with Michael Kirst, *The Political Web of American Schools* (Little, Brown, 1972).

**DOUGLAS YATES** is Assistant Professor of Political Science at Yale University and Assistant Director of Yale's Institute for Social and Policy Studies. He is the author of *Neighborhood Democracy* and *Street-Level Governments* (with Robert Yin). He is completing a study of urban policy making entitled *The Ungovernable City: The Politics of Urban Problems and Policies.* He also directs the Office of State and Local Studies at Yale and has worked extensively with both state and local governments.